WE BELIEVE

✛   ✛   ✛

WE BELIEVE

✦ ✦ ✦

Recovering the Essentials
of the Apostles' Creed

Michael Horton

WORD PUBLISHING
Nashville·London·Vancouver·Melbourne

Word Publishing
1998

Unless otherwise indicated, Scripture quotations used in this book are from
the Holy Bible, New Century Version, copyright © 1987, 1988, 1991 by
Word Publishing, Nashville, Tennessee 37214. Used by permission.

Scripture quotations noted NIV are from the Holy Bible: New International
Version®. Copyright © 1973, 1978, 1984 by International Bible Society.
Used by permission of Zondervan Publishing House. All rights reserved.

Book design by Kandi Shepherd

Library of Congress Cataloging-in-Publication Data

Horton, Michael Scott.
We believe : recovering the essentials of the apostles' creed / Michael Horton.
p.   cm.
Includes bibliographical references.
ISBN 0-8499-1408-6
1. Apostles' Creed. 2. Theology, Doctrinal—Popular works. I. Title.
BT993.2.H67   1998
238'.11—dc21
97-44342
CIP

Printed in the United States of America
8 9 0 1 2 3 4 BVG 9 8 7 6 5 4 3 2 1

To Lisa, proof to me that doctrine and life never have to part company.

CONTENTS

Contents

Preface

I wrote this book for the average layperson who wonders, often secretly, what really lies at the heart of Christianity and what might be said to one who, ruffled by the many challenges to biblical claims in our day, struggles to identify the edge of the envelope. *We Believe* reasserts the "bottom-line" of Christianity stated so clearly in the Apostles' Creed, affirming the importance of a return to the central concerns of Christianity.

We Believe follows the basic affirmations of the Creed within the history of redemption. In other words, we will trace each declaration of the Creed in its biblical development in history from Genesis to Revelation. Along the way, we will interact with representative critics of the Christian claims and relate those claims to our understanding of ourselves, as Christians, and of our world in this "postmodern" environment.

It is my hope that this book will be a useful resource for you as you seek to grow in your knowledge of, appreciation for, and gratitude to the God who has made us for himself.

THE APOSTLES' CREED

✦ ✦ ✦

I BELIEVE IN GOD THE FATHER ALMIGHTY,
MAKER OF HEAVEN AND EARTH,

AND IN JESUS CHRIST HIS ONLY SON OUR LORD;
WHO WAS CONCEIVED BY THE HOLY GHOST,
BORN OF THE VIRGIN MARY,
SUFFERED UNDER PONTIUS PILATE,
WAS CRUCIFIED, DIED, AND WAS BURIED;
HE DESCENDED INTO HELL;
THE THIRD DAY HE ROSE AGAIN FROM THE DEAD;
HE ASCENDED INTO HEAVEN, AND SITTETH ON THE
RIGHT HAND OF GOD THE FATHER ALMIGHTY;
FROM THENCE HE SHALL COME
TO JUDGE THE QUICK AND THE DEAD.

I BELIEVE IN THE HOLY GHOST;
THE HOLY CATHOLIC CHURCH;
THE COMMUNION OF SAINTS;
THE FORGIVENESS OF SINS;
THE RESURRECTION OF THE BODY;
AND THE LIFE EVERLASTING.
AMEN.

ONE

A Time to Stand: What Can an Ancient Creed Say to Us Today?

✦ ✦ ✦

"It was the best of times, it was the worst of times." When considering the world of today, the Christian is forced to agree with Dickens's oft-quoted summary of Victorian England. Perhaps it is only what C. S. Lewis called chronological snobbery that ascribes such significance to our generation. But despite the dangers of exaggerated importance, it is beyond doubt that those now living are witnesses to the passing of one age and the beginning of a new era. No branch of learning, no vocation, pastime, religion, or cultural endeavor is aloof to these enormous changes. Gone are modernity's conceited certainties; they are replaced by postmodernism's irrepressible cynicism.

From the universities to network news, the last two decades have been enlivened with talk of the revolution: The modern era has come to an end, the postmodern self is now in the ascendancy. Yet nobody is even sure that such a "self" exists. As Stephen Toulmin has shown, every age in which the tectonic plates of culture shift dramatically has led to an overwhelming sense of confusion and anticipation.[1] In 1611 the poet and preacher John Donne expressed the motion sickness of his generation as the so-called modern age achieved its majority:

For every man alone thinkes he hath got
To be a Phoenix, and that there can bee
None of that kinde, of which he is, but hee.
("The Anatomy of the World")

Between the two World Wars, William Butler Yeats explored the same sentiments, only this time with the anxiety that came from the failures of that world—failures that haunted Donne:

Things fall apart; the center cannot hold;
Mere anarchy is loosed upon the world; . . .
The best lack all conviction, while the worst
Are full of passionate intensity.
("The Second Coming")

As religious dogmatism was challenged by rationalistic and scientific dogmatism during the Enlightenment of the seventeenth and eighteenth centuries, it was thought that a new era of unlimited human potential would be unleashed. Finally, superstition would be beaten down under the feet of reason; reliance on one's own experience and conviction would drive out the barbarian tribes of religious and secular authority. Wars of religion would disappear in a world dominated by sensible agnosticism. Now truth was what scientists and philosophers knew, while religious people were allowed their opinions. The former claimed the public realm, and the latter were to be allowed whatever private religious opinion suited them.

But, of course, wars did not cease even after President Wilson's "war to end all wars." Utopian visions, aided by heavy machinery, claimed the lives of more people in one century than in all previous centuries combined. Christian eschatology was secularized into a vision of evolutionary progress, as reason-empowered men and women found new and efficient ways of making heaven on earth. But few people these days speak so triumphantly of the New Jerusalem. The mood is captured even in popular culture, as in Sting's admission that he has lost his faith in science, in progress, in politicians, and in the church that lent its aid to the modern plot.

In 1920 T. S. Eliot asked:

> Where is the Life we have lost in living?
> Where is the wisdom we have lost in knowledge?
> Where is the knowledge we have lost in information?
> The cycles of Heaven in twenty centuries
> Bring us farther from GOD and nearer to the Dust. . . .[2]

The Church and the Culture

The church itself is often captive to the culture. By trying to win the "cultured despisers," she has often kept her richest treasures in vaults. Ironically, just when the culture was reacting against modernity—including its prohibitions against the supernatural—the church was altering its creed to be in step with the times. This tendency to accommodate instead of confess the faith continues unabated. Eliot continues:

> And the Church must be forever building, and always decaying,
> and always being restored. . . .

Today the church is merely saying what the culture already hears from others: the Rotary Club, one political party or the other, therapists, marketing wizards, celebrities, and talk shows. We are like those in Milton's sonnet who fail to realize that "new foes arise, Threat'ning to bind our souls with secular chains." We want to be liked, to be popular and successful, to be photographed with all the right people and to win a spot in the limelight of popular culture. We want our churches to grow and to exercise influence. But it is always the difficult task of the church to ask itself the question posed by Eliot later in his poem: "Why should men love the Church?" After all:

> She tells them of Life and Death, and of all that they would forget.
> She is tender where they would be hard, and hard where they like
>   to be soft.
> She tells them of Evil and Sin, and other unpleasant facts.

But, we are told, our age is so unique. It is the era of techno-logical sophistication and the information superhighway. Not long ago, a pastor in Arizona was reported in *Newsweek* saying, "People today aren't asking about justification, sanctification, and similar questions." Hardly a rank liberal, he has nevertheless opted for a user-friendly religious approach that tries not to bore people with, well, Christianity.

Doubtless, this pastor would sign on the dotted line of orthodox doctrine, but it would appear that such commitments have little to do with his actual ministry. If we have to judge by the popular ser-mons, Christian best-seller lists, or by the shelf space given in Christian book stores to Christian doctrine and the relationship between truth and life, the church seems to have little interest in God's questions, much less his answers. Back to Eliot's poem:

The Church disowned, the tower overthrown, the bells up-turned,
    what have we to do
But stand with empty hands and palms turned upwards
In an age which advances progressively backwards?

The Seed of the Church

The Christian who is alert to God's clues in history knows that the pattern is always bad news followed by good news. The Gospel always has the last word over sin, death, and temptation—whether it be the believer's individually or the church's generally. It was, after all, into a world fallen as a result of the will to power that our race heard the surprising announcement of saving grace: The seed of the woman will crush the serpent's head. He who had beguiled the royal couple into seeking their own autonomy would himself be destroyed. And just as the world was looking upon the disfigured body of the crucified Messiah in disgust and mockery, God was act-ing for the salvation of his enemies.

A tiny band of disciples was huddled in a Jerusalem loft, expect-ing immediate arrest and execution, when the Holy Spirit came in power and turned a room full of trembling fishermen, ex-prostitutes, doctors, businesspeople, lawyers, and tax-collectors into a witnessing community whose teaching overthrew the powers of darkness. Eventually, their blood became the seed of the church. It was a time to stand, even in the arena as they died for the sport of cheering fans.

Yes, we are told, but we live in a period of religious pluralism, and there are enormous pressures to tone down the dogmatism of orthodoxy. Of course, the days of the martyrs were also dominated by religious pluralism. Had Christians claimed that Jesus was a way, or perhaps the best way, no one would have bothered with them. Had they suggested Christianity as the empire's ally in creating patriotism, morality, and civic virtue, they would have been welcomed and Jesus would surely have been added to the pantheon of Rome's faithful divine patrons. But their claim—the one that got them in trouble—was that Christ was the only saving revelation of God. They maintained that he alone held the key to history, to the understanding of self and society, sin and salvation, and that his historical resurrection will be followed by a historical return in judgment against all who refuse him.

"We are publicly accused of being atheists and criminals who are guilty of high treason," Tertullian wrote. In A.D. 177, Athenagoras reported, "Whenever the Christians proclaim that there is only one God and he is only known in Christ, a law is put in force against us." Rome concluded that their dogmatic claims to exclusive, public, final truth surely made them enemies of public peace and order. The Roman historian and official, Tacitus, surmised that Nero rightly persecuted the Christians "for their hatred of the human race."

Polycarp, a disciple of St. John, was urged by the chief of police to renounce his beliefs. "How could I blaspheme my King and Savior?" he replied. "Hear my frank confession," Polycarp told the official: "I am a Christian. If you are willing to learn what Christianity is, set a time at which you can hear me." Refusing his offer, the official offered one last warning, but Polycarp answered, "You threaten me with a fire that burns but for an hour and goes out after a short time, for you do not know the fire of the coming judgment and of eternal punishment for the godless. Why do you wait? Bring on what you will."

As he was brought into the crowded arena, the masses cried out, "He is the teacher of Asia! The father of the Christians! The destroyer of our gods!" When his body failed to be consumed by the poorly-lit flames, the executioner drove a dagger into the saint's breast.[3]

When everything is on the line, one has to determine whether one's convictions are worth dying for. Threats aside, this community of martyrs was created in the nursery of the apostolic church, where the believers gathered daily to listen to the apostles' teaching, to receive communion, and to worship God in prayer and song. Doubt affords little patience for persecution, but these were times of great advance for the church, in depth as well as breadth. People knew what they believed and why they believed it. And there they stood.

Heroes and Heretics

But when persecution turned to toleration after Constantine's reported conversion in A.D. 313 and eventually led to the empire's official adoption of Christianity, popularity had its price. "Christendom" became a confusion of popular myth and biblical claims, often secularized for the greater good of the empire. It was during this period that the church faced an onslaught of heresies. In 325, three hundred bishops assembled, representing the farthest reaches of Christian expansion by this date, as far away as Persia and from among the Goths. Among this godly assembly was a young man named Athanasius who would later become Bishop of Alexandria and defender of the faith. At issue was the Arian heresy, which denied the eternal deity of Jesus Christ and, therefore, the Trinity as well. Once the leaders of the Christian church agreed upon this common confession in a universal council, the Nicene Creed became the basis for instruction for new Christians and was required at their baptism.

This approach to settling doctrinal debate was first illustrated in the Council of Jerusalem, recorded in Acts, when the apostles reached consensus on the end of the Jewish requirements for Gentile converts and the full embrace of Paul's arguments in Galatians. Furthermore, the pattern of inserting creedal or confessional statements in the regular worship service was laid down in the Bible itself. As Jewish worship had included the Shema from Deuteronomy 6 ("Hear, O Israel: The Lord our God is one Lord; and you shall love the Lord your God with all your heart, and with all your soul, and with all your might"), Peter's confession ("You are the Christ") became the rock upon which Christ built his church (Mark 8:29). Among the earliest New Testament writings, Paul introduces official confessional statements in the liturgy as well (1 Tim. 3:16; 1 Cor. 8:6; 15:3–7). Some were in the form of hymns (Phil. 2:6–11; Col. 1:15–20). Furthermore, there were implicit Trinitarian affirmations in the New Testament (Matt. 28:19; 2 Cor. 13:14).

As early as A.D. 107 the Apostolic Father, Ignatius, drafted a widely used creedal statement against the Gnostic sects that denied the physical characteristics of Christ's person and work:

Be deaf, therefore, whenever anyone speaks to you apart from Jesus Christ, who is of the stock of David, who is of Mary, who was truly born, ate and drank, was truly persecuted under Pontius Pilate, was truly crucified and died in the sight of beings of heaven, of earth and the underworld, who was also truly raised from the dead.

About fifty years later, a summary emerged that expanded on that of Ignatius: "[I believe] in the Father, the Ruler of the Universe, and in Jesus Christ, our Redeemer, in the Holy Spirit, the Paraclete, In the Holy Church, and in the Forgiveness of Sins." Here we begin to see the form of our present Apostles' Creed emerging. These summaries of the faith were increasingly necessary as the apostles and their pupils were no longer living and the church was beset with errors.

Contrary to the medieval tradition that the apostles drafted the Apostles' Creed by divine inspiration after the Ascension, this time-honored summary nevertheless contained the basic elements of statements that were used around A.D. 100. It was actually the Nicene Creed (325) that became the first universally accepted official summary of the Christian faith, and that is why the major bodies—Eastern Orthodox, Roman Catholic, and Protestant—have traditionally embraced both creeds as containing the articles necessary for salvation.

A Creed for the Ages

Although the Reformation sought to purge the church of medieval superstitions and additions to apostolic Christianity, the Reformers staunchly defended the Nicene and Apostles' Creeds as necessary for a genuine Christian profession. Not only were they facing errors in the Roman Church, but there was also a revival of ancient heresies among the radical sects. The major Protestant confessions and catechisms follow the outline of the Apostles' Creed, and Calvin even patterned his famous *Institutes of the Christian Religion* on it.

In our own day the Apostles' Creed deserves renewed attention. It serves both a negative and a positive function: the former, by excluding the errors that are especially widespread in our day among the cults and liberal Protestants; the latter, by providing a way of instructing a new generation in the essentials. On the eve of the Reformation, parents could not teach their children the creed because they themselves did not know it. The same is largely true in our day, as Gallup and similar pollsters have made painfully clear.

Throughout this book, then, we will mine the treasures of our historic faith in an effort to mint coins for a new generation. We can win that generation by God's grace, but it will require a renewed commitment to the pursuit of truth and a vigorous application of that truth to our contemporary situation. Perhaps the collapse of the culture of modernity, like that of ancient Rome, will be an occasion for some surprising advances for the kingdom of Christ. Only a new age of faith can preserve us from the demise prophesied by Eliot's haunting poem:

> And the wind shall say: "Here were decent godless people:
> Their only monument the asphalt road
> And a thousand lost golf balls."[4]

To make a stand, we have to know three things: our biblical faith, our own time, and the differences between the two. It requires not only a knowledge of the truth, but a willingness to defend it at all costs, regardless of how the culture—or the church itself—may receive it. We have to believe in our deepest heart that the greatest crisis is not political, moral, or cultural, but spiritual—which is to say, theological. The fact that most Americans claim to be evangelical Christians is testimony to the fact that breadth is no substitute for depth. Furthermore, we can even say that heresy is not the worst thing that the church can face. While it is tolerated in both Roman Catholic and Protestant bodies today, heresy's dangerous claims often lead to greater clarity and conviction in Christ's church. Stirring the church to think more deeply about its confession, heresy is often turned, by God's grace, into a means of strengthening the church's witness.

If there is to be genuine recovery, we will have to abandon our obsession with symptoms and address the real crisis: the silencing of the clear Christian announcement. Whether by heresy, ignorance, distraction, or apathy, the Christian witness has been largely silenced. That is not to say that there is not a great deal of energy and zeal, not to mention resources, spent on activities that we call "evangelistic." But the saving message has been silenced. Sometimes it is altered and we end up with, in Paul's words, "another gospel which is no gospel." But frequently, the disease is subtler. Too often, the sword of the Spirit has dropped from the soldier's hand. In the conflict between the Spirit of Christ and the spirit of the age, perfectly sound churches can lose their nerve. And they have.

We have to know the Word and we have to be willing to use it. "Orthodoxy" encompasses both duties. It is not enough to sign on the dotted line, especially in our day of "cafeteria-style" Christianity. Like the early Christians, we must be willing to work our doctrinal confession of Christ with consistency into the fabric of our worship, evangelism, and our very lives.

Sitting is a lot easier than standing. One of the "deadly sins," sloth or laziness is too often tolerated in Christian circles. Outside observers and concerned voices within the church today have raised

the concern of anti-intellectualism. As preoccupied with the flicker-
ing images on the screen as any medieval peasant was dependent on
images instead of words, our age has given itself willingly to the
enterprise of "dumbing down." But losing our grip on what really
matters goes deeper than lazy thinking. Critics of this cognitive laziness are not "intellectualists" who want to make know-it-alls out of
everyone. The whole person is involved in this sloth.

It is not only that we do not think enough; we do not love
enough, and, what is more important, we do not love the right
things. C. S. Lewis writes, "Our Lord finds our desires not too
strong, but too weak. We are half-hearted creatures, fooling about
with drink and sex and ambition, when infinite joy is offered us,
like an ignorant child who wants to go on making mud pies in a
slum because he cannot imagine what is meant by the offer of a
holiday at the sea. We are far too easily pleased."[5]

The church, we hear, has to satisfy the needs of the people; it
cannot simply ignore the questions that people are asking today. Of
course, that's true. It isn't enough for the church to simply educate;
it must address itself to the whole person in the whole context of that
person's life. We must not ignore the connection between the text of
Scripture and the experience of men and women living today.

Questions of Life and Doctrine

But the problem is the one expressed here by Lewis. Our felt needs
are trivial. It is not only that they are human-centered but that the
pleasures of such religion fall far short of the everlasting peace that
comes from a sound understanding of the faith. We are so wrapped
up in tips for living, relationships, and success in life that we miss
the grander scheme of redemption from God's wrath. We are children "making mud pies in a slum" when we could be enjoying a
holiday at the sea. Our sin consists not simply in demanding that
God make us happy, but in being so oblivious to what real happiness is. We think we have all the answers, but we don't even know
the right questions.

Knowing what we believe is not just an intellectual thing,

though it is certainly that. We are loving someone or something with our minds and hearts, but is it God or is it ourselves? We are not only failing to love God with our minds, but also with our "hearts, souls, and strength." The classical affirmations in this book we will be considering are not merely there to fill our minds with wonderful thoughts, but are meant to revive our souls, cheer our hearts, and animate our hands.

Whenever people clamor for the practical and prefer to speak about the horizontal dimension—for instance, relationships and success—the unspoken truth is that they love God less than they love themselves and each other. Their interest in God is in using him as a means to ends rather than in glorifying God and enjoying him forever. Others focus on knowing all the correct doctrines. However, the doctrines have become the object of their worship rather than the divine person these doctrines are meant to describe. In both cases, Christians settle for less than God, and they worship and serve the creature rather than the Creator.

"Some take doctrine, others take life," we are told. But that is quite impossible. Show me a person who is content with a merely intellectual religion and I will show you an unfulfilled and pitiful man or woman. Equally, if I should meet a person who is quite happy to be occupied only with happy, joyful, pleasant feelings or energetic and zealous activities, it is easy to predict that such a person will end up resenting those feelings and despising those activities in due time. When the old product loses its luster, the obsession of yesterday will be quickly traded in for a new model promising greater self-fulfillment.

Both the dry intellectual and the wet sentimentalist are lazy. Both fail to love God well. You see, even if God did heal everybody, make everybody rich, and fix everyone's lives, self-centered religion would still be wrong—not because people would be demanding too much, but because they would be settling for too little. God wants to open the heavens of his spiritual riches in Christ and give us our inheritance as his children. He wants to tell us who he is and how he has saved us from his wrath. And here we are, asking him if he has any candy in his pockets!

The Arrogance of Ignorance

One of the great culprits in this whole enterprise is anti-intellectualism. In his Pulitzer Prize-winning book, *Anti-Intellectualism in American Life,* Richard Hofstadter points out that the evangelical faith built America's only indigenous intellectual tradition, but as Puritanism degenerated into revivalism, the nation lost its intellectual balance. While the Reformed evangelists of the Great Awakening were also presidents of Princeton and Yale, evangelists since Charles Finney have actually boasted in their lack of education. Evangelicalism has a legacy of anti-intellectualism that has not only crippled its witness to the watching world, but has opened the church itself up to the most remarkable reaches of stupidity and incredulity.

Anti-intellectualism is not humble. Humility says, "I don't know, but I'll have to look into that." But pride says, "I don't know, and that's OK." To conclude that things which are beyond my reach of knowledge, insight, or experience are not worth knowing is the height of arrogance. I am not the measure of all values, all truths, and all meaning. I am not the center of the universe.

Anti-intellectualism is also arrogant in its plea for balance. People often cry for balance whenever they do not want to take the time to think through their own point of view. Holding a so-called middle position saves us the hassle of having to actually employ critical skills. Circumventing thought processes, it is a mere act of will that attempts to pick up the slack of our lazy thinking. This plea for balance does not, however, keep us from claiming moral superiority for having the grace, moderation, and sophisticated detachment to stand above and outside the debate.

Furthermore, anti-intellectualism is arrogant in its intellectual egalitarianism. Egalitarianism is the spirit of our age that insists on everybody being equal. Positively, egalitarianism begins by insisting on equality before the law, but then it goes so far as to insist on equality in abilities, skills, and authority. Consequently, anti-intellectualism claims that one person's views are just as valid as another's—no matter how ill-conceived they may be—because all ideas, like all people, are created equal. Anti-intellectualism makes egalitarianism possible by "leveling the playing field." While in past ages, consulting wise elders and the books of the great thinkers was considered an act of humility, anti-intellectualism considers such consultation elitist. In such a time, the church should be standing apart from such worldly arrogance. Unfortunately she is often found at the helm of this ship of fools.

The Case for Orthodoxy

In this context, "orthodoxy" has become one of the most pejorative words in the contemporary vocabulary, and it is also one of the most often misunderstood.

As is the case with nearly anything, there are two extremes to be avoided. On one hand, there are those—we'll call them "experientialists"—who emphasize the personal act of faith. Becoming a Christian, for them, is chiefly a matter of making a decision. In many cases, in fact, public evangelistic events are staged in which there is little actual content of Christian truth proclaimed. The focus is on moving people to make a decision, become "born again," or rededicate their lives. But, at least in this extreme form, such an approach is a sublimated form of works-righteousness. While often resisting the temptation to turn other activities into works which somehow attain God's favor, the experientialist's temptation is to turn faith itself into its very opposite, a sort of meritorious decision or qualifying experience which enters a person into God's favor. But we are reminded in the Westminster Confession, that believers are justified (declared righteous before God) "not for anything wrought in them, or done by them, but for Christ's sake alone: not by imputing faith itself, the act of believing, or any other evangelical obedience to them, as their righteousness; but by imputing the obedience and satisfaction of Christ unto them, they receiving and resting on him and his righteousness by faith; which faith they have not of themselves, it is the gift of God" (Ch. XIII. 1). "Faith in faith" is an especially American heresy, since we are all raised with optimism and the "can-do" spirit that is effective in the marketplace but destructive in religion. We are not saved by believing, but by Christ; this is why we must have Jesus and his saving work held up before us constantly, rather than the bare imperatives to believe, to trust, to decide, to choose, and so forth.

At the same time, there is the opposite danger. Let's call it "intellectualism." Here I am not particularly thinking about a high IQ or academic sophistication, but the idea that faith is merely believing *that,* rather than believing *in.* It is the view that faith is in propositions rather than in a person. Instead of Jesus Christ being the object of faith, the doctrines *about* Jesus become our hope. This is hardly a living relationship with a person, so it is understandable that people with this defective view of faith show little personal interest in God or Christian faith and practice. They've given their assent to all the right things, and that is their religion. In fact, they will often fight vehemently for their orthodoxy, but in actual practice, their hearts are far from the One to whom their words refer.

Both are defective types of faith. The one is an act without an object; the other an object without an act. In one, nothing is gained; in the other, nothing is lost. What we have to realize is that genuine faith—as knowledge, assent, and trust—is the act of casting oneself on God's promise in Christ. Faith, this ability to say, "I believe . . .," in more than either an experientialist or intellectualist way, is a gift from God, but it is we who believe. God does not believe for us and the truths do not save us simply by being true. We have to take a risk.

Unlike the detached observation with which a biologist studies organisms under a microscope, the knowledge we have of God is personal, like the knowledge we have of other people. Without knowing something about a certain person, we can hardly entertain a relationship, and yet, knowing things about someone is not the same thing as knowing a person. Knowledge of truth is a means to a greater end, the end of actually enjoying God's fatherly goodness and forgiveness in Christ. In Christian faith, we do not study God and Christian truth as observers, but as players. It demands self-involvement, as we take our stand: "*I* believe . . ." *I* am taking personal responsibility for my reaction to this "good news." Here we risk ourselves, not merely in terms of being right, but in terms of being saved. God is *my* God. "Who do *you* say that I am?" Jesus asks.

"The word 'heresy' not only means no longer being wrong," wrote G. K. Chesterton early in this century. "It practically means being clear-headed and courageous."[6] In his book *The Heretical Imperative,* Peter Berger points out that today it is actually necessary for one to be "heretical." As Billy Joel said of honesty, orthodoxy is "such a lonely word," and it is "hardly ever heard" when everyone is "so untrue." What seems to matter is how things look, not how they are. After all, "Image is everything."

We don't normally build a fire in the middle of the living room or wherever we happen to feel like enjoying its warmth. But neither do we build a fireplace, stack the wood ever so neatly, only to stare at it and shiver. Correctly understood, orthodoxy builds and tends a fire that will drive out the darkness and safely warm the body and soul, even in the most gloomy weather. When our hopes are frozen and our hearts are hard, the Good Shepherd never fails to lead us to shelter. He himself gathers the wood ("Sanctify them by the truth— Your Word is truth" John 17:17), and makes us dwell in safety.

Take orthodox doctrine from me, and my fire will consume me; keep the doctrine from catching fire and it will remain cold and useless.

So let's stop settling for either the carefully stacked, but unused, woodpile or the glowing but uncontrolled fire. Further, instead of settling for too little, the trivial things that we call "practical" and "relevant," let us "fix our eyes on Jesus, the author and finisher of our faith" (Heb. 12:2), plundering our neglected resources, gathering the kindling of truth from Scripture's sacred pages. Then let us fan the flame until its brilliant glow can be seen from afar by homeless souls seeking warmth and light on a cold winter's night.

TWO

God in the Hands of Angry Sinners

✦ ✦ ✦

I BELIEVE IN GOD THE FATHER ALMIGHTY, MAKER OF HEAVEN AND EARTH.

"Give me something to believe in." That's the cry from a popular band, representative of a growing theme in rock lyrics these days. With the success of hits like "What If God Was One of Us," "Tell Me All Your Thoughts On God," and "Dear God," it is clear that a lot of young people want to hear about God these days. But how will they hear without a preacher?

As a fairly young person myself, I often notice people of my own generation talking about their lack of direction. When I listen long enough, I find they are asking questions about God. Many know that their confusion is deeper than the usual questions about career goals, marriage, relationships, and other things we regard as the most relevant topics for seekers. Often the complaint I hear goes something like this: "I used to go to church, but nobody told me why I should believe it all." Bored by the activities many youth directors and pastors thought were actually attracting young people, many are now convinced that if there are answers, the church is not the best place to find them. But they can't stop asking the questions.

Some years back, J. B. Phillips wrote that enormously popular little book, *Your God Is Too Small.* Among the false gods many people worship in place of the real one, Phillips described Resident Policeman, Parental Hangover, Grand Old Man, Meek-And-Mild, Heavenly Bosom, Managing Director, and other rivals. Satan's best tactic has not been his obvious heresies, but the gradual transformation of the biblical God into an idol of domesticated religion. Phillips's analysis is even more striking with age:

> No one is ever really at ease in facing what we call "life and death" issues without a religious faith. The trouble with many people today is that they have not found a God big enough for modern needs. While their life experience has grown in a score of directions, and their mental horizons have been expanded to the point of bewilderment by world events and by scientific discoveries, their ideas about God have remained largely static.[1]

Upon reaching adult discoveries (which seems to occur a lot sooner these days), many people who have been raised in the church either ignore the yawning chasm between their view of God and their experience of the world, or they jettison it all in favor of something else. "There are undoubtedly professing Christians with childish conceptions of God which could not stand up to the winds of real life for five minutes," Phillips writes. "If it is true that there is Someone in charge of the whole mystery of life and death, we can hardly expect to escape a sense of futility and frustration until we begin to see what He is like and what His purposes are."[2] Seeing what God is like and what his purposes are is precisely what this chapter will begin to address.

From Feeling Fear to Feeling Good

We are all allowed theories. One of mine goes something like this crude summary: The God of fundamentalism was so angry and relentless in his discipline, that the cross as the good news of God's forgiving and justifying grace stood in the shadows. The hymnist may have had the confidence that Christ "had hushed the Law's loud thunder" and had "quenched Mount Sinai's flame," but as far as many were concerned, that had little to do with the grim experience of growing up a conservative Protestant or Roman Catholic.

Gradually, however, a new generation (the postwar "new evangelicals") longed for a God of love and freedom. The difference between these two generations cannot be easily detected in systematic theologies or in the more theoretical publications, but it took shape in the pulpit and the pew. Tracts changed. Sermons and hymns changed. Popular Christian books changed. People wanted to know that God was friendly and approachable, accepting them just as they were: jeans, long hair, and all the rest.

But because this was largely a popular trend rather than an academic one, there was not a great deal of debate. To be sure, some fundamentalists retrenched and launched crusades against the emerging "neo-evangelicals," but in many cases the shift occurred even within fundamentalist churches, in spite of protests. And, no doubt, many older adults who had recalled the days of heavier hands were themselves rather relieved by the new emphasis.

Because this more positive emphasis was a popular trend, there does not seem to have been a great deal of interest in rethinking the doctrinal framework that produced such anxieties in the first place, or created the need for such new emphases. Instead of thinking through a richer theological perspective with the aid of reflections of wise Christians in other times and places, evangelicalism simply drifted into an outlook that was much more conducive to the spirit of the times. Just as Protestant liberals had accommodated their *theology* to modernity, evangelicals have tended to accommodate their preaching and popular diet to "felt needs." It is likely that secular sentimentalism, therapeutic and relational categories, subjectivity, and longing for direct, intense experience directed these trends rather than any doctrinal controversies that may have been acted out. And fundamentalism's lingering memory—both caricatured and real—offered the dark backdrop.

But the emerging generation does not know what it was like to find Mom and Dad at home after school, much less stern, seemingly omnipresent parents who served as analogies to God. If they have been exposed to evangelical churches, it is hardly dogmatism, but a doctrinal vacuum, that they encountered. Far more experience oriented than even their postwar parents, they are the "TV generation" and even churched teens today are more likely to know the names of the hapless castaways on *Gilligan's Island* than those of the twelve apostles.

It is not enough to explain where this generation is; the real question is whether this is where they should be. The church does not exist to conform, but to transform, beginning with the renewing of the mind (Rom. 12:1–2). In my own experience, younger Christians are fascinated with ultimate questions and many among the unchurched are attracted to communities of faith in which the doctrine, life, and worship are different from their daily routine. Why is it that so many twenty-somethings are turning out in droves for conferences on theology? Why are they looking for serious theology and liturgy in church services, seeking to be governed by Scripture, attempting to recover continuity with previous generations? Perhaps they are running, not from fundamentalist rigor, but from meaningless triviality.

Putting God on Trial

This does not mean, of course, that the generation I am describing will be running en masse toward biblical Christianity! If our fundamentalist era drove people to the image of a weak and rather helpless deity, the current direction seems to be toward putting God on trial. If children of fundamentalists rebelled against a cruel god in the sixties, the MTV generation appears to be reacting against evangelical sentimentality with a vengeance. If the deity of contemporary evangelical faith, worship, and life is "too small," they seem to say, it is time to put him on trial.

Like monarchs who only ruled because their tormented subjects were too afraid to speak out, idols are easily toppled when their weakness is discovered. A modern Bastille Day has arrived. And while many people are asking questions about God today, it is not without a certain tone of interrogation. This is understandable, given recent history. How, they ask, could a good God have allowed the Holocaust? Vietnam? The natural disasters that are portrayed for us on the nightly news?

However loudly lamented, the plague, which literally depopulated London in the seventeenth century, was met with confidence in providence. But today, even the slightest brush with tragedy is enough for the masses to set a trial date for the Almighty. Jonathan Edwards kindled the fires of the Great Awakening with "Sinners In the Hands of an Angry God," but today, as R. C. Sproul has noted, the script reads the other way around: God is in the hands of angry sinners. And often, strangely enough, it is not those who suffer the most today (for instance, the poor and marginalized in underdeveloped nations) who call God to account, but those of us from relatively privileged backgrounds.

Current Views of God

Two extremely persuasive alternatives to the classical view of God as "the Father Almighty" should be mentioned briefly. Shaped by the horrors of Auschwitz, one view is the theology of the suffering God. *Theodicy* is the defense of God in the light of evil, and the popular way of stating this problem is as follows: If God could end suffering but does not, he is not good. On the other hand, if God would like to end suffering but he cannot, he is not all-powerful. One of these attributes has to go; it's simply a contradiction to maintain both. A Christian theodicy attempts to face this dilemma.

In our day, God is often identified with the world, the Creator and creation fused. An extreme version of this has roots in the

German philosopher G. F. W. Hegel (1770–1831), who identified God with everything that is real and therefore rational. According to Hegel, history is God's self-realization, as Spirit progressively transforms everything by radical swings from thesis to antithesis, resulting in a higher synthesis. As appropriated by theology, this meant that the cross is symbolic of the death of everything (thesis) that is required for the resurrection of everything (antithesis), resulting in a new stage of history's (i.e., God's) self-realization. For Hegel, this process was marked by a cheerful optimism, but war and injustice on a massive scale challenged such so-called progress. In the 1960s, the "Death of God" theologians had argued this so forcefully that *Time* carried the cover story, "Is God Dead?"

Others have been more restrained. To them, while God is not dead, he is suffering. More recently, this view has become popular even in evangelical circles. In fact, *Christianity Today* addressed this view in its February 3, 1997 issue. Both of its articles on the subject advanced this view, one even arguing that the "error" of the classical view can be traced to the Chalcedonian Creed (A.D. 451).

Appealing to the biblical references in which God is described as "afflicted," "repentant," "pleased," and so forth, proponents of God's suffering do not accept the traditional interpretation that these are anthropomorphisms—that is, figures of speech in which God describes himself in human terms so that we can better understand his character.

Although hardly an orthodox theologian himself, Hans Küng offers a sound critique of this position, as it is "inspired more by Hegel than by the Bible." No one has attempted to grapple more with the Holocaust and suffering in general than Küng, but he correctly observes that we cannot do away with the "godness" of God in order to find an easy explanation of suffering. He writes,

> A look at scripture may sober up such speculative boldness. . . . Granted, in anthropomorphic language the Hebrew Bible some-times attributes the whole range of human feelings and attitudes to God. . . . But nowhere is the difference between God and human beings done away with, nor is human suffering and pain

simply declared to be the suffering and pain of God and thus transfigured. Nowhere does God's Godliness become ungodliness, his faithfulness unfaithfulness, his reliability unreliability, his divine mercy human pitifulness. For the Hebrew Bible, though human beings fail, God does not fail; when human beings die, God does not die also. For "I am God and not man, the holy one in your midst," states Hosea 11:9 against any humanization of God, although at this very point as elsewhere there is anthropomorphic talk of God's "compassion" on his people.[3]

As for this emphasis on God's unchanging character, the New Testament tells the same story. Jesus cries out to God, "My God, my God, why have you forsaken me?" for the suffering of the God-Man is not the suffering of the divine nature itself. Küng encourages us to, "emphatically protest against a masochistic, tolerant understanding of God according to which a weak God has to torture himself to resurrection by suffering and death if he is not to suffer eternally."[4]

If God is affected by that which occurs outside of himself, he is dependent on these factors for his pleasure or pain. He is therefore a victim of evil, along with the rest of us. It may help some people to learn that God feels their pain, but if it is at the expense of his invulnerability to change, frustration, despair, and suffering, God is no more helpful in a crisis than is the therapist or sympathetic neighbor.

If one is trapped inside the elevator of a burning building, a fireman outside the elevator who can break down the door is preferable to a fellow victim who is also trapped but understands the problem. Being omniscient, God knows our pain and hears our cries. And in Christ, God did experience our human suffering inasmuch as he was the God-Man. But as God, he was able to rescue us because he possessed the very attributes that we do not possess. Because he is in himself beyond suffering, he cannot be affected or hindered by anything that happens in the world. When he does act, it is out of strength, abundance, self-sufficiency, and freedom, not out of weakness, lack, dependence, or constraint. Although this may not fully resolve our curiosities about the problem of evil and suffering, it is good news to those who are actually suffering.

The second of the two modern alternatives to "God the Father Almighty" has its source in Karl Marx's critique of power and hierarchy which has been influential in liberationist and feminist theologies. Marx said that the criticism of religion as "the opiate of the people" was the point of departure for an unrelenting criticism of the status quo in every field. According to theologian Sallie McFague, for instance, Jewish-Christian patriarchalism which pervaded the early church, was the product of a monarchical conception of God.

A male king rules over a hierarchy of lesser powers, all of whom reign over women and other marginalized members of society. Thus, the theory goes, theology justified and produced hierarchical and patriarchal cultures. The picture represented in the "Hallelujah Chorus" of Handel's Messiah ("King of kings and Lord of lords," "for the Lord God omnipotent reigneth") is "a very dangerous one," writes McFague.[5] Of course, these attributions of monarchical sovereignty do not originate with Handel, but with the Scriptures themselves.

Closely related to the notion of a "suffering God," the alternative picture suggested by feminist theologians is that of a vulnerable deity who, unlike the "masculine" God of power and stoic indifference to feeling, is a fellow traveler. Process theology, even when it does not explicitly draw on feminist themes, is another popular expression of these basic ideas. God, proponents suggest, is not the king over all, but a lover who invites us to become co-creators, co-sufferers, and co-redeemers.

First, this is a complicated critique and deserves far more attention than we can give it here. It is true that the church has sometimes strayed beyond the biblical story to borrow from Greek philosophy in its defense of a God who does not suffer. To be sure, the church for centuries abused its authority with incredibly blatant exercises of tyranny and injustice. In many places, it still does today. American Protestantism and Latin American Catholicism remind us of the dangers of a church that loses its prophetic role by propping up the status quo in politics and society. But this critique engages in what logicians call "the genetic fallacy." That is, while the historical realities cannot and should never be denied, it is wrong to blame Christian theology per se unless there is a clear causal link.

Many of the examples cited (forced conversions of pagans, the Crusades, the Inquisition) actually took place in a setting in which theology revolved more around the veneration of Mary than around "God the Father Almighty." Nevertheless, this did not produce a feminist hierarchy. In many Catholic countries today, severe oppression of women continues to take place in cultures deeply committed to the cult of the Virgin.

Furthermore, Jesus was deeply critical of the social injustices of his day with respect to tyranny and oppression, breaking taboos with respect to women, foreigners, and social outcasts. And yet the Scriptures show us that God was his father, not his mother (or "parent"), and Jesus was God's Son, not a genderless child, and the sovereign God of the prophets and apostles was none other than the one to whom even Jesus acknowledged subordination in his earthly ministry. No one has ever proclaimed "God the Father Almighty" as forcefully (and as evangelically) as Jesus Christ.

The critique of God as both father and almighty has deep difficulties. Beyond the obvious biblical challenges, it is flawed even in its analysis of the problem. It assumes that patriarchy is inherently oppressive, never minding the many contradictory examples one can find in history. After all, since most societies throughout the ages have been patriarchal, how could one single this factor out as definitive? Christians have historically explained fallen societies in terms of fallen human hearts, not in terms of good people imprisoned in evil institutions. While certainly not minimizing the point that institutions as well as individuals are sinful, Scripture nowhere identifies patriarchy as inherently oppressive, despite the fact that many patriarchies have been so.

The divine patriarchy does not sanction unjust and oppressive systems of power; rather, it is precisely their judge. Who can ignore the indignation of God against the powerful who oppress the weak in society, including the poor, the alien, and women? As one example, we learn that in the civil legislation of Israel, women were given rights that did not belong to women in antiquity. It was a good Father who created, preserves, and saves, a Father who "is opposed to the proud but gives grace to the humble" (James 4:6), who tenderly cares for his children, and uses his power to reconcile the wicked to himself despite their sin and resistance.

Instead of projecting our modern experience of patriarchal societies and impoverished fatherhood on religion, we must allow the biblical story to reorient our very notions of fatherhood and power. We can sympathize with women and men who have been victims of inadequate and even destructive father images. It is no wonder so many women identify patriarchy with oppression, violence, and injustice. And we can never simply dismiss our personal experience from the process of interpretation.

But the sociological "is" does not reflect what of necessity has to be. Despite their enduring wounds, those whose fathers were absent, judgmental, or cruel can have their concept of "father" transformed by the story of an "Eternal Father, Strong to Save." The more we get to know God's redemptive actions in history, the greater our chances of overcoming the prison of our own narrow experience. Instead of abandoning these models, we must allow God's version to redeem our experience of fatherhood and sovereignty. To the weak and oppressed, a sovereign liberator comes as good news.

Critics are quite correct to point out that patriarchal religious views can create oppressive cultures. When we project our earthly father-images onto God, we set them in concrete. If this is what God is like, we reason, then who is to question? So if we happen to live in a culture in which men grow up thinking of women as objects or tools for their own ends, they will likely erect a chauvinistic deity to lend credibility to the projection. But this is sheer idolatry. Far from sanctioning destructive patriarchy, God's self-revelation judges it as nothing else could. If, for instance, one were to simply jettison the male images and substitute female ones, this would hardly be capable of solving the problem of violence against women. Only a Good Father can judge a bad one and show us what real fatherhood is all about. So both chauvinists who "project" their distorted masculinity onto God and feminists who try to meet this challenge by "projecting" their own unscriptural images end up engaging in idolatry. It is not our images, but God's word that must shape our faith and practice.

One reason why this affirmation can actually heal rather than reinforce malevolent parental relationships is that God's fatherhood is the source of all fatherhoods. At first, this sounds somewhat strange because we are used to working our way analogically from that which we know best (human relationships) to that which is more remote (divine relationships). But God built his intertrinitarian paradigm into our human psyche. The Son is eternally begotten by the Father and from both proceed the Holy Spirit. There was no time when the Son was not, and therefore, no time when the Father was not a father. Relationship is built into the very fabric of the Trinity. Thus, while in practice we cannot help but be influenced in our views of God's fatherhood by our earthly experiences, the Good Father can heal our broken images. He can do this because we learn that good fatherhood is not from good human fathers, but from God himself. After all, he invented the idea.

As we will see further in this study, the knowledge of "God Almighty" is hardly comforting by itself, especially when we know deep down that we are at odds with God and he is our judge. God is almighty in wrath, in justice, and in blinding glory. But when we add that intimate title *Father* to the equation, and by our incorporation into Christ can call him our Father, the unlimited power and indestructible will of God become good news to us: He is strong to *save*.

This is an important warning for some who seem to regard God's sovereignty as the center of the Christian message. As important as it is, this emphasis can only lead to fear, doubt, and despair unless it is read through the lens of God's saving will made certain in Christ through the promises of the Gospel. It is the Gospel that makes the affirmation of God's omnipotence welcome rather than fearful news.

But to take our mission field seriously, we will have to take our faith more seriously as well. And that means it is time to topple the idol of popular sentiment, repent of our trivial pursuits, and recover the grand vision of God that has always led to the most remarkable advances of Christ's kingdom throughout history. We must not only eliminate the idea of a graceless god, but also the idol of sentimentality. Neither is great enough to capture the hearts and minds of our disenchanted age, especially in the face of evil, oppression, violence, and death. More importantly, neither vision represents the God of the Bible.

Getting to Know the God Who Is There

Imagine a friend telling you that she has fallen in love with a man she has known for some time now. For weeks she has been mutely staring right through you, as if the fellow's face were projected on the wall behind you. Finally, she runs up to you as you are returning from shopping, nearly knocking the groceries out of your arms. "I'm in love!" she announces. "We're getting married!" During all of this time, however, you have continually asked her about this man. What is he like? What does he do? Where is he from? Who are his parents? But all you get are the blank stares. "I don't know," she finally answers. "I don't want to know about him; I just want to know him."

The rather silly scenario I am describing is a situation that most of us would regard as unlikely. We do not usually pit falling in love with someone against knowing something about that person. And if we were to see someone doing this, we would probably say that he or she is heading for disaster. We call such superficial enchantment puppy love or infatuation rather than mature, adult love. And yet, when we come to God, it seems that we are perfectly free to substitute emotion for understanding.

Throughout Scripture, we are called to experience God by way of some self-disclosure on his part about who he is and what he has done for us. Theology is a word that comes from two Greek words: *Theos,* God, and *logos,* reason. As biology is the study of life (bios), theology is the study of God. How can we say that we do not need theology? It is tantamount to saying that we do not need to know anything about God in order to be Christians.

Everyone needs theology, because everyone needs God. In fact, one could say without exaggeration that the whole Bible is concerned with theology, since everything in it is intended as God's self-disclosure in Christ. It tells us about his nature, his purposes, and his activity. If we do not love theology, we do not love God and we do not love the Bible. Happily for us, God has not left us to figure things out on our own, since our own imaginations are "idol factories." He has taken the initiative to speak to us and to show us what he is like. Because of his generous revelation of himself, we are able to take a brief look at some of God's attributes and actions.

God's Incommunicable Attributes

As great Christian minds have scoured the Scriptures, they have been able to discern a number of attributes—characteristics affirmed by God as belonging to his nature. These fall into two categories: incommunicable and communicable. The former are those attributes that humanity shares with God as his image bearers; the latter are those attributes that belong to God alone.

God Is Self-Existent and Self-Sufficient

First, God is self-existent and self-sufficient. One of the oldest questions in philosophy, and perhaps the most frequently asked question among children is, "Who made God?" The question is based on the dilemma as to whether there is anything in the universe that is eternal. If we say that nothing that we see could have come into existence without a cause, we eventually work our way back to God himself. So, who caused God to be? Aristotle insisted that God was the First Cause, the eternal being who causes all things to exist but who himself is uncaused and uncreated.

While these notions became increasingly trapped within Greek philosophy, the Scriptures do affirm the basic thrust of Aristotle's point. It is impossible for us to fully grasp God's self-existence because we do not have any analogous reference point in ourselves or in the world. For us, everything is in some way the product or effect of something else. However, when God revealed his name to Moses, there was no question that God's self-existence and self-sufficiency were not only true, but that God's whole nature could be summarized this way.

From the burning bush, itself a symbol in that it burned but was not consumed, God called to Moses, and in the course of conversation the patriarch asked, "Indeed, when I come to the children of Israel and say to them, 'The God of your fathers has sent me to you,' and they say to me, 'What is his name?' what shall I say to them?" "And God said to Moses, 'I AM WHO I AM.' And he said, 'Thus you shall say to the children of Israel, I AM has sent me to you'" (Exod. 3:13–14).

Far better than any philosophical speculation, God's own self-disclosure of his name offers the clearest expression of his self-existence and self-sufficiency. "To whom then will you liken God? Or what likeness will you compare to him?" (Isa. 40:18). When it comes to God's incommunicable attributes, there is no analogy of being.

We cannot point to another self-existent and self-sufficient person and say, "That is what God is like." Paul declared in Athens that, unlike the gods of Greek mythology, the true God is "not served by human hands, as though he needed anything, since he gives to all life, breath, and all things" (Acts 17:25). It is he, says the apostle, who has set the boundaries on his creatures: where they will be born, live, and die. The Graeco-Roman deities were glorified men and women, projections of the most powerful generals, the wisest rulers, and the most skillful athletes. But Paul challenges their view of God as "man writ large" by starting with God's self-existence and self-sufficiency.

God does not need anything from us, but we cannot take our next breath without him. "In him we live and move and have our being" (Acts 17:28 NIV). God is present to us in the world he made and sustains, but we are now sinners running like Adam and Eve through the forest to escape his presence. We at least know that much about ourselves. However, for those who have been adopted by God, the world becomes, in Calvin's words, "the theater of

God's glory," a place where God's omnipresence brings delight and wonder, replacing fear and dread.

This truth is put in the form of praise in Romans 11:34–36:

"For who has known the mind of the LORD? Or who has been his counselor? Or who has given anything to God that he should repay him? For of him and through him and to him are all things, to whom be glory forever. Amen."

It is difficult for us, especially in our day of the God who is too small, to really come to terms with the fact that God did not create us because he was lonely or because something was missing in himself. He enjoyed the eternal company of inter-Trinitarian fellowship, each person of the Godhead contributing inexhaustible pleasure, joy, and delight. Though, admittedly, it is deeply humbling, we must nevertheless recognize that if none of us had ever been born, God would be just fine. He created out of strength, not weakness; out of abundance, not lack; out of an excess of joy, not because he was unfulfilled.

We must beware of trying to understand God's incommunicable attributes by devising analogies to ourselves. We need our parents, our spouses, our friends, our children, our jobs, and so forth. But God needs no one and nothing for his eternal happiness. Everything for him is a question of wisdom and self-determined choice, while for us our decisions are always determined by a perceived need. Our Savior put it this way: "For as the Father has life in himself, so he has granted the Son to have life in himself" (John 5:26). We have life from God, but God has life in himself.

God Is Immutable

A second incommunicable divine attribute is immutability. A mutation is a change from one thing to another. To attribute immutability to God is to say that he never changes. Many modern theologians have attacked this and related attributes as owing more to Greek philosophy, with its celebration of static, unchanging, perfect being, which opposes growth and evolution. But is this really the reason for centuries of commitment to this teaching?

First, Greek philosophy has never been at one on this point, although Plato and the disciples of Stoicism exercised an enormous influence over Western thought. It must be acknowledged that some formulations of such attributes do sound a great deal more like philosophical speculation than biblical self-disclosure, but Scripture does indeed declare that God is immutable: he never changes.

The divine name, "I AM WHO I AM," not only points to God's self-existence, but to his changeless character. He did not say, "I AM BECOMING ABSOLUTE BEING," as Hegel, Whitehead, and many other modern philosophers and theologians would have preferred. The Psalmist notes that while God changes the ancient heavens and the earth as a nurse changes diapers, he himself does not change: "They will perish, but you will endure; yes, they will all grow old like a garment; like a cloak you will change them, and they will be changed. But you are the same" (Ps. 102:26).

In fact, "same" here is the Hebrew name translated in Exodus 3 at the burning bush: "I Am." Thus, the qualitative distinction between God and all that he has made is measured by the fact that everything changes, while he remains what he has always been and will always be.

God declares of himself, "I the LORD do not change" (Mal. 3:6). He says Israel can take comfort in this (v. 7). After all, if he did change, he would certainly have broken his covenant with his disobedient people and consumed them with fire by now! Paul refers to the nations as exchanging the glory of a changeless, perfect God with that of a changing, imperfect deity (Rom. 1:22).

This is, after all, the point of God's immutability. If he is changing in his very essence and being, it suggests that it is possible for him to move from imperfection to perfection, from a lack of knowledge to fullness, from a lack of love or mercy to a plenitude of grace, from a lack of power over a particular situation to victory over rival forces. These points, which Paul attributes to Greek idolatry, are actually being argued explicitly even in evangelical circles these days. This argument challenges the opening confession of the whole Christian faith: "I believe in God the Father Almighty."

James insists that with the true God "there is no variation or shadow of turning" (James 1:17). For the Greek Stoics and Plato, change was itself negative: that which is perfect never changes, while changing things are inherently inferior (because they're changing). This is not the biblical defense of God's immutability, however. For instance, in sanctification the believer is being changed gradually into the image of Christ. In the case of creatures (as well as historical movement), change can be both good and bad, depending on the direction.

In what direction does God change? Either toward greater perfection or away from it. If we deny God's immutability, we have to do away with his perfection as well. Thus, the biblical argument for God's immutability is not some preference for "that which does not change," as in Greek thought, but hangs on the conviction that God is beyond improvement.

There are, of course, passages that suggest that God does change. For instance, we read of God "repenting" that he had ever created humanity. This expression is used in other places as well. It might well be asked what of the Scriptures that speak of God's coming and going, judging and forgiving, condemning and then showing mercy when the people turn to him? Do these not clearly indicate change? Of course, they do. But what kind of change? In each of these cases, there is a change in God's relation to his creatures, but never is change ascribed to his being. Although he himself does not change, his voluntary involvement with creatures who do change means that his actions in this ever-changing realm of history can only be described for us in these terms.

When Scripture, therefore, speaks of God repenting or changing his mind, we are forced to one of two conclusions. Either we can say that Scripture contradicts itself, which is impossible for those who take it as God's own self-disclosure, or we can say that God is speaking in anthropomorphisms, as if he were a human being.

God often speaks this way so that we will understand him, the way a parent speaks to a child. For instance, when the Scriptures speak of coming under God's wings for refuge, as in Ruth 2:12, we understand the author to be describing a truth about God in a way that is not literally true. God is not a giant bird, and the author does not expect us to believe that he is one. Even though it is said in a context of historical narrative rather than poetry, it is intended as a figure of speech, the way America is referred to as a melting pot. The reality is that God is tender and covers us with his saving mercies as if he were a bird. Because God's changeless character is not something that we find in ourselves, God appropriates rich metaphors and similes from the natural world and everyday experience in order to help us know him.

Similarly, Scripture attributes change to God because there really are changes in his relations within human history, due to the fact that we change and are part of an ever-changing historical world. But the fact of the matter is that he is not like us in this respect: "I am not a man that I should change" (Mal. 3:6).

God is infinite and eternal and he is perfect in all his attributes, without change or improvement. As he was in the beginning, he is now, and shall be forever. We, on the other hand, are fickle, and as prone to change as the weather. One minute we are in love with someone or excited about a new job, the next minute we are disenchanted and depressed. It is good to know that the One in whom we have placed our trust is not like us in this respect.

God Is All Knowing, All Powerful

Third, God is omniscient and omnipotent. That is, he knows everything and he has power over everything. We may know some things and have control over others, but God's wisdom and power know no limitations. God does not have to arrive at knowledge through reason or observation. Rather, he possesses all knowledge in himself in every moment (Job 37:16).

God's knowledge is not like ours, either in content or in mode. In content, it is perfect and infallible knowledge: God cannot possibly err in his knowledge of what will come to pass. In mode, it is immediate and intuitive. In other words, unlike us, God does not arrive at an item of knowledge. He knows the end from the beginning in one act of reflection:

> Remember the former things of old, for I am God, and there is no other; I am God, and there is none like Me, declaring the end from the beginning, and from ancient times things that are not yet done, saying, 'My counsel shall stand, and I will do all My pleasure. . . . Indeed I have spoken it; I will also bring it to pass. (Isa. 46:9–11)

Scores of biblical passages relate God's foreknowledge of the future actions of creatures. Prophecy rests on the belief in God's foreknowledge: "Behold, the former things have come to pass, and new things I declare; before they spring forth I tell you of them" (Isa. 42:9). Furthermore, God not only knows the future; he controls the future. His omniscience and omnipotence are in perfect harmony. In fact, it is because he has decreed everything that comes to pass that he knows the future in every detail. Hardly a passive spectator, merely knowing future acts of his creatures, God is actually the active architect of history. He is "God, the Father Almighty, Creator of Heaven and Earth." Even the results of a throw of the dice are determined by God already in every case (Prov. 16:33).

The prophecies of Scripture rest on this assumption: that God not only knows the past, present, and future in every detail, but that he does so precisely because he has decreed the end from the beginning according to his own secret counsel. As the Westminster Shorter Catechism puts it, "The decrees of God are his eternal purpose, according to the counsel of his own will, whereby, for his own glory, he hath fore-ordained whatsoever comes to pass" (VII).

Paul writes, "In [Christ] we have also obtained an inheritance, being predestined according to the purpose of Him who works all things according to the counsel of His will . . ." (Eph. 1:11).

If this is true, how can humans have any free agency? This has been the question that has puzzled theologians and philosophers for ages. Yet, God seems to think that it is enough for us to know that he is sovereign and that we are responsible. God always gets his way, but in such a manner that human agency is not undermined or destroyed. While Scripture does not seem to resolve this mystery, some theorists choose to reject either divine sovereignty or human agency. This option for either position is not available to us, however tempting it may be.

It is actually God's unlimited sovereignty that makes human decisions and activity both meaningful and possible. If God had not planned the future in every detail, there would be no reason to believe that his promises would be fulfilled, that salvation would triumph over destruction, or that life would gain victory over death. Our actions take on meaning because they are part of a larger plan that we ourselves do not even comprehend:

> Beating my wings, all ways, within your cage
> I flutter, but not out.[6]

As the ocean is to fish and the skies to birds, God's sovereignty is the environment that creates meaningful history for us. Within that ocean, there is seemingly limitless freedom, but it is always the ocean and not something else. Fish cannot be something other than fish, and creatures—even those created in God's image—cannot be the Creator. When they try to achieve this rank, they plunge themselves into misery. Only a God with perfect wisdom and goodness can so order the universe and history that even those things we may mean for evil purposes God intends for good ends (Gen. 50:19–20).

God can only work all things together for good (Rom. 8:28) because he has control over every variable in the equation. This should comfort us in the realization that there is nothing that happens purposelessly or meaninglessly, even though it may seem that way to us. To know that there is a point to it all, even if we do not yet know how particular pieces of the puzzle fit, is a great assurance when life's storms reach our shore. Those who reject God's providential control over every event do not thereby gain freedom, but find themselves in slavery to some form of determinism: chance, fate, the power of others, or their own self-will.

We have to realize that there are tremendous odds against our believing in God's providence today. It's one thing to confess it verbally, but quite another to experience it as an anchor deep in the soul. The Enlightenment left us with the belief that the phenomenal realm (that which we can observe with our senses) and the noumenal realm (that which lies beyond our experience) are divided by an ever-expanding gulf (more about this in a later chapter). God must exist as a first cause, and perhaps even intervene from time to time, but scientific laws are the governing structures of day-to-day existence, so far as we can see. That was how the argument has gone for the last three hundred years.

Because of this "God of the gaps" outlook, the tendency has been to either swallow up nature in grace or grace in nature. In other words, many have concluded that if God's existence, attributes, and activity cannot be actually observed by the microscope or telescope or in repeatable experiments of observation, if he does exist he must not be active in daily affairs. In reaction, others have argued that God is so active that the miraculous is God's normal way of involving himself in human matters.

In the process, the doctrine of providence has been lost. We need to recover the sense that God is just as active in the normal routine of non-miraculous events as he is in the creation of the world, the Resurrection, the New Birth, and the Second Coming. The birth of a child may not be miraculous, following as it does the common natural causes established by God, but it is a remarkable instance of God's activity even in non-miraculous details of life. His Word not only created the world, but keeps every element and atom intact and on course (Col. 1:16–17). We do not have to claim the miraculous in order to recognize God's fatherly hand in the most ordinary circumstances of daily life.

God Is Everywhere

Another incommunicable attribute of God is his omnipresence. Omnipresence is the truth that God is everywhere and fills the whole universe. After all, he is spirit and is not limited to a particular spatio-temporal place. It's difficult for us to conceive of God as a person when he is not really like any person we have ever known, so we project images of God that more nearly reflect our own relatives.

In the popular imagination, for instance, God is sometimes viewed as "the man upstairs," a grand old patriarch with a long white beard. But God is different from any person. Just as he does not possess a physical body (apart from the Son's incarnation), God is present everywhere. Thus, according to Romans 1 and 2, God's invisible attributes of power and majesty are everywhere on display. This means that we must outgrow the popular image of God as located in a particular place "up there," remote from this world. God is as present on the streets of New York as he is in the highest heavens. There is no place where God is not. Even in hell, God is present in judgment.

In spite of the curse of the fall and our own sinfulness, we know that God exists. But this sense of his universal presence sometimes becomes an occasion for us to turn away from the true God and to worship ourselves through the idols of our imaginations, hearts, minds, and hands. Because of this sense of God's universal presence in the beauty of nature, we identify God with the creation, confusing the Creator and creature. But the Christian faith insists—against those who push God out of this world (deists) and those who regard him as indistinguishable from it (pantheists) or indwelling it somehow (panentheists)—that the God who is present everywhere is nevertheless distinct from the cosmos which he has made. Our minds must be restrained here, for this is where explanations give way to humble adoration of God's mysterious hiddenness.

God's Communicable Attributes

There are characteristics that we share with God by virtue of the fact that we were created in his image. Unlike rocks and trees, we were created by God for a personal relationship with him. As Adam found no suitable wife among the animals until God created a wife from his own body, so God created for himself a being who could share enough common characteristics with him that genuine communication and free, meaningful interaction could take place with the work of his hands.

God Is Holy

First among these communicable attributes is God's holiness. As we possess intelligence, knowledge, and the ability to rule without being omniscient and omnipotent, so we were created in holiness. But God's holiness is not only quantitatively different from that with which he endowed humanity in creation, it is qualitatively different. In God's presence, true holiness strips us of our pretenses. Only in God's holy presence did Isaiah become overwhelmed with the sense that not only others, but he himself, was "undone" because of his sin (Isa. 6). In the same way, Peter said to Jesus, "Depart from me, for I am a sinful man" (Luke 5:8). Even if there had been no fall from grace and our sins had not separated us from God, there would still have been a distance between Creator and creature.

To say that God is holy is to say that he is different from any other being in existence. From the Hebrew verb, "to be separate," holiness refers initially to God's uniqueness. In this sense, God's holiness is the summary of all his attributes. As for his incommunicable attributes, he is entirely distinct from his creatures. Even according to his communicable attributes—those shared by humanity in creation—God possesses these characteristics in himself and unchangeably. He is distant and separate from everything he has made. This is not meant in spatio-temporal terms, since we recall that God is spirit and fills the heavens and the earth. Unlike the "blind watchmaker" of modern thought, God is intimately involved in every detail of earthly life. Nevertheless, his involvement is distinct from that of any creatures.

But holiness has another connotation, that of moral perfection. It is in this sense that Adam and Eve were created in the likeness of God. This moral perfection is concerned chiefly with relationship, not with actions, although the latter are expressions of the former. To be holy and righteous in one's actions is first of all to be in a right relationship and set apart for the purposes and interests of this relationship.

"Truly, this only I have found," the Preacher concluded. "That God made man upright, but they have sought out many schemes" (Eccles. 7:29). Created for intimacy with God, humanity rejected this holiness that belongs to God by eternal essence. Instead of being separate from the animals and set apart to the Lord, they wanted to be gods themselves and instead became like the animals.

God Is Good

Again, in one sense, only God is good, as Jesus observed (Mark 10:18). Although humanity was created good, Adam and his posterity have chosen to be bad. But God is goodness itself and he possesses it as an eternal and unchangeable choice that flows from his perfect nature. As a good Creator, God gives life, breath, food, water, shelter, and every good and perfect gift to every living creature (Ps. 145:9–16; James 1:17). He is the Lord of rain and harvest, taking pleasure in the happiness of our youth, the joy of marriage and lovemaking, the comfort of old age, and full homes at holidays.

To say that we believe in "God the Father Almighty, Creator of Heaven and Earth," is not simply to say that we believe in a proposition, but that this affirmation leads us to a person. He is the Almighty Creator, but he is also Father. Before we talk about the Fall and the relation of humanity to God after judgment was pronounced, we have to realize that God created all things good, for that is the only way God can himself create things. He is kind and does not hold grudges. He is patient and more anxious to provide blessings than curses.

At the same time, God is just and is angered by the presence of anything that violates his perfect character. Too often, we pit God's attributes against each other, as if, for instance, we had to choose between God's omnipotence and goodness or between his just wrath and his fatherly kindness. But that is our problem, not God's.

While in his eternal peace, enjoying the obedience of his heavenly hosts before the fall of Lucifer and his angels, God was perfectly happy not to express his wrath. Unlike his holiness, righteousness, perfection, love, omnipotence, justice, and goodness, God does not exercise wrath perpetually and without interruption. Rather, this is expressed by God when his attributes are affronted and his holiness has been mocked. Although we may find it almost impossible to talk about God's wrath, the Scriptures are clear on this divine expression.

It was their awareness of God's holiness, and the anger that must express itself when that holiness is violated, that caused Adam and Eve to flee from God's presence. But they only knew they had violated God's holiness because they had originally been created in holiness themselves. Where God's footsteps in creation had once been a source of comfort and purposeful existence, now they were signs of judgment. Instead of enjoying the divine presence, every corner of the glorious world that witnessed to God's majesty was now a hell to humanity.

This has been human nature ever since the Fall: to flee from God and his wrath. In the midst of Israel, God determined to show himself as holy. Not even the slightest deviation in sacred worship was tolerated. We recall the fire that immediately consumed Aaron's priestly sons when they offered unauthorized fire before the Lord (Lev. 10:1–7), and the judgment that claimed so many lives in Korah's rebellion (Num. 16).

Psalm Two is the first of the many "war songs" that anticipate the judgment that will be executed by the Messiah. God is pictured there as laughing in heaven, mocking the machinations of the pagan nations. The Father says to the Son:

> You shall break them with a rod of iron; you shall dash them to pieces like a potter's vessel' . . . Now therefore, be wise, O kings; be instructed, you judges of the earth. Serve the LORD with fear, and rejoice with trembling. Kiss the Son, lest he be angry, and you perish in the way, when his wrath is kindled but a little. (vv. 9–12)

But God is not arbitrary in his wrath, like a cruel monarch who bullies his subjects. In his goodness, God himself undertakes to defeat those forces that have set themselves up against his reign, forces that enslave the masses and create injustice. It is important for us to know that the One who is exercising his wrath is the good, just, long-suffering Creator. The execution of his wrath, therefore, is good news for those who are oppressed by God's enemies.

> Before your pots can feel the burning thorns, he shall take them away as with a whirlwind, as in his living and burning wrath. The righteous shall rejoice when he sees the vengeance; he shall wash his feet in the blood of the wicked, so that men will say, "Surely there is a reward for the righteous; surely he is God who judges the earth." (Ps. 58:9–11)

The believer knows that he deserves God's wrath as much as the vilest sinner. "By your wrath we are terrified," the Psalmist declared (Ps. 90:7). Why? "You have set our iniquities before you, our secret sins in the light of your countenance. For all our days have passed away in your wrath; we finish our years like a sigh . . . Who knows the power of your anger? For as the fear of you, so is your wrath" (vv. 8–11).

God speaks of pouring out his wrath as if it were a chalice of bitter wine (Hos. 5:10). In case anyone supposes that this is a difference between the Old and New Testaments, it was our incarnate Lord himself who spoke most directly about God's wrath and judgment. In the midst of describing God's incomparable love in sending his Son, we read, "He who believes in the Son has everlasting life; and he who does not believe the Son shall not see life, but the wrath of God abides on him" (John 3:36). Throughout the New Testament we read of divine wrath and the last judgment to come at the end of the age.

God Is Infinite and Personal

Finally, God is personal. He is not a force, a principle, a mere ground of being or first cause, but is "God the Father Almighty, Creator of Heaven and Earth." To a certain degree, forces, like machines, can be controlled. At least we can predict their moves, but God is not a passive power source somewhere in the universe. He is both infinite and personal, eternal and yet more actively involved in time and space than all of us put together. He is transcendent—completely different from us—and yet he has condescended to create us in his image and to enter into a relationship with us by speaking and acting in history. C. S. Lewis observes how unsettling it is to discover that the God who exists is personal:

> An "impersonal God"—well and good. A subjective God of beauty, truth and goodness, inside our own heads—better still. A formless life-force surging through us, a vast power which we can tap—best of all. But God Himself, alive, pulling at the other end of the cord, perhaps approaching an infinite speed, the hunter, king, husband—that is quite another matter. There comes a moment when the children who have been playing at burglars hush suddenly: was that a real footstep in the hall? There comes a moment when people who have been dabbling in religion ("Man's search for God!") suddenly draw back. Supposing we really found Him? We never meant it to come to that! Worse still, supposing He had found us?[7]

Although God the Father is not a *human* person, he is a *person* and possesses the identities of individual, personal existence. Therefore, we address him as, "Father," as our Lord taught us to pray. Ludwig Feuerbach, Karl Marx, and Sigmund Freud were among the modern thinkers who argued that "God" was nothing more than a projection of the longings of the alienated self. Despite their agnostic cynicism, there is a certain truth to that point. This is why our imaginations are "idol factories": we do project ourselves into our view of God. We do this for at least two reasons, I suppose.

First, we want to create God in our image because we are sinners and want a god who will serve, not judge, us.

But second, we cannot help but seek out analogies to help us relate to this God who is described in Scripture. Theologians call this the *analogia entis,* or analogy of being. While God is different from us, there are some similarities due to the fact that we were created in his image. Therefore, it is not entirely inappropriate that we employ analogies of God from our own experience, as long as we rein them in and test them by God's own self-disclosure in Scripture. No human being is more formative in our analogy building for God than our own earthly fathers.

I am confident that one of the reasons I have taken up theology as my favorite subject is that my father was a positive analogy. When I pray, "Our Father in heaven, hallowed be thy name," I do not first have to stop and distinguish the good Father in heaven from my images of a terrible childhood, as many people do. The crisis of fatherhood in our society, much lamented by secular as well as religious groups, is not without its effects on our understanding of God.

As anthropologists have demonstrated, people in every culture look for things around them to serve as analogies for unseen truths. In pastoral ministry I have seen a good number of people raised by abusive or absent parents who have nevertheless been able to find healing through a biblical doctrine of God. They have learned to understand God's wrath as something other than arbitrary, unjust abuse and have been able to relate it to his goodness, justice, and holiness.

All of these attributes (as well as others we have not considered) are essential if we are going to confess that we believe in "God the Father Almighty, Creator of Heaven and Earth." He is God, and there is no other. He shares his power and glory with no one and is dependent on no one and nothing for his happiness, life, joy, or the fulfillment of his plans. He does all things well and no one can thwart his purpose.

In spite of this unlimited power and majesty, however, God is also infinitely good and loving. He does not use his power unjustly or cruelly, neither does he close his eyes in the face of rebellion or transgressions against his holy character. His love is never subversive of his justice; his fatherly goodness is never expressed in a way that violates his holiness and sovereignty. He is never one of these things against the others, but is all of these things at one and the same time.

To reduce God to love or wrath, to goodness or sovereignty, to mercy or holiness, is to worship another god altogether. We worship the true God when we have before us the One who is only God because he possesses all of these attributes together, without imperfection or improvement or alteration. The Preacher reminds us how important it is for us to work out our theology before the crises of doubt and suffering assail us in life's struggle:

Remember your Creator while you are young, before the days of trouble come and the years when you say, "I find no pleasure in them." When you get old, the light from the sun, moon, and stars will grow dark; the rain clouds will never seem to go away. At that time your arms will shake and your legs will become weak. Your teeth will fall out so you cannot chew, and your eyes will not see clearly. Your ears will be deaf to the noise in the streets, and you will barely hear the millstone grinding grain. You'll wake up when a bird starts singing, but you will barely hear singing. You will fear high places and will be afraid to go for a walk. Your hair will become white like the flowers on an almond tree. You will limp along like a grasshopper when you walk. Your appetite will be gone. Then you will go to your everlasting home, and people will go to your funeral. Soon your life will snap like a silver chain or break like a golden bowl. You will be like a golden pitcher at a spring, or a broken wheel at a well. You will turn back into the dust of the earth again, but your spirit will return to God who gave it. (Ecc. 12:1–7)

THREE

How Can We Know God?

I BELIEVE IN JESUS CHRIST,
HIS ONLY SON, OUR LORD.

"Where is your Father?" the Pharisees demanded of Jesus.

To the Pharisees' ears, Jesus' response was outrageous: "You know neither me nor my Father. If you had known Me, you would have known My Father also. . . . You are from beneath; I am from above. You are of this world; I am not of this world. Therefore I said to you that you will die in your sins; for if you do not believe that I am he, you will die in your sins" (John 8:19–24).

Later Jesus had a similar conversation with his own disciples: "If you had known Me, you would have known My Father also; and from now on you know Him and have seen Him."

These were astonishing statements. Not only did Jesus claim to be the only one through whom the Father could be known, but he also claimed that seeing him was equivalent to seeing the Father.

In spite of such a clear declaration, Philip had a follow-up question: "Lord, show us the Father, and it is sufficient for us."

Jesus replied, "Have I been with you so long, and yet you have not known Me, Philip? He who has seen Me has seen the Father; so how can you say, 'Show us the Father?'" (John 14:7–9).

What does it mean to know God? The Pharisees thought they knew God. After all, they were zealous for good works, anxious to keep up the rituals and regulations that had accumulated in Jewish tradition. But Jesus told them that they did not, in fact, know God at all. Although claiming to be children of Abraham, they were actually, Jesus said, children of the devil (John 8:39, 44). Thinking themselves Israel's spiritual guides, they were really blind and destitute of any righteousness. They were enemies of God.

With Jesus' uncompromising assessment in mind, it would seem that this business of knowing God is rather more difficult than some of us may believe. Who doesn't think he or she knows God? Sometimes this presumed knowledge of God is expressed in explicit forms, as in Joseph Campbell's *Hero of a Thousand Faces*. Sometimes it is stated implicitly, as in public nonsectarian prayer. In either case, the natural assumption is that God is a general entity out there who can be known apart from the particular self-revelation of God in Scripture and apart from the person and work of Christ. However, throughout the Scriptures we are introduced to Jesus Christ—both by promise and fulfillment—as the One in whom and through whom God is made known. It is not complicated or difficult: one just has to know the right person. In short, no one knows or worships God but through Christ.

At various times in Israel's history, the temptation was great to follow the nations in both their religious and their cultural habits. The nations kept their gods up close. They could touch and see them. Why did Israel have to worship a God who was invisible and could not be touched? "You cannot see My face," God told Moses. "No one can see Me and live" (Exod. 33:20).

But the promise was that one day God himself would become flesh, and in that day his servants would touch him with their hands, see him with their eyes, and hear him with their ears. And now, a carpenter from Nazareth was announcing, "He who has seen Me has seen My Father. . . . Most assuredly, I say to you, before

Abraham was, I AM" (John 8:58). Jesus was claiming, in his very person, the attributes described in the previous chapter. He was God incarnate: "And the Word became flesh and dwelt among us, and we beheld His glory, the glory as of the only begotten of the Father, full of grace and truth" (John 1:14). Therefore, John could declare, "That which was from the beginning, which we have heard, which we have seen with our eyes, which we have looked upon, and our hands have handled, concerning the Word of life— the life was manifested, and we have seen, and bear witness, and declare to you this eternal life which was with the Father and was manifested to us—that which we have seen and heard we declare to you, so that you may have fellowship with us; and truly our fellowship is with the Father and with His Son Jesus Christ" (1 John 1:1–4).

How far this is from an ambiguous notion of "god"! As Paul told the Athenians, so we must declare to our culture: "The God whom you worship as 'unknown,' I will explain to you" (Acts 17:23). And that explanation revolves around God Incarnate. Unlike Greek philosophical speculation, God's self-disclosure is public, unmistakable, and unsophisticated. If one wants to know what God is like, he or she must look no further than Jesus Christ. He is God on display. No one can see the face of God's naked majesty, but in Christ God has hidden his majesty and has clothed himself in humility. He is God among us.

All other physical representations of the invisible God are like golden calves. But, appropriating an early Christian hymn, the apostle Paul reminded the Colossians that:

> Jesus is the image [*eikon,* from which we get the word *icon*] of the invisible God, the firstborn over all creation. For by Him all things were created that are in heaven and that are on the earth, visible and invisible, whether thrones or dominions or principalities or powers. All things were created through Him and for Him. And He is before all things, and in Him all things consist ["hold together"]. And He is the head of the body, the church, who is the beginning, the firstborn from the dead, that in all things He may have the preeminence. For it pleased the Father that in Him all

the fullness [of the Godhead] should dwell, and by Him to reconcile all things to Himself, by Him, whether things on earth or
things in heaven, having made peace through the blood of His
cross (Col. 1:16–18).

Imagine that: Jesus Christ, like us in every respect except for
sin, was nothing less than "the exact representation of the invisible
God"! We only worship the true God by way of this person, this
particular manifestation of God in our flesh and in our world history of time and space. Our age is not very interested in theological
precision. "God," for most Americans, is an important person in
whom to believe, but it does not seem to make much difference
who he is or whether the one we worship as God is the correct one.
Often it is considered dangerous for a person to die an atheist, but
less concern is expressed about the eternal status of the person who,
though believing in "God," has rejected Christ.

It's important for us to realize that Jesus Christ is not simply the
most perfect expression of the divine nature, but that he is God.
Apart from him there is no God but mere idols of our imagination.
Even conservative Christians sometimes give the impression that
it does not matter whether the children in public schools pray to
the God and Father of our Lord Jesus Christ, or to Allah, the
"Higher Power," Krishna, the finite god of the Mormons, the non-
Trinitarian deity of Jehovah's Witnesses and Protestant liberals, or
the divine inner light. The concern is simply that there is some public recognition of the place of "God" in society. "Maybe it isn't traditional Christianity," wrote one pastor, "but it's sure a step in the
right direction."

But in both the Old and New Testaments, anything other than
worship of the true God is called idolatry, and idolatry is never a
step in the right direction. It is a bad thing to worship a general
"God." We are simply going to have to realize that Christianity
does not consider religion benign and honorable, but makes public
claims that directly counter the claims of every rival. From the
Christian perspective, religion is no less dangerous than atheism.

To seek to know or worship God in any way other than through the person and work of Jesus Christ is to invite wrath and confusion. It is a particular God who is described for us by God himself in Scripture and history.

Christ is the key to knowing God. Apart from him, there would be no world, no human speech, no relationship with God. In fact, apart from the Son there would be no God at all, since the only God who really exists is the Trinity: one in essence, three in person. This is why Scripture describes God by revealing Christ in promise and fulfillment, from Genesis to Revelation. We know God by seeing him in action, and the whole biblical story is about his action in Christ, foreshadowed in promise and accomplished in fulfillment. It is not "God," but this God—Yahweh—who is the object of our worship. It is not by personal experiences or by speculating or spinning a web of reasonable opinions about God that we come to know the true Creator and Redeemer, but by locating divine action in history.

As with ourselves, God is best known by his involvement in personal relationships to which he attaches his authority. In other words, God is known as he reveals himself in Scripture, not as we "find" him ourselves. The question is not, "What should God be like, given our experiences or philosophical premises?" but "What has God actually shown himself to be like?" This is why Jesus Christ—and not philosophical speculation—must be our guide to the Godhead. Not even the Bible itself is to guide us to the Father apart from Christ. Although our Savior is everywhere in Scripture, it is possible to read even God's inspired Word in a way that ignores Jesus' central role. This was our Savior's chief critique of the way the Pharisees read the Scriptures (John 5:39–40).

God is not to be thought of apart from Christ for two reasons: He is the eternally begotten Son, the second person of the Holy Trinity, and to talk about "God" is to refer to the Trinity. Second, it was the Son—not the Father or the Holy Spirit—who became man and revealed God to humanity. This leads us to the heart of our affirmation in this line of the Creed: "His Only Son, Our Lord."

The Eternal Son

Israel's creed was summarized in the Shema: "Hear, O Israel! The Lord our God is one" (Deut. 6:4). They were to have no other gods (Exod. 20:3). While monotheism (belief in one God) lay at the heart of biblical religion, the triunity of God was maintained from the very beginning. To be sure, it becomes clearer with successive chapters of redemptive history; nevertheless, even in the opening act of the drama we see God acting in the triune Godhead. The Father speaks the Word, while the Holy Spirit is hovering over the face of the waters (Gen. 1:2–3; John 1:1–3).

When we come to the creation of Adam, we read, "Then God said, 'Let us make man in Our image, according to Our likeness'" (Gen. 1:26). Three interpretations have been offered here concerning the use of the plural, "us" and "our." Some argue that the reference is to the plural of majesty—the "royal we." God here is speaking as a royal personage. The problem with this interpretation is that it depends entirely on a convention of English history and language. We have no evidence that ancient Near Eastern rulers adopted a similar grammatical convention, so this interpretation does not seem plausible.

A second option is that the use of the plural refers to God and his angels, the heavenly hosts. But unless we are willing to say that creation in God's image is really creation in the image of God and the angels, this interpretation runs into problems. Furthermore, this image is expressed in dominion, which belongs properly to God and not to angels. Later in Genesis we are confronted with the Angel of Yahweh (Jehovah) who is described as both Yahweh himself and distinct from Yahweh (Gen. 16:7–13; 18:1–21; 19:1–28).[1]

Finally, the next verse announces, "So God created man in His own image; in the image of God He created him; male and female He created them" (v. 27). It would seem, therefore, that God is referring here to himself alone, but to himself as a plurality of persons. This third interpretation seems most consistent with the narrative as with the rest of Scripture: We have, in other words, the first reference to a plurality of persons within the one Godhead.

The real support for the Trinity, as for any other revelation of God's nature, is to be found in divine action, not in abstract contemplation of the divine nature. Thus, the doctrine of the Trinity, though revealed somewhat obscurely in the Old Testament, is clearly disclosed in the work of redemption as it culminates in the sending of the Son and then the outpouring of the Spirit.

First, the New Testament recognizes the Old Testament's identification of Israel's Redeemer as none other than Yahweh himself and then applies this identity to the man Jesus Christ (Matt. 1:21; Luke 2:11; John 4:42; Gal. 3:13; 4:4–5: Phil. 3:20; Titus 2:13–14). As Louis Berkhof points out, the Old Testament presents Yahweh as indwelling the hearts of his people (Ps. 74:2; 135:21; Isa. 8:18; 57:15; Ezek. 43:7–9; Joel 3:17, 21; Zech. 2:10–11), while the New Testament applies this specifically to the Holy Spirit who indwells his church (Acts 2:4; Rom. 8:9–10; 1 Cor. 3:16; Gal. 4:6; Eph. 2:22; James 4:5). God sends the Son (John 3:16; Gal. 4:4; Heb. 1:6; 1 John 4:9), and both the Father and the Son send the Spirit (John 14:26).

At our Lord's baptism, there is the voice of the Father, pronouncing his benediction on the Son, with the additional presence of the Holy Spirit in the form of a dove. An even more direct reference to the Trinity is found in the baptismal formula, where the sacrament is to be performed in the name of the Father, and of the Son, and of the Holy Spirit (Matt. 28:19). First Corinthians 12:4–6, 2 Corinthians 13:14, and 1 Peter 1:1 refer to the Father, Son, and Holy Spirit as well.

In his own life and ministry, Jesus was aware of his eternal Sonship. In Matthew 11:27, he says of himself, "All things have been delivered to Me by My Father, and no one knows the Son except the Father. Nor does anyone know the Father except the Son, and the one to whom the Son wills to reveal Him." The Great Commission proceeds from Christ's own person: "All authority has been given to Me in heaven and on earth" (Matt. 28:18). Clearly, this is a violation of the heart of Israel's faith (i.e., monotheism), unless Jesus Christ is actually who he claimed to be: God the Son in the flesh.

"No one has ascended to heaven," said Jesus, "but he who came down from heaven, that is, the Son of Man who is in heaven" (John 3:12). We see once more the importance of coming to know God through his historical actions when Jesus says, "My Father has been working until now, and I have been working" (John 5:17). It was not that the Father was on holiday, but that the Son's role in redemptive history had now taken on more direct significance. The Father plans our redemption, the Son secures it, and the Holy Spirit applies it.

Liberal Protestants have sought to explain such passages away by saying that Jesus understood himself to be God's Son in the same way that we are all children of God. But our Lord's original audience had no trouble understanding his meaning: "Therefore the Jews sought all the more to kill him, because he not only broke the Sabbath, but also said that God was His Father, making Himself equal with God" (v. 18). This was simply not the sort of announcement that young Jewish men went about town making! It was not perceived as a benign, friendly reference to the universal fatherhood of God and brotherhood of man, but as a declaration of nothing less than equality with God.

And how did Jesus respond to their perception? Did he say, "Wait a minute! You have misunderstood me"? Not at all! He said:

> For as the Father raises the dead and gives life to them, even so the Son gives life to whomever He will. For the Father judges no one, but has committed all judgment to the Son, that all should honor the Son *just as* they honor the Father. He who does not honor the Son does not honor the Father who sent Him. (vv. 21–23, emphasis added)

Those two words, "just as," are unmistakable: Jesus was claiming that he is equally worthy of divine worship as the Father himself. "Therefore, if the Son makes you free, you shall be free indeed" (John 8:36). The presence of Jesus among us is the very presence of Yahweh himself, our Creator and Redeemer who undertakes personally to rescue us. Jesus Christ was and is "the image of the invisible God" (Col. 1:15). This leads us to second affirmation in this line of the Creed.

The Sovereign LORD

Matthew's Gospel describes a remarkable scene:

> While the Pharisees were gathered together, Jesus asked them, saying, "What do you think about the Christ? Whose Son is he?" They said to him, "The Son of David." He said to them, "How then does David in the Spirit call him, 'Lord,' saying: 'The LORD said to my Lord, "Sit at My right hand, till I make Your enemies Your footstool"'? If David then calls Him 'Lord,' how is He his Son?" And no one was able to answer Him a word, nor from that day on did anyone dare to question Him anymore. (Matt. 22:41–46)

Knowing about his earthly lineage, the Pharisees recognized that Jesus belonged to David's house, as Scripture prophesied concerning the Messiah. But Jesus presented them with a puzzle: In Psalm 110:1, David is referring to a future Son who is nevertheless already in existence as his Lord! How could David call one of his descendants "Lord"?

No wonder the Pharisees were tied up in knots in the face of this theological question! They had acknowledged that Jesus was a descendant of David, but to identify him as David's "Lord"? That would be to identify Jesus as nothing less than the Messiah, he who sits at the Father's right hand until all his enemies are made his footstool. Whatever their conclusion about Jesus, the Pharisees had to grant the argument that David's future messianic descendant (whoever that might be) was his present, existent Lord.

As we have seen, Jesus elsewhere identified himself as the "I am" of the Old Testament (John 8:48–59), the self-existent, self-sufficient, omnipotent, omniscient, holy, just, loving, jealous, merciful, wrathful, good God of Abraham, Isaac, and Jacob. Astonished by this announcement, the Jews demanded, "Are You greater than our father Abraham, who is dead? And the prophets are dead. Who do You make yourself out to be?"

Our Lord replied by saying that the Father honors him. Furthermore, he said, "Your father Abraham rejoiced to see My day, and he saw it and was glad. . . . Most assuredly, I say to you, before Abraham was, I am" (vv. 53–58). Once again, the Jews had no trouble understanding Jesus' claims: "Then they took up stones to throw at him; but Jesus hid himself and went out of the temple, going through the midst of them, and so passed by" (v. 59).

The Jewish leaders understood Jesus far better than today's liberal Protestants do. The Jesus proclaimed by the liberals is quite benign: He is simply a preeminent example of someone who possessed a God-consciousness to the full, hardly the sort of claim that would ruffle too many feathers.

The New Testament affirms the Old Testament faith in one God (for instance, 1 Cor. 8:6; 1 Tim. 2:3), but clearly declares, "For it pleased the Father that in Christ all the fullness of deity should dwell . . ." (Col. 1:17). We are told to wait patiently "for the blessed hope and glorious appearing of our great *God* and Savior Jesus Christ" (Titus 2:13). In the earliest New Testament writings, the apostolic witnesses to our Savior's divinity clearly forbade the tendency of modern theologians to separate the Jesus of history from the Christ of faith. This, as if Paul's "invention" of Jesus as God was different from the Jesus Christ who was described by the disciples themselves.

If one wishes to deny Jesus' divinity, the Gospels must also be surrendered. More than that: the Old Testament, too, is similarly insistent that the One who would come and secure redemption would be no less a person than Yahweh himself. Christianity stands or falls on the divinity of Christ, as did the Old Testament anticipation.

If Jesus is not who he claimed to be, he is not a helpful guide or a singular example for what it means to be a child of God. Rather, he is one of the greatest charlatans in history, a self-deluded man who was in fact guilty of the highest blasphemy, just as many of the Jews claimed. Nothing that our Lord says about himself, or that the apostles say about him, is unrelated to this claim to divinity.

Therefore, those who take what they want from the New Testament (the Beatitudes, the Sermon on the Mount, etc.), have no reason to believe that their cherished remains of Christianity have any more validity than the ravings of a religious huckster.

When the New Testament, therefore, attributes the title "Lord" to Jesus Christ, the purpose is clearly theological. It is not good manners, but an affirmation of Christ's divinity that leads the apostles to address him in this way. We must always keep in mind that the apostles themselves were Jews. In fact Paul was a Jew of the highest religious and academic order. Each knew what "Lord" meant as a title of address, and they boldly applied it to Jesus of Nazareth.

Jesus was the same Lord who spoke the world into being (John 1:1) and who upholds it by his power (Col. 1:17). It was he who appeared in his preincarnate state to saints in the Old Testament. To simultaneously affirm belief in one God (1 Tim. 2:5) and the belief that Jesus is God (Titus 2:13) is to confess faith in the Son's lordship as a necessary expression of his nature, not merely as an exercise of a role. There is one God, but three persons in the Godhead: trinity in unity.

What Does This Have to Do with Us?

The early Christian martyrs went to their deaths not because of an experience they'd had, nor because of moral principles or religious and philosophical ideals, but because of an announcement of God's personal involvement in human affairs. It was not a "God-in-general" they had in mind—the nameless, faceless "Unknown God" of Athens. It was this particular God who is known in Jesus Christ. Their lives hung in the balance of two words, *Christos Kyrios,* "Christ is Lord."

If they had simply renounced this claim concerning the universal lordship and deity of Jesus Christ, they could have believed, claimed, or practiced whatever they wished. They could have gone on seeking converts, helping to build moral fiber, and get on with their interesting, if mysterious, rituals. All they had to do was to give up this stubborn particularity—the conviction that Jesus was the only embodied self-revelation of God, Savior, and Lord, the only true way of salvation. All they had to do was deny that, apart from him, all people were eternally lost. Everything hung on this single issue, both the Christian witness and their own lives.

Today, something far more subtle than lions and lunatic emperors threatens this central Christian affirmation. Our "Babylonian captivity" takes the form of modernity, the spirit of the age that has so shaped the world in which we live. When the Enlightenment convinced men and women that religious truth claims belonged to the realm of the mystical, "otherworldly," and unknowable, much of the church reduced "truth" to the level of mere "opinion." "For me, Jesus is Lord," has replaced the uncompromised confession of the martyrs. Jesus' title became "my personal Lord and Savior," rather than the Lord and Savior. In other words, objective claims of truth were reduced to subjective claims of experience.

Earlier this century, William James said that the test of a religious truth claim is "its cash-value in experiential terms." In other words, will it work? Pragmatism makes sense as a way of justifying claims only if there is no access to historical, scientific, or rational explanations. And that is precisely what the modern mind concludes about religious claims. Indian missionary and bishop Lesslie Newbigin describes this shift from truth to opinion:

> It is certainly not more than a hundred years since children in Scottish schools learned at an early stage the fact that "Man's chief end is to glorify God and to enjoy him forever." This was as much a fact as the movement of the stars and the Battle of Bannockburn. Today it is not taught as fact. It may be included in a syllabus of religious studies, along with the beliefs of Buddhists, Hindus, and Muslims, for it is a "fact" that some people do have these beliefs. But it is not itself a fact: it is a belief which some people hold.[2]

The chasm between "We know" and "We believe" grew wider in German philosopher Friedrich Nietzsche's subversion of right and wrong in favor of the will. Thus, personal choice reigns. "Values" replace "truth" and "preference" replaces "facts." Modern thought has concluded that either our minds discover or impose a structure on reality (rationalism, idealism) or are blank slates upon which reality writes its truths (empiricism). It is not just the gulf between God and the observable world that is assumed in modernity, but a gulf between the knower and that which is known (i.e., subject and object).

Where rationalism and idealism promised a knowledge of everything, postmodern thinkers who are now repudiating this failed enterprise often revel in "playful" agnosticism with respect to any ultimate truth and meaning. It is reflected in a healthy appreciation for human finitude, but it also takes the form of skepticism: the belief that one cannot really know anything except for one's own subjective feelings and opinions. In other words, it is not just religion that is removed from the realm of truth to that of opinion. This fallacy applies to all knowledge.

That, of course, may work for philosophers and social scientists, anthropologists, literary specialists, and other theoreticians. But even these people go on reading history books as if they conveyed some accurate details of other times. They are still consulting scientific journals for the results of experiments and studies. Common sense operates at a deeper level than sophisticated speculation, and no one can escape it—not even the philosophers who regard common sense as an outdated notion.

Various philosophers of science have led some helpful discussions on this topic in recent years, many of them influenced by Michael Polanyi.[3] How can a modern or postmodern relativist even level charges of inadequacy or foolishness? There are certain things that even the most dedicated scientist assumes before he or she can even begin to doubt other things. For instance, has it ever been proved that the world exists objectively and not simply as a projection of the human mind? We believe that other people exist besides ourselves. But can anyone prove this assumption?

Has an experiment ever proved that the world is rational and open to critical investigation? How can we be certain that rules of logic are true? How can we trust our senses to perceive reality? Scientists advance because they assume these things, and it is only by presupposing these unproved assumptions that they can then begin to investigate and doubt other things. Those who begin and end with doubt, therefore, have no basis for doubt itself. One must believe some things are true in order to doubt or disbelieve in other things.

To be sure, we cannot know everything, and even that which we do know is only known to us in part. This, after all, is affirmed in Scripture: "For now we see in a mirror, dimly, but then face to face. Now I know in part, but then I shall know just as I also am fully known" (1 Cor. 13:12). Nevertheless, to know in part is not to know nothing at all.

The Gospel According to Kant

Immanuel Kant was perhaps the most important modern philosopher. Kant believed that there was an invisible realm to which none of us has access. That realm, which includes God, cannot be observed empirically nor proved rationally. Nevertheless, we have to believe in it: otherwise how could we believe in morality? Newbigin is helpful on this point:

> To the Kantian one may put the question: "How do you know that the unknowable noumenon exists?" And to the one who says that the whole truth of God cannot be disclosed in Jesus Christ, the Christian may fairly ask, "What is the source of your knowledge that this is so?" How does the doubter know so much about the unknowable? . . . But seeking is only serious if the seeker is following some clue. . . . The relativism which is not willing to speak about truth but only about "what is true for me" is an evasion of the serious business of living. It is the mark of a tragic loss of nerve in our contemporary culture. It is a preliminary symptom of death.[4]

Christianity cannot exist as an opinion, for it is a claim to universal truth; public truth, not private sentiment. Unlike other religions, Christianity goes out on a limb when it insists that its claims about what God is like, what we are like, and how God reveals himself and saves are historical in nature. When, for instance, a Buddhist claims belief in Nirvana, or when a Hindu claims belief in reincarnation, these are not argued on the basis of knowledge to which everyone has access. In order to be a Muslim one must simply accept that Mohammed is the prophet of God and the Qu'ran is inspired. But Christianity says that something happened in history that belongs to the public record, like any other historical event.

The life, death, resurrection, ascension, and return of Jesus Christ are not spiritual or moral lessons that are useful even if they never really happened. And their historical character is what makes the religious truth claims valid. If I told you that I had discovered a cure for cancer, when in fact I actually had only discovered how gullible the public is when it comes to a cure for which we desperately search, there would be no way to put a positive spin on my bogus announcement. My students might defend my claim by saying that it represented the universal longing for such a cure and, after all, it gave the world a renewed hope for what could be if we all worked hard enough. But nothing could save such a false announcement from the scorn and mockery of the public.

Similarly, when the stakes are so high, Jesus and his apostles (even the prophets who predicted their existence centuries earlier) cannot be forgiven if the historical claims are false. There is no salvaging the Christian religion by appeals to universal reason or experience being somehow illustrated by these claims.

Modern liberalism insists that what is important in religion is ideas—universal truths that stand above and beyond the historical claims of the Bible. God may or may not have created the world out of nothing; there may have never been a historical Adam who was created in God's image and plunged the race into judgment and depravity; the Exodus may never have really happened except in the lively religious imagination of ancient Jews; a Jewish rabbi may never have been bodily raised from the dead in first-century Palestine. Nevertheless, modern liberals insist, these "myths" are important because they illustrate something that is true and significant: ideas, principles, longings, and hopes. The Bible may be more a revelation of the religious aspirations of human beings than a revelation of God's character and activity in history. However, they assert, that does not mean that it is an insignificant guide to the moral and religious life.

But we cannot apply criteria of judgment to a religion that resists such criteria as alien. Christianity bases all its claims on public events. If these events did not happen, there is no reason to believe that Christianity is a reliable guide to anything except the misguided reflections of a remarkably deluded sect. We will see this in further detail when we discuss the Resurrection.

The claim of Jesus Christ to be the eternal Son of the Father and Lord of the universe is not merely a declaration of private belief; it is a statement of public truth. In a world whose view very much resembles the pluralistic relativism of ancient Athens and Rome, we find that our message is still "foolishness to Greeks and a stumbling block to Jews." Nothing has changed on that front and we must still be willing to stake our lives on those two words, *Christos Kyrios*. Apart from that confession, nothing else is important.

"In Faith, through the Holy Spirit"

In May of 1934, a group of Lutheran and Reformed pastors and theologians gathered to confess the faith in the face of opposition that was not unlike the fires confronted by the first century martyrs. Their gathering was called the Confessional Synod of the German Evangelical Church, convened because the group believed that it was only by confessing the faith that the salt would not lose its savor and become part of the ungodly Reich of Adolf Hitler.

At this point, the Evangelical Church of Germany, dominated by liberalism and pietism, had come to regard doctrines as divisive obstacles to genuine Christian experience and national unity. Many of its leading theologians and leaders mocked Christian truth claims with their own claims to universal knowledge through philosophical idealism and rationalism. And their "enlightened" version of

Christianity as religious and moral sentimentalism made it possible for them to officially adopt the Nazi dogmas, to embrace Hitler as the leader, and to change the name of the Evangelical Church to the Reich's Church.

In opposition to this apostasy, the Confessing Synod drafted the Barmen Declaration. The preamble declared, "In opposition to attempts to establish the unity of the German Evangelical Church by means of false doctrine, by the use of force and insincere practices, the Confessing Synod insists that the unity of the Evangelical Churches in Germany can come only from the Word of God in faith through the Holy Spirit."

The Synod's first article insisted, "The inviolable foundation of the German Evangelical Church is the gospel of Jesus Christ as it is attested for us in Holy Scripture and brought to light again in the Confessions of the Reformation. . . . We are bound together by the confession of one Lord of the one, holy, catholic, and apostolic church," they said.

When one of the leaders of the Confessing Synod met with Hitler, he informed the dictator that the church has only one king and one messiah. Arrested shortly thereafter by the Gestapo, Pastor Martin Niemöller was acquitted by the court, but was then immediately sent to Sachsenhausen and Dachau as Hitler's "personal prisoner." Although he was liberated by the Allied troops in 1945, a number of other Confessing pastors did not fare so well. Among them was the martyr Dietrich Bonhoeffer.

"My Jewels . . . My Festive Dress"

For the leaders of the Confessing Synod, confessing Christ as God's Son and our Lord was not merely a matter of official assent to church teachings. It involved the personal embrace of Jesus Christ himself. In a sermon on Jesus' parable of the wedding garment, Niemöller attacked the idea that the great enemy of Christianity is atheism and immorality. "That is a man-made thought, but it will not do the moment God approaches us: 'Friend, how camest thou in hither not having a wedding garment?'"

The garment is not a matter of indifference to him. We must repent—put off our old garment of self-righteousness, which is really sin, and believe in Christ—which is to wear his righteousness instead. "Dear friends," Niemöller said, "that is the real temptation for us church Christians:

> I do not speak of those who come to church to hear something special or interesting, something that is not in the newspapers. "Verily they have their reward." Nor do I speak of those who come to spy, to catch the Lord Jesus Christ and to nail Him to the cross. They too have their reward. I am thinking of us who come again and again and cannot make up our minds to say good-bye to our own self-righteousness, so that we may give ourselves up wholly to the merciful grace of God. "Many are called but few are chosen." Do we belong—no, do you belong—no, do I belong to those chosen few, who build their hope and their trust wholly upon grace, because they know that Christ the Lord won God's grace for us on the cross? May God help us, we pray, to believe and to learn to profess our belief:
>
> > "Christ's precious blood and righteousness
> > My jewels are, my festive dress.
> > Clad in this glorious robe of grace
> > Boldly I'll stand before God's face."[5]

At the end of the day, to confess, "I believe in Jesus Christ, [God's] only Son, our Lord," is not merely to know the truth and to accept it as public truth, but to trust in the person who comes to us wrapped in the promises and declarations of Scripture. The devil is quite orthodox. Unlike those he seduces, he never questions the deity or lordship of Christ as objective truths, for even now the rattling chains that bind him to his dark cell remind him of these truths. But faith *in* is more than faith *that*. Many will be condemned on the last day who believed the correct doctrine, but never allowed those precious truths to lead them by the hand to the person about whom they spoke so eloquently.

Do we trust in Christ as both the universal Lord and our own Redeeming King? His eternal deity must banish all rival princes to exile. His claim to the royal title over heaven and earth must receive our fullest homage. Individually, this means that we must declare war on our own sinful hearts and continue in that battle, however often we fail, until we are safe on the other side of the front. Corporately, it means that we must dethrone the forces of modernity that work against the kingdom of Christ even as they promise to us the kingdoms of this world.

No longer can we allow politics, marketing methods, pragmatism, and the claims of consumerism, therapy, or abstract religious experience and speculation to reign in the church. As our supreme prophet, Christ's word alone is to be believed and obeyed. As our supreme priest, his redeeming, justifying, and sanctifying work alone must be relied upon. As our supreme King, his revealed will alone must guide and direct the mission and methods of the church.

As he liberated his people from Egyptian bondage and led her by his sovereign command, so too we can only believe in Jesus Christ, owning him as God's Son and our Lord, because he has taken us for himself as his covenant people. Surrounded by the cloud of witnesses in the heavenly arena, may we also receive God's grace to confess, "Jesus Christ is Lord," by the power of the Holy Spirit, to the glory of God the Father.

FOUR

What If God Were One of Us?

. . . WHO WAS CONCEIVED BY THE HOLY GHOST AND BORN OF THE VIRGIN MARY.

A top hit on the pop rock charts in 1996, Joan Osborne's "What If God Was One of Us" wondered aloud what it might be like to run into God on a bus. What if he were "just a slob like all of us," trying to get home after work? Do you really believe that God was one of us? Has it settled in that the Almighty Creator and Ruler, the Eternal Son and Sovereign Lord, has actually become and remains this very moment "one of us"?

A Tale of Two Seeds

The amazing story of Jesus' incarnation begins in the early chapters of Genesis. When she gave birth to her first son, Eve named him Cain ("Here He Is") probably thinking that he was the promised son who would crush the serpent's head and roll back the curse. After judgment has been pronounced, the Gospel is warmly announced: "And I will put enmity between you and the woman, and between your seed and her Seed," God told the serpent. "He shall crush your head, and you shall bruise His heel" (Gen. 3:15). From that moment on, the serpent began his historic struggle to defeat the advance of the messianic line.

If he could somehow hide in the shadows to bring nations against the covenanted lineage and intercept even one link in the chain of succession to the Seed, perhaps he could overthrow God's redemptive intentions. Better yet, if the evil one could only corrupt the line of descent by leading the dynasty of faith into apostasy and intermarriage with the sons and daughters of unbelief, there would be no one left to carry forward the messianic hope.

We see examples of both strategies in the next few chapters of Genesis. In Genesis 4, Cain murders Abel, God's first prophet after Adam's fall, as Jesus himself acknowledged (Matt. 23:35). "By faith, Abel offered a sacrifice that was pleasing to God" (Heb. 11:4), so Cain slays his brother out of anger.

Has Lucifer succeeded in making a mockery out of God's promise? Not at all. In Abel's place God sends Seth, which means, "Elect One." Seth would carry the torch to another generation. And when the two genealogies are set side by side at the end of the chapter, Cain's line is described by its worldly accomplishments in the city of man, while Seth's line is distinguished by the announcement, "Then people began to call on the name of the LORD" (Gen. 4:26).

In spite of the new hopes raised by a new son, Seth's family line eventually became less interested in God than in worldly success. As the generations passed, they grew increasingly corrupt. "Now it came to pass, when men began to multiply on the face of the earth, and daughters were born to them, that the sons of God saw the daughters of men, that they were beautiful; and they took wives for themselves of all whom they chose" (Gen. 6:1–2).

Eve had taken the fruit "when she saw that it was pleasing to the eye and desirable to make one wise." And now the sons of God saw that the daughters of men "were very beautiful." Children were born from these unions of Sethites and Cainites and the people were no longer holy, set apart to the Lord. Had the serpent triumphed at last?

Noah was one "son of God" who was still faithful to the covenant of grace. Although he was a sinner who could only stand before God because of divine mercy, Noah "walked with God." "By faith Noah, being divinely warned of things not yet seen, moved with godly fear, prepared an ark for the saving of his household, by which he condemned the world and became heir of the righteousness which is according to faith" (Heb. 11:7). Satan had lost yet another match.

After the flood, Noah's son Ham was expelled from the covenant family as Cain had been, but Noah's believing son Shem became the heir of the promise. God also promised to bring Shem's brother Japheth's descendants into the tents of Shem. Here we have an early promise to bring the Gentile nations into the church. Shem became the father of the Semitic peoples, but his line too eventually became corrupt until there was only one man left: Abram. God found Abram in Ur of the Chaldeans, a land full of superstition. This godly line, including Abram's father, had now become so apostate that it had adopted the pagan worship of the moon.

God called Abram out of this darkness and made him the patriarch of the dynasty of faith. From Genesis 12 to 20, we see Abram wandering between faith and unbelief. Although God had promised him a son to inherit the promise, Abram was quite old and his wife Sarai, in her late nineties, had been barren throughout their marriage. In unbelief, they took their salvation into their own hands and turned to their slave Hagar for procreation, with Ishmael as their offspring. Notwithstanding their efforts, God had made it clear that the promise was to provide the promised seed by Sarah, not by Hagar.

God placed before Abram tokens of his faithfulness in spite of the patriarch's infidelity. He showed Abram the starry hosts and told him that his offspring would be as innumerable. While Abram was asleep, God appeared to him in a vision, taking part in a legal ceremony that was common in the ancient world. When treaties were concluded, the representative of both parties would walk together between animals that had been cut in half, each side of the carcass placed on either side of the aisle.

In this way, they were calling down the same fate upon their own heads if they were unfaithful to the compact. But in Abram's vision, God was walking between the halves alone. Taking all of the burden of salvation upon his own shoulders, God was by this ritual calling down all of his own curses upon his head if the promise in any way failed to be fulfilled. Despite these reassuring tokens, and the sacrament of circumcision, Abram was still willing to lie his way to the promise rather than trust in the Lord who provides. And yet, this did not change God's determination to provide in spite of Abram's sinful wavering and Sarai's unbelief.

In Genesis 17, Abram ("father") became Abraham ("father of many"), and Sarai was Sarah. Finally Isaac was born (Gen. 21). "For Sarah conceived and bore Abraham a son in his old age, at the set time of which God had spoken to him" (v. 2). That phrase, "at the set time of which God had spoken to him," was repeated in connection with the greater Son to come (Gal. 4:4). God's timetable of redemption was set in motion before the creation of the world and was now being made manifest in history.

As Ishmael and Isaac grew up together, the time came when God commanded Abraham to send the elder son away from the covenant community. He was not the son of promise, but the son of bondage, and the two covenants—one by grace, the other by works—could not be confused (Gal. 4:21–31). The two lines of descent once more come into sharp contrast and as Cain had persecuted Abel, the seed of Ishmael would become the age-old enemies of Israel's peace. But just as it seemed that the covenant was secure and the succession of the promised messiah protected, God commanded Abraham to take his son to Mount Moriah and sacrifice him there (Gen. 22). Although Isaac was Abraham's son of promise, his only son, the patriarch by now had learned to trust in *Yahweh-Jireh,* "The Lord Will Provide."

Although the command seems to flatly contradict the promise, Abraham trusted God that the promise would win out in the end. However God decided to solve this problem, Abraham was convinced that he would. When they reached the place of sacrifice, Isaac asked his father, "Where is the lamb for the burnt offering?" Abraham replied, "The Lord will provide the lamb." He did not know how God's command could fail to extinguish the bright light of the promise, but he trusted in his covenant-keeping Savior.

Just as the knife was descending, and Abraham was about to sacrifice his son, the angel of the Lord intervened and ended the ordeal. A ram caught in a bush suddenly appeared and took Isaac's place on the altar of sacrifice. It would be on this very mountain that David would receive his audience with God and that Solomon would build his splendid temple. And on this very spot, a place of crucifixion in Roman times, another "ram" would be sacrificed in the place of sinners. God's people lived in the future hope of that divine name, Yahweh-Jireh, "The Lord Will Provide."

Isaac had two sons also, Esau (his firstborn) and Jacob. God had chosen Jacob as the heir of the promise, even though it seemed to flatly contradict human reason once again. First of all, in the ancient world, the firstborn son always received most of the family inheritance. Second, Esau was morally superior to his younger sibling. Jacob was a schemer who was, as the saying goes, "tied to his mother's apron strings."

Jacob was hardly a likely candidate for sainthood. Esau was not quite as smart as Jacob, but he was hardworking and loyal to his father. Nevertheless, God decreed "Jacob have I loved, and Esau have I hated" (see Romans 9). The covenant of grace is never merited, but is freely given by God's own merciful will to whomever he chooses.

One night, while running from his brother, Jacob fell asleep and had a dream. A ladder extended—not from earth to heaven, but from heaven to earth. Angels were ascending and descending this ladder. God himself stood above it, renewing his covenant oath to Jacob and his offspring. After waking up, Jacob exclaimed, "Surely this is the House of God and the Gate of Heaven" (Gen. 28:17). Ages later, Jacob's long-awaited heir would refer to himself as this ladder, this house of God and gate of heaven, with angels ascending and descending (John 1:51).

Again and again we find the warfare between the spiritual descendants of the serpent and the heirs of promise acted out with such intensity that the reader waits in breathless anticipation to learn the outcome. Esau's descendants, like Cain and Ishmael, sought the destruction of the chosen seed.

Although Joseph was the second youngest of Jacob's sons, he received a vision from the Lord proclaiming him the heir, and Jacob accepted this as God's will. Out of a jealousy reminiscent of Cain's, Joseph's brothers threw him into a well, expecting never to hear from him again. Had the serpent triumphed? Not at all, for eventually Joseph's brothers came to Egypt begging for relief from a famine only to discover that the prime minister is no less than their persecuted sibling. "You meant it for evil," Joseph tells his brothers, "but God meant it for good" (Gen. 50:20).

The Continuing War

By the time of Moses, the family of God was in Egyptian slavery but was growing in number. Worried that their slaves might become so numerous and mighty that they would threaten Egyptian security, Pharaoh commanded that every son born to the Hebrews be thrown into the Nile, while the daughters were to be spared.

How could the covenant line prevail against this wholesale slaughter? Would there be a single son of promise left to carry the line of succession to the Messiah? One Jewish woman, upon giving birth to a son, placed him in an ark of reeds next to the river's bank. Pharaoh's daughter discovered the floating box, spared the infant's life, and became his adopted mother.

Eventually Moses became the patriarch of the covenant of grace, leading the church out of Egyptian slavery through the Red Sea, across the desert toward the Promised Land. Yet, even after being liberated by God's redeeming grace, Israel rebelled in the wilderness. Even at the foot of Mount Sinai, while God was giving his Law, Israel was engaging in drunken revelry around a golden calf.

Throughout Israel's wilderness experience, God was judging and saving, separating the "sheep" from the "goats," purifying a people for himself who would carry on the covenant succession. God allowed Moses only to see the Promised Land before he died. The blessing of leading the people in was to be given to Joshua, whose name means, "The LORD Is the One Who Saves."

After God commissioned Joshua to cross the Jordan and claim the Promised Land, Joshua sent spies ahead to survey the territory. "So they went, and came to the house of a prostitute named Rahab, and lodged there" (Josh. 2:1). As Pharaoh's daughter had protected Moses from the massacre of Israel's sons, so Rahab protected the spies from the king of Jericho. Rahab informed the spies that news had reached them that God had delivered Israel from Egypt. "I know that the LORD has given you the land . . .," she said. "And as soon as we heard these things, our hearts melted; neither did there remain any more courage in anyone because of you, for the LORD your God, he is God in heaven above and on earth below" (Josh. 2:8–11).

Rahab was instructed by the spies to hang a scarlet cord from her window, so that when Israel conquered the land, she would be saved. Already we see the promise of Gentile sinners being incorporated into the church. Centuries later, Rahab was honored in Matthew's genealogy as an ancestor of Jesus (Matt. 1:5). And in Hebrews 11:31 she is included in the succession of the covenant, an adopted daughter of Israel, justified by faith.

Now in the Land, Israel was governed by judges who were also God's prophets. But even in the Promised Land God's people grew corrupt, as "everyone did what was good in his own eyes" (Judg. 21:25). A whole new generation had forgotten God's saving grace (Judg. 2:7–11). Abimelech organized a massacre of his own brothers in order to secure his place as ruler of Israel. Hired assassins slaughtered the "first family," all seventy sons of Jerubbaal. "But Jotham the youngest son of Jerubbaal was left, because he hid himself" (Judg. 9:5). From his mountain hideaway, Jotham cried out for judgment and finally one day, a woman dropped a stone from a tower and crushed Abimelech's head, a harbinger of things to come for Lucifer himself. Through Jotham, a seed was once again preserved for the Lord.

Later, after all that God had done to prove that he was her king, Israel wanted human kings like the surrounding nations. Her first king was Saul, a man of divided sympathies. When the young shepherd David defeated Goliath and received the approval of God and the people, Saul was filled with jealous rage and persecuted David, seeking to murder God's appointed ruler. Once more, God interrupted the enemy's designs and preserved his messianic line. David was anointed king, and he won numerous battles in the Lord's strength as he drove the idolaters from the Land of Promise. He even won Jerusalem for Israel.

Before long, however, even David, "the man after God's own heart," fell into grievous sin, committing adultery with Bathsheba. Worse yet, he sought to cover up his sin by purposely sending his loyal officer Uriah, Bathsheba's husband, to his death during battle (2 Sam. 11). As a result, David's royal house became a source of great heartache and misery even after the king had confessed his sin and obtained God's mercy.

Again and again the messianic line was threatened, more by apostasy within than by enemy forces without. King Ahab instituted Baal worship in Israel, even sacrificing his firstborn son and placing his corpse in the foundation of the pagan temple (1 Kings 16). Ahab's wife Jezebel massacred God's prophets, but a young prophet named Elijah was hidden in a cave.

Proclaiming God's judgment was not a popular thing in Elijah's day, and he escaped from Queen Jezebel to the wilderness. He prayed, "I have been very zealous for the LORD God of hosts; for the children of Israel have forsaken your covenant, torn down your altars, and killed your prophets with the sword. I alone am left; and they seek to take my life" (1 Kings 19:10). Through this one man, God drove out the prophets of Baal and eventually condemned Ahab. In spite of Israel's unfaithfulness, God was still loyal to his covenant.

Who Is the Real Hero?

In the foregoing saga, we have left out many other key figures in redemptive history. But there is enough here to make the point underscored by the writer to the Hebrews after he listed the successors in this dynasty of faith:

> And what more shall we say? For the time would fail me to tell of Gideon and Barak and Samson and Jephthah, also of David and Samuel and the prophets: who through faith subdued kingdoms, worked righteousness, obtained promises, stopped the mouths of lions, quenched the violence of fire, escaped the edge of the sword, out of weakness were made strong, became valiant in battle, turned to flight the armies of the aliens. Women received their dead raised to life again. Others were tortured, not accepting deliverance, that they might obtain a better resurrection. . . . They were stoned, they were sawn in two, were slain with the sword. . . . And all these, having obtained a good testimony through faith, did not receive the promise, God having provided something better for us, that they should not be made perfect apart from us. (Heb. 11:32–40)

What is this apostle telling us, when he says that these heroes did not receive the promise? Like Eve, who thought she had given birth to the Messiah only to discover that Cain was the first antichrist, and like Moses, who led Israel through the wilderness but never himself crossed into the Promised Land, the Old Testament saints were saved by looking forward to the fulfillment of the promise. We, however, belong to the age of fulfillment itself! Only together with us do these men and women of promise actually inherit the true resting place. Only in our company do they experience the arrival of the seed of the woman, the Son of man, the Son of Abraham, and Son of David, and the heir of salvation.

Finally, it becomes clear: The Old Testament is not about heroes of faith at all. After all, even the best among them were (and are) corrupt and weak in both faith and obedience. The real hero of this story is God himself, who is faithful to his promise in spite of every obstacle.

The serpent did not take this well. As in the days of Ahab, a wicked king sat on Israel's throne. Herod was a petty feudal lord who ruled Palestine by the permission of Rome. He had received word from foreign dignitaries that one had been born who would become the "king of the Jews." These foreign rulers, known popularly as the "wise men," had come to worship the child. Unwilling to surrender his title to an unknown child, Herod devised a plan. Like Pharaoh's massacre of Israel's male sons, Herod slaughtered all the male children in and around Bethlehem, certain that this would eliminate any future problems.

But once again, the divine plan eluded the serpent's strategies. The Lord had already commanded Joseph to take Mary and the child to Egypt until Herod's death. Thus Numbers 24:8 and Hosea 11:1 were fulfilled: "Out of Egypt I called my Son." Just as Isaac had been born to Abraham and Sarah "in the fullness of time," so "when the fullness of the time had come, God sent for His Son, born of a woman, born under the law, to redeem those who were under the law, that we might receive the adoption as sons" (Gal. 4:4). A Christmas carol celebrates the "little town of Bethlehem" where "the hopes and fears of all the years are met." World history had arrived at the birth of its most central figure: Israel's long-awaited Messiah.

Belief in the Virgin Birth

Until the modern age, Christians everywhere and in all places have staked their claims about the Messiah on the Old Testament promise and New Testament announcement of his virginal conception. It is better, by the way, to speak of the virginal conception than the virgin birth. There was, after all, nothing supernatural about Christ's birth: he was born in the ordinary way, no differently than any other healthy child who has been brought into this world. But the Christian claim is that in Nazareth, where the Holy Spirit came to Mary, God became a zygote in the uterus of a Jewish virgin who was pledged to be married to Joseph.

After carefully listing the genealogy of Jesus Christ from Abraham, Isaac, and Jacob, through Judah, and then finally leading to Joseph, Mary's husband, Matthew says that before the consummation of their marriage Mary was "found with child of the Holy Spirit" (Matt. 1:18). At first Joseph assumed that Mary was not a virgin. But an angel of the Lord appeared to him in a dream, saying, "Joseph, son of David, do not be afraid to take to you Mary your wife, for that which is conceived in her is of the Holy Spirit. And she will bring forth a son, and you shall call his name JESUS, for he will save his people from their sins" (vv. 20–21).

Luke similarly reports the angel's announcement: "And behold, you will conceive in your womb and bring forth a son, and shall call his name JESUS. He will be great, and will be called the Son of the Highest; and the Lord God will give him the throne of his father David. And he will reign over the house of Jacob forever, and of his kingdom there will be no end" (Luke 1:31–33).

Frightened, Mary asked how this will happen. "And the angel answered and said to her, 'The Holy Spirit will come upon you, and the power of the Highest will overshadow you; therefore, also, that Holy One who is to be born will be called the Son of God'" (v. 35).

It is important, first of all, to note that the question, "Can we still believe in the virgin conception?" assumes a great deal of modern baggage. It is like asking, "Can we still believe in tooth fairies or Santa Claus?" But has science discovered anything at all that would throw doubt on the historic claim of the virginal conception of Christ? To be sure, there have been assumptions in the modern world that presuppose the impossibility of miracles, but are these assumptions themselves proved by any scientific or historical discovery?

One of the ways of dealing with this question is to discuss the external, historical evidences for Christian truth claims, and to trace those evidences back to this particular claim. We can apply one of the most powerful arguments within the biblical text itself: fulfilled prophecy. While the Bible is full of a rich variety of literary genres and tropes, its most outstanding feature is its narrative quality. In other words, the Bible tells stories. And these stories are not treated as myths that are intended to illustrate some more important point: the story is their point.

Against the Pharisees, Jesus said, "You search the Scriptures, for in them you think you have eternal life; and these are they which testify of me. But you are not willing to come to me that you may have life" (John 5:39).

He was, of course, referring to the Old Testament Scriptures, just as he was when he opened up the Scriptures on the Emmaus Road with the grieving disciples there. "And beginning at Moses and all the Prophets, he expounded to them in all the Scriptures the things concerning himself" (Luke 24:27). They too had known these Scriptures, and yet they failed to see that they all pointed to the events that they themselves had just experienced. It was a terrific case of missing the forest for the trees.

Once we truly grasp the message of the New Testament, it is impossible to read the Old Testament again without seeing Christ on every page, in every story, foreshadowed or anticipated in every event and narrative. The Bible must be read as a whole, beginning with Genesis and ending with Revelation, letting promise and fulfillment guide our expectations for what we will find there.

We have already seen that the Old Testament anticipated a Messiah who was no less than Yahweh himself, God the Son and yet also the Son of man. The Gospel writers, especially Luke, labor to make the point that Jesus Christ is not only fully God, but fully human as well. To be sure, Israel was looking for God himself— "Immanuel: God with Us"—but this coming Redeemer also had to be from a particular line of genealogical descent. He was not only to sit at the Father's right hand in heaven, but on the throne of his father David, as a legal descendant of the royal house. God had faithfully preserved a royal seed, and he was born king of the Jews regardless of imperial permission.

The Old Testament itself required a Messiah who was legally descended from God's chosen royal line. He had to be not only God by nature and human by appearance, but both God and man by nature. Not only was this expected in the biblical narrative, but it was required by the theology of the Old Testament. As Anselm argued in the eleventh century, the Savior had to be God in order to achieve our salvation by paying an infinite price and rising again, but he had to be man in order to be a true legal representative of Adam and his chosen seed. Only God *could* save, but only a man *should* save. It was, after all, humanity that owed the debt. In his person, therefore, we have the union of two distinct natures, divine and human, so that the child of Mary was nothing less than God and nothing less than man.

If the biblical narratives are intended merely to illustrate higher moral or spiritual truths, then it is not only possible but commendable to distinguish the universal truths of reason and experience from the reports of actual, historical events that happen to be miraculous. One should, in that case, keep the higher lesson and disregard the historical claims.

It bears repeating: Christianity rests not on philosophical ideas outside of the text, but on the authority of the claims themselves. They either actually happened or there is no Christian faith: those are the only choices (1 Cor. 15:14–19). To say that these events did not happen—that, for instance, the virginal conception is impossible for enlightened people to believe—is at least honest, even if it is hopelessly committed to circular reasoning. But to deny these reports while claiming to derive some benefit from them sufficient to call oneself a Christian is impossible to defend, given the nature of the story itself.

There is no recourse to sentimentality here: we cannot say that we believe in Jesus the way we believe in Santa, by believing in that which he represents. A version of the Christian story that eliminates the virginal conception is already a different story altogether. If one chooses not to accept these reports as describing something that actually happened, then the story has exhausted its potential. It will not yield higher dividends. But this is good news for those who realize that what they need most is not a great hero or example, but a second Adam, "to fulfill all righteousness," so that sinners could be reconciled to God.

The Two Natures of Christ

While the Creed of Nicea (A.D. 325) established the consensus concerning the Son as God, controversies continued concerning the deity and humanity of Jesus Christ: Is he equally God and man? Was his humanity swallowed up into his deity, or vice versa? Or were both natures so divided that the identity of Jesus as a single human being was threatened, as if his humanity and deity were like two boards glued together?

On one side of the debate stood the Eutychians, who said that the two natures were mingled. On the other stood the Nestorians, who said that the two natures were separated. Other heresies along the spectrum included Apollinarianism, which tried to evade the difficulty by simply denying Christ's true humanity. The Docetists, influenced by the Gnostic heresy which regarded matter as evil, had already argued that Jesus was not fully human, but that he only appeared to have a human body. (It's this heresy that John attacks, in 1 John 1:1–4; 4:1–3.)

What all of these answers shared was a satisfaction of human curiosity. As with the doctrine of the Trinity, we are not satisfied to simply accept something that we cannot totally comprehend. Here we need to distinguish between *comprehending* the truth and *contradicting* the truth. To say that God is One and Three is a contradiction only if we say that he is both in the same way and at the same time (i.e., God is One in person and Three in person). But that is not what Christianity teaches. Instead, it teaches that God is One in *essence* and Three in *person.*

Similarly, it is not a contradiction to say that Jesus is both fully God and fully man. It is, however, incomprehensible. We cannot fully get our cognitive arms around it. We understand it enough to assent to it, but not enough to satisfy our curiosity. It is just at that point that the orthodox are willing to keep silent before the mystery (since it isn't a contradiction), while heresies are carried aloft on the wings of speculation.

The best summary of the biblical material on this topic is the Creed of Chalcedon (A.D. 451):

Following, then, the holy fathers, we unite in teaching all men to confess the one and only Son, our Lord Jesus Christ. This selfsame one is perfect both in deity and also in humanness; this selfsame one is also actually God and actually man, with a rational soul and a body. He is of the same reality as God as far as his deity is concerned and of the same reality as we are ourselves as far as his humanness is concerned; thus like us in all respects, sin only excepted. Before time began he was begotten of the Father, in respect of his deity, and now in these "last days," for us and on behalf of our salvation, this selfsame one was born of Mary the virgin, who is God-bearer in respect of his humanness.

We also teach that we apprehend this one and only Christ—Son, Lord, only-begotten—in two natures; and we do this without confusing the two natures, without transmuting one nature into the other, without dividing them into two separate categories, without contrasting them according to area or function. The distinctiveness of each nature is not nullified by the union. Instead, the "properties" of each nature are conserved and both natures concur in one "person" and in one hypostasis. They are not divided or cut into two prosopa, but are together the one and only and only-begotten Logos of God, the Lord Jesus Christ. Thus have the prophets of old testified; thus the Lord Jesus Christ himself taught us; thus the Symbol [Creed] of the Fathers has handed down to us.

The two natures of Christ should not be confused, transfused, or comingled on one hand (the Eutychian temptation). Neither should they be divided or separated (the Nestorian temptation). The divine and human natures remain distinct, but not separate: union without confusion.

Each nature possesses the attributes appropriate to it. Jesus' humanity means that he not only has a human body but a human mind and soul. He is not a deified man. But then he is also not a humanized God: even as he lay in Mary's womb for nine months and walked along the streets of Galilee or Jerusalem, he continued to fill the heavens and the earth according to his omnipresent and omnipotent Godhead. If we are willing to accept and joyfully embrace this mystery, our curiosity may not be satisfied, but we will avoid the easy way out which is provided by heresy. Such remarkable truths are matter for praise rather than for speculation.

What About Today?

We live in a superspiritual era. Whereas the modern age has consistently eroded public confidence in the supernatural, postmodern reactions have unleashed a maelstrom of "spiritualities." But spirituality is no better friend of the Apostles' Creed than atheism. By affirming that God became fully human in the womb of Mary, to the point of sharing her human ancestry (and legally, Joseph's as well) and the physical characteristics that go along with that, the apostolic eyewitnesses dealt a serious blow to superspiritual religion. However, various groups in every age, whether the ancient Gnostics, medieval Manichean sects, radical Anabaptists, and enthusiasts on the fringes of American Protestantism, have had problems with the idea that God became a man.

First of all, they insist, the body is intrinsically evil. Furthermore, aren't we supposed to be saved from the body and from this world? It just does not seem spiritual enough. But the Scriptures are quite explicit here. We are alienated from God not because of our physical existence, but because of our guilt and rebellious hearts. God became flesh in order to save us, both our souls and bodies, and to make all things new in heaven and on earth.

We are also reminded by this biblical truth that God comes near to us. It is he who always takes the initiative. Like Adam and Eve, we are always running from God. But he catches up to us. Finally, after millennia of human history, God the Son actually laid aside his majesty, power, happiness, and wealth to become low and weak through suffering and poverty.

In the beginning we saw the importance of recovering a healthy sense of God's distance from us: his exalted status that makes him worthy of worship. "I believe in God the Father Almighty, Creator of Heaven and Earth" establishes this Creator-creature distinction, but not a Creator-creature dualism. God and human beings are not opposites: it is not because we are fully human that we are at odds with God, but because we are sinfully human. In rebellion against God, we rebel against our true humanity. By taking on our humanity, God restores its dignity and splendor.

The fact that God became fully human underscores the fact that the problem lies not in our humanness, but in our sinfulness. In Christ, the Creator-creature distinction remains—even within himself, the divine and human natures retain the proper qualities belonging to each. Nevertheless, Christ's incarnation ends forever false dualisms between the divine and the human, the sacred and the secular, the soul and the body, God and the world. In this doctrine, we see the nearness of this exalted God: "Immanuel: God with Us."

Toward the close of the last century, the German nihilist Friedrich Nietzsche announced God's alleged death, and by the late 1950s and early 1960s a band of radical American theologians announced the divine funeral. It is important to realize that the "god" who actually died was not Immanuel. It was, instead, the idol of modern men and women who wanted to remove the real God from the scene. Western humanists had devised a distant deity who created, but then stepped aside and left things to natural laws—laws they could then discover and control.

The "god" of modern men and women was a deity who gave birth to its own sons: "progress," "optimism," "triumph," "race," "class," "nation," "ideology," "morality," and any other ideas that would justify, in Nietzsche's words, "the will to power." No wonder Westerners, waking up with a hangover the morning after the party that has left their home in rubble, decided to put God on trial or to simply lynch him in an act of mob violence.

This helpless and remote idol, of course, was not the God who is actually there. Far from the God of Abraham, Isaac, and Jacob, or of Athanasius, Luther, and Calvin, he was the creation of modern people who wanted to be gods themselves. Thank God, *that* god really is dead!

It is also important for us to know that there is no characteristic that belongs to us as human beings that did not belong to our Redeemer, except sin. Far from a distant judge who cannot sympathize with our weaknesses, Jesus Christ faced the same threats, hopes, fears, dreams, temptations, joys, pleasures, and disappointments that we experience throughout our lives. There he is, providing the best wine for a wedding reception, enjoying the company of friends among the moral and social outcasts, screaming out at death with tears streaming down his face as he suffers at his friend's grave. *God* with us, to be sure. But God with *us*. For Christians, "What if God were one of us?" is no idle question. God was one of us. That is reality. It is a claim upon which we are willing to stake our very destinies.

FIVE

Behold, the Lamb!

+❖+   +❖+   +❖+

HE SUFFERED UNDER
PONTIUS PILATE, WAS CRUCIFIED,
DIED, AND WAS BURIED;
HE DESCENDED INTO HELL.

At the heart of most religions is a moral code. At the heart of
Christianity is a cross, planted in the middle history. The ancient
equivalent of the modern electric chair, in its day the cross was a
symbol of defeat rather than victory. So why does the death of
Christ continue to be viewed as salvation-bearing by Christians?

Waiting for Godot

In his 1952 play, *En Attendant Godot* (Waiting for Godot), Irish nov-
elist Samuel Beckett placed his two central characters, Estragon and
Vladimir, in a music hall where, throughout the entire play, they are
(as the title suggests) waiting for the arrival of someone named
Godot. Making the most of the boredom, they carry on a dialogue

that highlights the tragic despair of human existence. Godot never arrives, and the play ends in resignation to hopelessness.

This motif, so characteristic of existentialism, is actually quite familiar to readers of the Bible. It is evident in Moses, a weary hero who strikes the wilderness rock in his frustration, with the result that God refuses to allow him to enter the land before his death. Much later, we see, during Israel's Babylonian captivity:

"The harvest is past,
the summer is ended,
and we are not saved!"

Jeremiah weeps for his people:

"Is there no balm in Gilead,
Is there no physician there?
Why then is there no recovery
for the health of the daughter of my people?"
(Jer. 8:20, 22)

God works his plans out in history, not all at once, but in stages. And that means that the humans involved have to wait to see his word fulfilled.

From the very beginning of the initial Gospel announcement, depicted by God's clothing of the disgraced couple in the skins of a sacrificial animal, a pattern of worship is established: Only by the sacrifice of a substitute can one appear before God. Abel revealed his faith in the future Lamb of God by offering the first-born of his flock, while Cain chose his own way of worship.

"By faith Abel offered God a better sacrifice than Cain did. By faith he was commended as a righteous man, when God spoke well of his offerings. And by faith he still speaks, even though he is dead" (Heb. 11:3–4 NIV).

As Jesus commended Abel as the first prophet of the Messiah (Matt. 23:35), so Cain is the first antichrist, the first persecutor of the Christ's church. In this ancient story the whole of redemptive history is already swirling around the question: How can sinners stand in God's presence without being consumed by his wrath?

We have seen how, in calling Abraham to carry forward God's redemptive program, God promised him a son from Sarah's barren and aged womb. In the ceremony of the animals cut in half, God accepted the burden for the curses in the event that Abraham and his heirs should be unfaithful.

God fulfilled the first stage toward the greater realization of this promise with the birth of Isaac, and with his miraculous provision of a sacrificial ram at the instant of Abraham's obedient sacrifice of his only son. Indeed, the Lord had provided the lamb for the burnt offering, so the patriarch called the place, "The LORD Will Provide." "As it is said to this day," we read in Genesis 22:14, "'In the Mount of the LORD it shall be provided.'"

In later years, the whole ritual life of the nation of Israel revolved around a bloody altar, where the high priest offered sacrifices that redeemed the people, and foreshadowed the Lamb to come.

From Joshua to David, the forerunners of the Messiah set out to drive the serpent from the garden, as Adam failed to do in Eden. Leading the army of Israel, God secured the nation's place in his holy land and once again there was heaven-in-miniature, a holy space on earth where God dwelled among his people. God's kingdom was identified as the nation-state of Israel and wherever his people went out in battle, he was the true King whose arm secured victory. The purpose of Israel was to mirror heaven. Israel's earthly worship was to mirror the heavenly choir; the earthly king was to merely reflect the righteous king of heaven. All this was made possible by the earthly sacrifices that foreshadowed the Lamb of God who would descend from paradise and bear away God's wrath in his own person.

And yet, like Adam, Israel failed as the servant of the Great King, and she was exiled from the divine presence. Again, the kingdom of God was removed to heaven, the worshipers were carried off as foreign prisoners, and the absence of the Spirit from the temple left the land cursed with thorns. Just as the cherubim had been placed at the eastern gate of Eden, barring re-entrance to fallen humanity, so these angelic princes guarded the eastern gate of the temple. Without the presence of God, Israel was simply another nation and the prophets of the exiles place the blame squarely on Israel, not on her foreign invaders.

One notices from reading the prophets that the most important factor in God's withdrawal from among his people had to do with worship. Repeatedly, Israel would seek more "user-friendly" gods like those of the nations, idols that would bless and never judge. They could follow their sinful ways without being constantly confronted by the I AM of the Exodus and Mount Sinai.

Nevertheless, God's covenant of grace is eternal. While his covenant with the nation of Israel, as with Adam, was conditioned on obedience, individuals were only redeemed by the unconditional promise made to Adam and Eve and repeated throughout biblical history. The Messiah would fulfill the obedience that Adam and Israel failed to attain. He would secure salvation. He would establish an eternal kingdom whose endurance would not depend on the fickle hearts of fallen men and women. "I will make a covenant of peace with them; it will be an everlasting covenant. I will establish them and increase their numbers, and I will put my sanctuary among them forever. My dwelling place will be with them; I will be their God, and they will be my people" (Ezek. 37:26–28 NIV).

Behold, the Lamb!

Finally, the day dawned. "Godot" arrived!

John the Baptist had the unspeakable honor of being the herald of the glad tidings that had been prophesied from the time of Abel: "Behold, the Lamb of God who takes away the sin of the world!" (John 1:29). Jesus was not only the Lamb, but also the high priest.

In Hebrews 10:3–4, the writer assures us that the sacrifices of the Old Testament could not actually take away sins, but could only cover believers who were awaiting the true sacrifice. "But when this priest had offered for all time one sacrifice for sins, he sat down at the right hand of God." At last, the writer observes, Jeremiah's prophecy is fulfilled: "'Their sins and lawless acts I will remember no more.' And where these have been forgiven, there is no longer any sacrifice for sin" (Heb. 10:11, 17–18 NIV).

This is the kingdom of God on earth! John the Baptist announced that the kingdom was at hand (Matt. 3:2), but Jesus said that with his appearance the kingdom had arrived (Matt. 12:28), and began preaching "the good news of the kingdom" (Matt. 4:23). Now Ezekiel's prophecy is fulfilled: God's people will never have to fear exile again, because the Great King has secured God's presence among his people forever by his own blood. Just as the temple curtain, which separated the people from God, was torn from top to bottom at the Crucifixion, so we enter into the Holy of Holies through the torn flesh of the Son of God.

Christ Jesus is high priest and sacrifice, vicar and victim, the one who leads us in worship and the one whose own worship and obedience have won us a place at the Father's table in his kingdom. As his blood spoke a better word than that of Abel, and provided full relief from sin's guilt and tyranny that the blood of lambs and goats could never secure, a bold entrance was opened into the Holy of Holies. We enter there, clothed not in the fig leaves of our own camouflage or the filthy rags of our own righteousness, but in the perfect righteousness of the obedient Son, the Second Adam, son of Abraham, son of David, and savior of the world. Real sins have been truly satisfied in the face of a real judgment by the provision of a real atonement—an atonement that leaves us without guilt before a holy God whose eyes are too pure to behold iniquity.

Caught in the Cross Fire

In spite of this amazing news of forgiveness and full pardon, the Christian gospel message continues to offend the natural self-love that dominates our age. While Christians have been willing for centuries to go to their deaths with the comfort that the scandal of the cross yielded blessings that far outweighed the world's scorn, it would seem that the testimony to this announcement is fading.

Once and for all, the Lamb of God was slain on the altar of sacrifice for God's forgiveness of all our sins. However, seemingly for a second time, he continues to be sacrificed on the altar of apostasy for the world's forgiveness of all our dogmas. This, despite the warning of the writer to the Hebrews about the unhappy end of those who seek to crucify Christ afresh (Heb. 6). We are living in a period of such widespread rejection of the Cross within the professing church itself that the distinction between the believing church and the unbelieving world is becoming increasingly difficult to discern.

It is remarkable to see individuals who have taken oaths to defend the Apostles' Creed attacking each of its articles. Do we regard someone as an accurate representative of Islam if he or she rejects the chief articles of that religion? Do we seek a faithful description of Buddhist teaching from someone whose career has been marked by a devotion to "debunking" Buddhist claims? Yet today, we have pastors, missionaries, seminary professors, denominational bureaucrats, and others, whose salaries are paid by many genuine disciples of Christ, unblushingly attacking the very teachings they gave their word to defend.

One rather colorful example these days is John Shelby Spong, the outspoken Episcopal Bishop of Newark and author of *Rescuing the Bible from Fundamentalism.* Of course, fundamentalism is the shibboleth attached to anyone who happens to believe what Christians have claimed for nearly two millennia. I quote Bishop Spong here not because he is a reputable scholar, but because he represents the sentiments of some mainline church leaders with regard to the issues that concern us in this chapter:

> But who is Christ for us? . . . To talk of a Father God who has a divine-human son by a virgin woman is a mythology that our generation would never have created and, obviously, could not use. To speak of a Father God so enraged by human evil that he requires propitiation for our sins that we cannot pay and thus demands the death of the divine-human son as a guilt offering is a ludicrous idea to our century. The sacrificial concept that focuses on the saving blood of Jesus that somehow washes me clean, so popular in evangelical and fundamentalist circles, is by

and large repugnant to us today. To see human life as fallen from
a pristine and good creation necessitating a divine rescue by the
God-man is not to understand the most elementary aspect of our
evolutionary history. To view human life as depraved or as vic-
timized by original sin is to literalize a premodern anthropology
and a premodern psychology.[1]

These are arguments? No, they are dogmatic assertions, the very
sort of splinters that the writer claims to observe in his believing
neighbor's eye. But they are widely believed as the only conclusion
that any rational modern thinker could hold. If the Christian doctrine
of sacrifice and satisfaction through Christ's death and resurrection
is so irrelevant, why is there so much vitriolic rhetoric against it?
Why don't they just ignore it, as many do in our own circles today?

It is not that the Christian doctrine of Christ's redemptive sacrifice is irrelevant or meaningless. It is precisely because of its impact
that contemporary theologians and unbelieving ministers attack it so
stridently. But when, for instance, Bishop John Shelby Spong tells
us that "the sacrificial concept that focuses on the saving blood of
Jesus" is "a ludicrous idea to our century" and "repugnant to us
today," what are we to do but reply with the apostle, "The message
of the cross is foolishness to those who are perishing" (1 Cor. 1:18)?

If Spong does not accept the biblical record at face value, surely
he is familiar enough with church history to notice that Greek philosophy has always spurned this Jewish model and has attempted to
subvert it with precisely the model that Spong and more sophisticated modern theologians insist upon. So what in our modern age
makes the Cross uniquely repulsive? Is this the first time men and
women have been offended by this message, which Paul even
called, "the offense of the cross"? Surely not. But modern hubris
reckons that we have new and compelling reasons for our unbelief.

Interestingly enough, reasons are precisely what one finds missing from such literature. Clearly, if one accepts the modern view of
human nature, he or she will see the self as basically innocent, only
in need of further transformation and development toward deeper
consciousness and fulfillment. The paradigm of seekers needing

recovery through the meeting of felt needs replaces that of sinners needing rescue through the saving work of Christ.

As Philip Reiff, Christopher Lasch, and a host of secular scholars have observed in recent years, our culture is saturated with "self," and the triumph of the therapeutic orientation has rearranged the priorities and the message of the church as well as of society. Thus, the notion of an indulgent parent who sees her duty as making sure her child is happy and developing positive goals has shoved aside the biblical self-portrait of a God whose love can never be spent at the price of divine holiness and justice.

It is precisely in the Cross where we see God's holiness, justice, and righteousness embracing his mercy, forgiveness, and loving grace. How can we claim to love God, while we despise his holiness? How can we say that we worship a good God, if we attack the very suggestion that God's wrath requires satisfaction so that his justice must be adequately served?

It would be bad enough if the attack on the Cross were confined to liberal Protestants, but the therapeutic orientation has saturated the evangelical world as well.[2] When asked to identify the Cross chiefly in terms of the satisfaction of divine wrath or as a demonstration of divine love, many Christians today are more likely to find the latter far more attractive. In February, 1990, *Christianity Today* featured a cover story on a so-called "evangelical megashift," from the classic Protestant sin-and-grace model to a more relational approach.

Because they are critical of classical theology, many "megashift" proponents suggest that God should be thought of more as a loving parent who seeks the welfare of his or her children than as a judge whose standards must be perfectly met. In fact, it is argued that the historic Western theological paradigm, shared by both Roman Catholics and Protestants, is basically flawed in both its conceptions of God and of the nature of salvation.

A highly legal culture in which relationships were often defined by contracts, Roman society left a deep imprint on developing Christian theology. God himself came to be seen as a sort of Caesar figure, an imperial judge who keeps track of infractions, and the courtroom picture began to tightly define the way the church spoke of salvation. Once we return to the biblical text, we will quickly see that the courtroom gives way to the family room, that God is viewed as a loving parent who seeks to nurture and guide his wayward children rather than as a judge whose character demands punishment of sin.

There are a number of strengths of this position. First, as we observed in the first chapter, it is possible that fundamentalism was so marked by a stern severity that the image of God as judge swallowed everything in its path. Perhaps we are merely reaping the whirlwind of one-sided emphases on the other side. Nevertheless, it is probably just as likely that this "megashift" has more to do with the therapeutic orientation of our narcissistic culture.

The great concern of our lives in modern America is, "How can I be happy?" We will do almost anything, pay almost anything, to be happy. We pamper ourselves, dote on ourselves, and our greatest fear seems to be that somewhere, somehow, we will be unhappy. Who will take care of us: The government? Our family? The church?

We see this reflected in the criminal justice system, where felons are often treated as victims of society. Maybe, we fear, what they need is our compassion, not our punishment! Rehabilitation makes sense in that sort of approach, where the demand for punishment itself is viewed a sign of sin and wickedness these days. Similarly, we wonder, how can hell heal people? How can that lead to a happy ending and rehabilitate the wayward? The notion of God requiring the judgment of sinners at all—even if it does fall on the head of a representative substitute—is repugnant to many.

Words of Worship

The triumph of the therapeutic in religion that has assisted in this "megashift" can be illustrated in the content of some of contemporary praise music. With notable exceptions, much of contemporary worship music is shaped more by therapeutic and relational than theological and doctrinal categories. An example of the hymnidy shaped by the later is Augustus Toplady's "Rock of Ages" (1776):

Not the labors of my hands
Can fulfill Thy law's demands;
Could my zeal no respite know,

Could my tears forever flow,
All for sin could not atone;
Thou must save and Thou alone.

Nothing in my hand I bring,
Simply to Thy cross I cling;
Naked, come to Thee for dress,
Helpless, look to Thee for grace;
Foul, I to the fountain fly,

Wash me, Savior, or I die!

Rock of Ages, cleft for me,
Let me hide myself in Thee;
Let the water and the blood,
From Thy riven side which flowed,
Be of sin the double cure,
Cleanse me from its guilt and pow'r.

These words are tender, moving, and warmly pastoral: God is pictured here as both just and merciful, but his judgment of sin in the person of Christ as our substitute is central. One certainly does not need a degree in theology to appreciate this hymn, for it is a "folk song" of the people of God, a song of Zion. Yet it is pregnant with thoughts of redemption.

By contrast, many of contemporary "praise choruses" celebrate *me* and my personal experience with a dangerously familiar diety. Take for instance the refrain of a popular worship song which speaks of falling in love with "Him over and over and over again."

Certainly we do have a relationship with God in Christ, but clearly the biblical focus on the object of faith—Jesus Christ and his saving work—has shifted to the individual and his or her experience.

Few contemporary evangelicals would want to say that they find the cross offensive, so what often happens is more subtle: The cross is defined differently. Instead of being the settlement of divine justice in a legal or courtroom setting, it is merely the demonstration or exhibition of divine love. Instead of being a propitiatory sacrifice (because propitiation requires the idea of wrath, and few believe in God's wrath anymore), it must be seen as a healing of broken dreams and shattered lives.

But that brings us to the second assumption of this "megashift" that has so much to do with the perspectives provided by churches, worship, evangelism, and a host of related issues: Is the classical evangelical, indeed, the Christian model shaped by secular Roman legal traditions rather than by Scripture? To answer that, we need to go to the text of Scripture.

Biblical Roots of the "Legal" Model

Reflecting back on the whole teaching of the Old Testament, the writer to the Hebrews summarized it in this manner: "Without the shedding of blood there is no remission of sins" (Heb. 9:22). The whole focus of Israel's history was on the Lamb of God, the coming One who would bear her guilt and carry away her sins into the wilderness, as the scapegoat commanded in Israel's ritual worship foreshadowed. No one can read the Old Testament without seeing the central prominence—indeed, obsession—with this sin-bearing substitute. God commanded Moses, "For the life of a creature is in the blood, and I have given it to you to make atonement for yourselves on the altar" (Lev. 17:11 NIV).

Throughout Scripture, we recognize the centrality of this need for a sacrifice to appease divine wrath, a substitute to bear the burden of guilt on our behalf. The very idea of atonement assumes that there is alienation between God and the sinner. Propitiation makes no sense as a concept unless we believe that there is a person who is angry and whose wrath somehow must be appeased, propitiated.

We have already observed that the sacrificial system that presupposes God's wrath against sinners, as well as his love, and finds a way of satisfying that wrath is derived from biblical rather than Roman legal customs.

But why is God angry with us? It is not simply because he is constitutionally difficult to get along with, but because there is some serious barrier standing in the way of our fellowship. Although he is far more long-suffering and patient than we are when attacked, God is angered by something in particular, something that offends him so greatly that he cannot bear to look upon us.

The Old Testament picture, far from representing a departure from the legal model, actually creates the pattern for Israel's own legal procedures. God commands his people to "maintain justice in the courts" (Amos 5:15; Zech. 8:16) because there is a correspondence between the kingdom of heaven and the kingdom of Israel. But justice requires a standard, and God gave Israel that standard in his Law. The revelation of his own personal ethical character, God's Law is not a suggested pattern but the criterion by which all judgments must be made. "The soul that sins shall die" (Ezek. 18:4).

Humanity was created in God's own image to reflect the good Creator's own personal character. Adam, however, chose to plunge himself and his entire posterity into the guilt and corruption that pervades our lives and experience. It is so "natural" to us now, that we consider our sinful condition normal. "I'm only human," we say of our folly. But sin is not the result of our humanness; it is not the way things were supposed to be. That realization makes us able to recognize the enormous dilemma this presents to a loving God who is also just and holy.

God's Law is not an arbitrary standard, but the revelation of his own unchanging character. The presence of the Ark of the Covenant in the midst of Israel, in which the tablets of the Law were carefully kept, was equivalent to the presence of God himself among his people (1 Sam. 4:21).

As Israel's landlord—the great King—God is often portrayed as the imperial judge who summons his people to court. If anything,

these Old Testament courtroom scenes have more to do with ancient
Near Eastern treaties. Again and again, especially in the prophetic
books, God's trouble with Israel takes the form of a courtroom trial.
Similar to the "Hear ye, hear ye," of the old English courtroom
announcing the arrival of the judge, God's assumption of his judgment seat is announced with solemnity, as in Hosea 4:1: "Hear the
word of the LORD, you children of Israel, for the LORD brings a
charge against the inhabitants of the land." This is followed by the
public reading of the charges against the people, concluding with a
verdict and the sentencing: Israel is again to be sent into exile from
the Land of Promise for her sins. This is her status until her faithful Savior once more saves her from her captors and forgives her
sins through a sacrifice of atonement.

Even in purely secular terms, and especially for its time, the
Jewish legal system was advanced. According to one Jewish ency-
clopedia, there are 613 commandments in the Old Testament. It is
not Moses or the judges who impose these laws on Israel, but no
less than Yahweh himself. This legal or covenant relationship by
which God condescends to engage in a personal relationship with
his people is not a projection of the experience or religious insights
of the people themselves. It's an expression of God's personal character. Sin is not a vague concept, nor are acts of disobedience
regarded as "mistakes" that God easily overlooks. A violation of
God's Law demands eternal punishment: nothing could be clearer
from a simple reading of the Old Testament.

In Psalm 2, the portrait of the messianic king brings to mind
Michelangelo's "Last Judgment" in the Sistine Chapel. In Psalm
11:4–7 we read,

> The LORD is in his holy temple;
>   the LORD is on his heavenly throne.
> He observes the sons of men;
>   his eyes examine them.
> The LORD examines the righteous,
>   but the wicked and those who love violence
>   his soul hates.

> On the wicked he will rain
>> fiery coals of burning sulfur;
>> a scorching wind will be their lot.
> For the LORD is righteous,
>> he loves justice;
>> upright men will see his face. (NIV)

"Who can stand before you when you are angry?" the Psalmist asks. "From heaven you pronounced judgment, and the land feared and was quiet—when you, O God, rose up to judge, to save all the afflicted of the land." And then there follows a deeply unsettling line: "Surely your wrath against men brings you praise" (Ps. 76:7–10 NIV).

Sinners in Need of Mercy

Nevertheless, God is kind, gracious, and slow to execute his wrath throughout the Old Testament. There is no "bad God" of the Old Testament to pit against a "good God" of the New Testament. In both, God is simultaneously just and merciful, full of wrath and full of love. From Genesis 3, where wicked Adam and his descendants are promised eternal life by relying on the coming Seed of the woman, mercy is held out, but on God's terms. Sinners must renounce their own "righteousness" and cast themselves entirely on God's mercy. Only by the shedding of blood can their sins be forgiven, for justice must be served. God cannot be merciful at the expense of his holiness. The measure of his mercy is not that he overlooks our sin, but that he who cannot overlook sin nevertheless took sin upon himself to suffer and die for the satisfaction of his holy character.

For the proponents of the therapeutic, relational view, the real problem is education: If we only knew how much God loved us, we would turn to him. But according to Scripture, the problem is far greater. We are born enemies of God, under divine wrath, bearing the curse, judged guilty. The cross cannot merely serve as a lesson in God's love, for we are "dead in sin" (Eph. 2:1) and our mind and will are enslaved to our sinful nature (1 Cor. 2:14; Rom. 6:6).

Viewing Christ's death merely as an illustration of divine love is impossible. Suppose a husband wanted to show his wife how much he loved her by putting a gun to his head and pulling the trigger. Obviously, such an act would be an example of violence, not of love. Similarly, self-sacrifice actually accomplishes little unless it pays a redemptive price. In dying for us, Christ not only demonstrated his love; he actually bore the guilt for our sins and carried God's judgment and curse, justly meant for us in his own body. It is only a testimony of divine love because it actually turns aside divine wrath.

The New Testament witness, therefore, relates to the Old Testament as the promise to fulfillment. Jesus Christ is the Lamb of God, the sin-bearing substitute for sinners. God is the same in the New Testament, warning us that we are "storing up wrath against [ourselves], for the day of God's wrath, when his righteous judgment will be revealed" (Rom. 2:5 NIV).

No one addressed the subject of God's wrath and the reality of judgment more clearly than Jesus Christ. In fact, he expressed it in legal terms. In John 3:8, the courtroom scene is painted once again: "Whoever believes in him is not condemned, but whoever does not believe *stands condemned* already because he has not believed in the name of God's one and only Son" (NIV, emphasis added).

The language of "condemnation" and "standing condemned" evokes the courtroom image, as the defendant stands to hear the verdict pronounced. As if this were not enough legal language, Jesus adds, "This is the verdict . . ." (v. 19). We find this terminology all the way to the end of the Bible, with "the wrath of the Lamb" executing a final judgment. On that day, the Father and the Son sit in judgment. "For the great day of their wrath has come, and who can stand?" (Rev. 6:16–17 NIV).

The Law, however, can only condemn; it cannot save. "What the law was powerless to do, in that it was rendered weak by our sinful nature, God did by sending his Son in the likeness of sinful man. . . ." (Rom. 8:3). Why? To teach us how much God loves us or to motivate us to turn to God? Paul continues,

What the law was powerless to do . . . God did by sending his Son in the likeness of sinful man to be a sin offering. And so he condemned sin in sinful man, in order that the righteous requirements of the law might be fully met in us. . . .

Thus, enemies have become friends (Rom. 5:10). However, we miss this great announcement if we fail to appreciate the fact that we were enemies before this decisive act was applied to us.

This is what the Creed means when it affirms, "He descended into hell." Although this line has been the occasion for a great deal of controversy over our Lord's postmortem adventures, that should not be the point. In Isaiah's famous prophecy, the Messiah is seen as one who "bore our griefs and carried our sorrows." He was:

smitten by God and afflicted, . . . wounded for our transgressions, . . . bruised for our iniquities. The chastisement for our peace was upon him, and by his stripes we are healed. (Isa. 53:4–5)

Our peace required his chastisement, and in order for us to be accepted by God in heaven's court, he had to experience the anguish of hell, which is God's rejection. "Yet it pleased the LORD to bruise him." Why on earth would this unparalleled grief please God? It is because he would be made an offering for sin. Bearing the iniquities of his people, the God-Man would secure the eternal relationship that the Father so indefatigably worked to achieve in spite of our sin and resistance.

How remarkable, therefore, for us to demand of God an account for suffering, evil, sin, pain, and death! It is we who, in union with our father Adam, have turned his paradise into foretaste of hell. It is we who seek to go our own way and live for ourselves, treating God's patience with mocking contempt. It is we who deserve not only the wages of sin in this life, but for all eternity. And yet, it is God who suffers for us. God not only pronounces the sentence of justice, but finds a way to bear the burden of justice himself.

Forsaken by His Father

You see, at the end of the day, it was not the mockery and loathing of men, nor the law and judgment of Rome, that Jesus feared. We recall the messianic prophecy in the psalm concerning Judas's treason: "I can endure the treason of my friends, for at least you are with me, My God." And yet, on this night, the Son is alone in hell. Not even the Father is his friend. Nobody loves the Son in this hour. His heart, a reservoir of boundless joy and friendship, is broken. He is the enemy both of his wicked creation and of his righteous Father. The reason Jesus shuddered at the thought of the crucifixion had less to do with the physical torture involved (although it undoubtedly included this) than with the far greater fear of becoming everything he hated most in his deepest being.

He who was the truth would become the world's most inveterate liar. He who was too pure to look upon a woman to lust would become history's most promiscuous adulterer. The only man who ever loved with pure selflessness would become the most despised villain in God's universe. He would become a racist, a murderer, a gossip, slanderer, thief, and tyrant. He would become all of this not in himself, but as the sin-bearing substitute for us.

At last, the moment came: God turned his face of wrath toward his bleeding, dying Son, and made him drink that cup of rejection to the last drop. See here the price of your redemption: God must hate his own sinless Son, the joy of his eternal heart, so that he may love you justly. The Father must become the enemy of the Son, the avenging angel who slaughters the firstborn Son in the dark Egyptian night of his captivity.

In that moment, with the sin of the world crushing his soul, Jesus looked for the Father, with whom he had enjoyed eternal intimacy and indescribable love, and found no one there to comfort him. Forsaken by the world because of its sin, and forsaken by his Father because he had become sin for us, Jesus cried out, "My God, My God, why have You forsaken me?" so that we would never have to speak those dreadful words. "No man can see me and live," God warned Moses. Yet we have seen God himself, impaled on a tree as the self-offered, curse-bearing substitute for sinners, enthroned in shame and suffering. Instead of being consumed by God's holy presence we now look to him and live—forever.

> Dar'st thou, poor Worm, offend Infinity?
> And must the Terms of Peace be given by Thee?
> Then Thou art Justice in the last Appeal;
> Thy easie God instructs Thee to rebell:
> And, like a King remote, and weak, must take
> What Satisfaction Thou art pleased to make.
> But if there be a Pow'r too Just, and strong
> To wink at Crimes and bear unpunish'd Wrong;
> Look humbly upward, see his Will disclose:
> The Forfeit first, and then the Fine impose:
> A Fine thy poverty cou'd never pay
> Had not Eternal Wisedom found the way:
> And with Coelestial Wealth supply'd thy Store:
> His Justice makes the Fine, his Mercy quits the Score.
> See God descending in thy Humane Frame;
> Th'offended, suff'ring in th'Offenders name:
> All thy Misdeeds to him imputed see,
> And all his Righteousness devolv'd on thee.
>
> (—John Dreyden, "On Religion")

The Cross was the cup of eternal wrath, distilled from the anger that had been building up since the sin of Adam, concentrated into one terrible drink. The Son drank the cup of wrath, so that we could drink the cup of salvation. And when he had finished his cup, there was not even a drop left for us who gratefully receive the benefit of his death.

In truth, it was not the Jews or the Romans who crucified Jesus Christ. It was God the Father who drove the spear into the side of his only Son, so that out of that sacred wound would flow the blood that would wash away the sins of his church. It was this cup—the "cup of wrath" (Isa. 51:17)—that caused our Savior's forehead to yield bloody sweat in the eve of his crucifixion. His hell gained our heaven; his curse secured our blessing; his incalculable grief brought us immeasurable joy. By being made God's enemy on the cross, he made us friends.

And so it was, on a day much like any other on the banks of the Jordan, that while John was baptizing, preparing the highways for the Messiah, his own cousin appeared. "Behold," John announced, "the Lamb of God who takes away the sin of the world" (John 1:29 NIV).

The writer to the Hebrews said that Christ's blood speaks a better word than did Abel's. Why is that? One cries out day and night for vengeance from the earth, while the other cries out day and night for God's mercy and grace from heaven. It is precisely in Christ's sin-bearing that we are spared the retributive justice we deserve.

Is this cross of propitiation the center of our preaching, worship, evangelism, and fellowship today? Are we driven regularly in our public worship to feel God's judgment of our pretended goodness, and then to sense God's full acceptance of us based solely on Christ's atoning sacrifice? Do we "love to tell the story"? May it not simply be the story of what has happened to us, what we feel or what we think. Let us recall and retell the story of what really happened to our Savior on a Roman cross, outside the city gates of Jerusalem.

SIX

Can We Still Believe in the Resurrection?

✛ ✛ ✛

ON THE THIRD DAY HE ROSE FROM THE DEAD.

Etched in my memory from childhood are those lines from a familiar Easter hymn in evangelical circles, "He Lives": "You ask me how I know he lives? He lives within my heart." In spite of the warmth that such sentiment offers, it hardly fits the bill sketched out by the apostle Peter: "Always be prepared to give an answer to everyone who asks you to give the reason for the hope that you have" (1 Peter 3:15 NIV).

In a recent informal survey of evangelical Christians, nearly everyone agreed with the statement, "It is more important for me to give my personal testimony than to explain the doctrines and claims of Christianity." That is remarkable, especially given the fact that not even the eyewitnesses of Christ's saving acts gave much attention in the New Testament to their own experiences and feelings. "What Jesus Means to Me" or "How Jesus Changed My Life" are simply not notable headlines on their accounts.

The testimony that concerns biblical Christians is that of eye-witnesses who observed events upon which we cast our hope for eternal life. "That which was from the beginning," says John in 1 John 1:1, "which we have heard, which we have seen with our eyes, which we have looked upon, and our hands have handled, concerning the Word of life"—this is the Christian's confidence. "That life was manifested, and we have seen, and bear witness, and declare to you that eternal life which was with the Father and was manifested to us—that which we have seen and heard we declare to you, that you also may have fellowship with us; and truly our fellowship is with the Father and with his Son Jesus Christ" (1 John 1:2–4).

It is much easier for Christians to adopt the Enlightenment view, championed by Immanuel Kant, in which the phenomenal (earthly and observable) realm is separated from the noumenal (heavenly and unknowable). Questions of reason and science are based on facts, while religious claims are a matter of "faith." And yet faith is defined in Scripture as requiring confidence in these events to which eyewitness testimony is given. Faith is not a synonym for nonsense, nor does it belong to a nonrational, non-historical, nonintellectual realm of blind leaps and sheer acts of will.

Far from separating faith from the rigorous questions that belong to reason and history, Christianity makes public claims that must stand the test of any other. In fact, the burden of proof rests on the Christian to make the case for the biblical faith, with the Resurrection as its cornerstone. Because God became flesh, the noumenal became phenomenal.

That is not to say that our faith is founded on reason, for only when reason receives the light of revelation is it capable of guiding us into such marvelous truth. It is one thing to say that the Resurrection can stand up to questions, but can it confront doubts? That is what this chapter will attempt to address, for everything else in the Christian faith depends on this historical event.

A Claim to Public Truth

In order to tackle the question of the Resurrection as a legitimate truth-claim, we must first have some idea of the motive in asking the question. It is not difficult to find a contemporary theologian who will deny the Resurrection on the basis that it is simply irreconcilable with the enlightened modern mind. One can even read volumes from major modern theologians who make such assertions without even the slightest attempt at defending their position with arguments. For them, it is enough to say that the supernatural worldview is untenable, case closed.

Existential theologian Rudolf Bultmann appropriated the German distinction between *Historie* and *Geschichte,* the former referring to actual historical events, the latter referring to "salvation history." This, of course, makes sense if one buys Kant's division. Implicit in that sort of distinction, of course, is the notion that there can be a form of history that is not historical!

What does it mean to say that certain things that happened in the past never really happened? Either they did or they didn't. But Bultmann and others forged a powerful school of modern theologians who wanted to get behind the historical claims of the Scriptures to discover the real idea. In other words, regardless of whether it happened in real history or not, what did the claim, "Jesus rose from the dead" actually create in the experience of the early Christian?

While assuming that the Resurrection is not a historical event like the Battle of the Bulge, Bultmann would say that the idea or experience behind that claim is what is important: Has Jesus risen in my heart? Have I experienced the "Christ event," the encounter with Christ here and now which creates a new way of existence? It's the present moment that counts, he would claim, the crisis event in which Christ meets me now in my experience, not whether the apostles were reporting factual history. This sort of sentiment is common not only among liberal theologians, but it often appears implicitly in evangelical circles where despite belief in the Resurrection, individual experience is made central.

We will deal with the question of whether it is possible for biblical claims such as the Resurrection to have any meaning unless they happened as reported. But first, it is important to ask why such unlikely interpretations of fairly plain reports are so attractive. Of course, there is a practical consideration: Avoid the social acrimony often directed at such bold declarations of miraculous activity, and yet enjoy a spiritually edifying experience based on their "meaning." In doing so, one can be an intelligent, late twentieth-century man or woman and yet give attention to the "things of the heart."

A well-balanced modern is dogmatically secular, and yet romantic and sentimental. He or she wants to experience "the magic of believing" while not really believing in things that "simply do not happen." Here we have arrived at the real hurdle for the modern mind: Such things as a resurrection simply do not happen. They can be written off entirely because we have already judged them to be impossible.

Of course, there is no rationale for this position. A rationalist or empiricist for instance, would (according to his or her own principles) have to be able to test the premise, "Resurrections do not happen," in order to conclude that the Resurrection of Christ is a farce. Yet no philosopher has been able to offer a compelling argument for such a premise.

David Hume, the empiricist who dealt most with this subject, simply concluded that miracles do not happen. This is quite an astonishing conclusion for a man whose life was devoted to ridding philosophy of a priori judgments of a case. Resting on "the universal experience of humanity," empiricists like Hume concluded that resurrections were out of keeping with the normal experience of ordinary men and women. Of course, that conclusion presupposes flawed premises. First, it assumes that David Hume is omniscient, knowing every experience or combination of experiences ever to have surfaced in the history of the human species. His claim is similar to the dogmatic assertion, "There is no intelligent life except on our planet," in spite of the fact that we do not have exhaustive knowledge of the universe.

Of course, there was a time when the common, everyday experience of the masses was that the world was flat. Only a fool would have questioned such an obvious deliverance of sense-experience. But other observations overthrew this assumption and now we can hardly imagine what it would be like to experience the world as flat.

What accounts for this in our case? We've seen too many photographs of our planet from space. Universal human experience is, therefore, dependent on the conditions of one's own time and place. What if the revelation of God in Christ, particularly the Resurrection, is, like those photographs, the new information that overthrows our previous assumptions? If so, it makes it impossible for us *not* to believe in the phenomenon of a bodily resurrection.

How can Hume say that miracles do not happen unless he is unlimited in his access to the experience of every creature in all times and places? There have been plenty of people down through the ages and all around the world who would pit their experience against Hume's, siding confidently with belief in the miraculous. Some, to be sure, would be superstitious and credulous. But if "universal experience" is the test of truth, Hume has tremendous problems rendering as universal his own experience as a secular philosopher. Indeed, his experience represents only a handful of like-minded colleagues.

The second assumption is that the miraculous contradicts the ordinary experience of people. But if a miracle were simply an ordinary phenomenon, why would one even distinguish it as a miracle? It is true by definition that miracles do not ordinarily happen, but it is one thing to say that they do not happen in normal circumstances and quite another thing to say that they cannot happen. Empirical observation is sufficient to conclude the former, but not the latter. What experiment has yet been conducted that has proved such a sweeping claim? These are not arguments, of course. These are the unsupported assertions of the modern mind.

Bultmann suggests that it is quite impossible for people who use electric appliances, who listen to the radio, to believe in events described in Scripture. In his view, one does not even have to offer devastating criticisms of Christianity and its historical claims, since the existence of radios and microwave ovens has something to do with the impossibility of believing in a resurrection from the dead. But the conclusion does not follow from the premise.

Meanwhile, the Resurrection is also among Bishop John Spong's targets:

> We would never in our day of space travel and knowledge of the vastness of the universe try to assert that the God experienced in Jesus has been reunited with the God who was presumed to dwell just beyond the sky by telling the story of the cosmic ascension. . . . We today do not think in natural/supernatural categories. God is not for us a human parent figure. We do not see human life as created good and then as fallen into sin. Human life is evolving, not always in a straight line, but evolving nonetheless into higher and higher levels of consciousness. We do not need the divine rescuer who battles the demonic forces of a fallen world in the name of the creator God. . . . That worldview has passed away.[1]

So what is the essence of the gospel according to Spong? "In the words of the popular commercial, it is a call to be all that one can be."[2] Following David Hume in his blind dogmatism against the miraculous, modern thinkers seem to think that such assertions are self-evident: "Miracles do not happen, because this is not the sort of universe where that sort of thing happens."

Truth or Superstition?

This is often where even the best minds end up, even though they would cite the same flaw in their opponents as an example of unthinking fundamentalism. With Bultmann, the Resurrection is reduced to pious myth with existential possibilities. Not because someone found the bones of a first-century Palestinian rabbi buried in Jesus' traditional tomb, but because the reigning view of knowledge is that of a straight line of progress leading from ignorance to enlightenment.

Ages of faith are really ages of superstition, we are told, and we have long since learned that things once attributed to supernatural forces actually have perfectly natural explanations. Of course, this is partially true. Magic and superstition have, in many important cases, given way to better explanations through advances in medicine, physics, and other disciplines. And there is no reason to look for miraculous explanations where non-miraculous ones will suffice. After all, God is lord over the ordinary, too.

We owe a debt of gratitude to researchers, many of them Christians, who preferred to develop a vaccine rather than attribute disease and plague to evil spirits. It is too easily forgotten that Christian scientists pioneered modern medicine, and their aversion to idolatry and superstition has led precisely to those advances and leaps of progress for which secular ideology would like to take credit. But to say that there can therefore be no miraculous events at all is to say that one has knowledge of every event that has ever occurred in history.

Boston University sociologist Peter Berger has exposed the fallacious logic of these positions. First, he says, there is a hidden double standard: The past can be relativized simply by explaining the misconceptions of the ancient worldview. "The present, however, remains strangely immune from relativization," Berger writes.

> In other words, the New Testament writers are seen as afflicted with a false consciousness rooted in their time, but the contemporary analyst takes the consciousness of his time as an unmixed intellectual blessing. The electricity- and radio-users are placed intellectually above the Apostle Paul.[3]

As Berger points out, this sort of reasoning is useful descriptively, but is hardly an argument against the miraculous. It is helpful to know why modern men and women find it difficult to believe in the supernatural, but once we have a better grasp of those sociological factors we still do not have a compelling reason not to believe in the supernatural. It might help my doctor to learn that I have an irrational fear of needles, but that does not make such fear less irrational. Berger says, "We may agree, say, that contemporary consciousness is incapable of conceiving of either angels or demons. We are still left with the question of whether, possibly, both angels and demons go on existing despite this incapacity of our contemporaries to conceive of them."[4]

Thus, Berger suggests that we begin to "relativize" our own context. In other words, perhaps the biblical worldview—clearly opposed to superstition but frankly supernatural—is the sane outlook after all, and we moderns are the ones who have the irrational worldview. Given the fact that centuries of rationalist and empiricist skepticism have not been able to offer a single compelling argument against miracles in general, or the Resurrection of Christ in particular, why should we continue to give our blind allegiance to unsupportable modern dogmas? (It is hardly surprising that Hume's radical empiricism led him to radical skepticism about knowing empirical reality at all.)

In questioning the modern worldview we will find that we are not alone. Happily, this modern dogmatism that simply asserts naturalism is itself being challenged. Even the events about which we do have some knowledge—even a great deal of knowledge—often hold unanswered questions.

Thomas Kuhn, in his groundbreaking study of scientific revolutions, argued that the modern notion of science as a progressive advance of knowledge is outdated. Instead, he says, each major scientific theory goes through various phases. As a theory, which makes sense of the observations of a wide range of scientists is advanced, old paradigms are either adjusted or discarded, and the new major theory creates a new paradigm. The history of science is not a gradual amassing of factual data, but a constant and somewhat chaotic series of paradigm revolutions.[5]

While Kuhn's interpretation is not universally accepted,[6] it is difficult to find philosophers of science (or of anything else) who embrace the sort of outlook exhibited by Hume. Spong and a great many theologians are still operating with these modern notions of knowledge based on modern science. More recently, philosophers of science are much more open to regarding science itself as a tradition, a community of discourse, in which members of various disciplines work on their specific projects. Occasionally they come up with an "explanation" that makes the most sense of a lot of data across these sub-disciplines. With this approach, there is no such thing as an uninterpreted "fact" or an unbiased observation.

Irrational Rationales

By even suggesting, as Spong does, that the "modern consciousness" somehow prohibits a particular religious claim, the advocate of modernity betrays the fact that his presuppositions are not only guiding, but determining, his investigation. In fact, his is not an investigation at all, but an appeal to power. It is not an argument, but a presupposition. One does not have to be convinced by it, since it is expected that every rational person would accept it on authority. This is the very authoritarian dogmatism that modernity claimed to have overthrown!

Too often we assume, often without knowing that we are assuming, that science has a right to dictate as a supreme authority. Awed by the practical achievements of science (technology, medicine, natural sciences), we do not even realize that we are treating all statements that claim scientific authority as worthy of belief, even if there is no evidence or proof. It is, after all, as possible to have blind faith in the authority of science as it is to have blind faith in the authority of the church.

But if science is not simply a description of reality in terms of brute facts, shorn of any interpretive framework and uprooted from any prior assumptions, what keeps this kind of thinking from degenerating into relativism? Among other things, it is the point made by Kuhn and others that one piece of data can overthrow a paradigm.

The scientist comes to the lab each day with pet hypotheses that are themselves somehow shaped by a constellation of other beliefs, many of them unquestioned. One day somebody notices some anomaly, something that does not fit the picture, and in spite of presuppositional biases, he or she is forced to acknowledge this new datum as a contradiction of previous research, even if that research is his or her own. A new theory is often required to make sense of this major interruption, a theory that may have been rejected long ago as entirely implausible.

Often, scientists have stumbled onto a major discovery while actually looking for something else. Like Columbus, who accidentally discovered the Americas while searching for a route to India, many advances are serendipitous. And, like it or not, a new discovery or observation—though never divorced from the beliefs and assumptions of the discoverer—has the power to overturn the scientist's most cherished beliefs.

What does all of this mean? First, it means that science in particular and knowledge in general cannot be viewed as a straight line of progress from ignorance to enlightenment. We have amassed far more data, and have at our disposal sophisticated instruments of observation that previous generations lacked. But it is still possible for a theory advanced by an obscure Greek philosopher or by an Arab mystic to account for the data better than more recent explanations.

Second, it means that the scientist or philosopher no longer has a bird's-eye view from which to look down objectively on all data. Everyone, including the most careful physicist, pursues his or her work with presuppositions and expectations of what he or she will find. Those presuppositions may blind them to important data that contradict their hypotheses. However, a piece of data occasionally comes along that brings down the house of cards: not only cherished hypotheses, but reigning theories. The result is a paradigm shift, a revolution in the way we understand reality.

Paradigm shifts occur in religion also. The Reformation is often referred to by historians as a "Copernican Revolution," because the recovery of an accurate working text of the New Testament by Renaissance philologists led inadvertently to a massive reevaluation of the meaning of salvation. That revolution in the church led to sweeping changes in every discipline, and it contributed significantly to the rise of modern science itself. But the religious event I want to examine has to do with a more fundamental revolution: the Resurrection of Jesus Christ.

Unexpected Findings

A legal scholar by the name of Simon Greenleaf, founder of the Harvard Law School, set out to disprove the Resurrection claim. A denizen of the "modern consciousness," Greenleaf was certain that simple, sustained attention to the claims of the New Testament, with regard to both the internal witness of the Gospels and the external testimony of secular historians of that period would finally put to rest lingering Christian beliefs. He came to his task with the purpose of refuting the bodily resurrection of Jesus Christ.

As a lawyer, Greenleaf was impressed with the idea of pursuing his project along the lines of legal inquiry. After all, the Bible makes public claims, and the best test of such claims is to try them in court. He would show the obvious examples of collusion of the writers that typically mark attempts at creating a powerful lie, and he would demonstrate the implausibility of the reports and their inherent contradictions.

As Greenleaf went deeper and deeper into his investigation, he grew increasingly uneasy. Thinking that further investigation would yield further evidence against the Resurrection, he only found it working in the opposite direction. Finally, the distinguished legal professor concluded the very opposite of his intention: Jesus Christ did, in fact, rise from the dead. It was not the most satisfactory conclusion in view of his "modern consciousness." But as a lawyer, he could not see how any of the other alternatives— either suggested throughout history or contemplated by himself— yielded an explanation of the evidence anywhere near as convincing as the New Testament claim.

Here is an actual case of Kuhn's "paradigm shift" taking place. Perhaps Greenleaf would have claimed "neutrality" and "unbiased, unprejudiced investigation" for himself if, in fact, the case had yielded different results. And yet, by his own admission, Greenleaf went into this investigation with the intention of discrediting a hypothesis. He ended up concluding that it was true "beyond any reasonable doubt."

We should have no difficulty admitting that we all have presuppositions and that no one simply "observes," "investigates," or "knows." We are always looking for something to support our point of view. And it is often the case that we will find just about anything we want—but not always. This is just one of those "not always" cases.

The Resurrection is among those rare stories that can overthrow our most cherished opinions. Unlike any other historical event, this event, if it did occur, is the most significant revolution or "paradigm shift" imaginable.

First, if Jesus lent his authority to the Old Testament and to the apostles as his eyewitnesses and deputies, the reliability of the entire canon of Christian Scripture is established by the Resurrection.

Second, the Resurrection establishes Jesus Christ as the Lord of history, who has won the right to interpret its past, present, and future.

Third, the Resurrection establishes the certainty of salvation for believers and of judgment for unbelievers.

Fourth, the Resurrection establishes the supernatural character of the church and its witness to God's saving events as public truth.

In the last part of this chapter, let us take a look at some of the evidence for the Resurrection, from both internal (i.e., biblical) and external (i.e., secular) sources.

Internal Evidence for the Resurrection

As Yale theologian Hans Frei insisted, the Resurrection is such a central part of the Bible's narrative plot that the whole story rises or falls with it, leading him to conclude, "To consign the resurrection to the category of myth is a typical species of modern laziness. . . ."[7] As we have seen in connection with the Incarnation, it is impossible to take anything in the Bible seriously if its central plot is dismantled. The eyewitnesses do not make claims about their own experience or offer ideas illustrated by these claims. Rather, they insist upon the Resurrection the way a witness gives testimony in a court of law.

According to the story itself, the Resurrection happened. And if it did not happen, there is nothing bigger or better behind it. Where liberalism might describe Christianity in terms of the attractive but disposable box of historical claims housing the jewels of religious experience—meaning, ideals, aspirations, and so forth—that makes the story someone else's story. In this case, it becomes the liberal's story, a late twentieth-century tribute to morality and progress. If the Resurrection did not happen, the story is no longer valid in any sense beyond its literary interest.

Even apart from and before the question of historical reliability, the more immediate question concerns the internal integrity of the narrative. Before we even ask, "Is it true?" we need to ask, "What is it?" We need to come to the Bible as it tells this story of Israel and Jesus and allow it to simply speak for itself. The apostle Paul makes this point: "And if Christ has not been raised, our preaching is useless and so is your faith. More than that, we are then found to be false witnesses about God, for we have testified about God that he raised Christ from the dead. . . . And if Christ has not been raised, your faith is futile; you are still in your sins. Then those also who have fallen asleep in Christ are lost. If only for this life we have hope in Christ, we are to be pitied more than all men" (1 Cor. 15:14–19).

Paul hangs everything on this claim to a historical, bodily resurrection of Jesus Christ. If it proves false, Christian preaching and faith are useless; its apostolic eyewitnesses have intentionally misled countless people on the most important subject; and—also important—we are still in the mess in which we found ourselves before this happy delusion, still in our sins. Whether one believes its claims or not, this is Christianity.

If Christianity is embraced merely for what it provides in this life, it is not the case, says Paul, that we should shrug our shoulders and say, "I'm glad it helps people." That's because the apostles never made its validity consist in its therapeutic value. If it fails to make good on its claims, it fails to make good on everything. There is no consolation prize, says the apostle, for those who embrace Christianity without the Resurrection.

The notion of resurrection in general, and the Messiah's in particular, is not a New Testament invention. Isaiah's "Suffering Servant," after his atoning death, "will be raised and lifted up and highly exalted" (Isa. 52:13 NIV). Throughout his earthly ministry our Lord pointed to his death, burial, and resurrection. After the Transfiguration, Jesus told his disciples, "The Son of Man is going to be betrayed into the hands of men. They will kill him, and on the third day he will be raised to life" (Matt. 17:22–23 NIV).

When the Jews demanded a miraculous sign, Jesus answered, "Destroy this temple, and I will raise it again in three days." As John observes, "But the temple he had spoken of was his body. After he was raised from the dead, his disciples recalled what he had said. Then they believed the Scripture and the words that Jesus had spoken" (John 2:19, 21–22 NIV).

In another report in which the Pharisees demand a miraculous sign, Jesus offered only "the sign of the prophet Jonah." He said, "For as Jonah was three days and three nights in the belly of a huge fish, so the Son of Man will be three days and three nights in the heart of the earth" (Matt. 12:39–40).

Clearly, Jesus was either remarkably self-deluded or he really believed that he was going to die and rise again. There is no via media on this point, any more than there would be if I were to announce to a crowd that I am the president of the United States. If I am not what I claim to be, I would not be regarded as possessing any authority whatsoever, especially when it comes to questions of ultimate truth, meaning, or morality.

If Jesus did not fulfill the mission that he clearly understood to define his whole purpose, he is not a good moral example we should wish our children to emulate. If he was not raised, we can only conclude that he did not come to demonstrate God's universal love, or to exhibit moral virtue and inspire us to lead lives of self-sacrifice, but rather to make absurd claims for himself. According to the Scriptures, Jesus did demonstrate God's love and he did model self-sacrifice for us, but far more is claimed and therefore far more is at stake.

Jesus did not view his mission as that of bringing universal peace and understanding (Matt. 10:34), nor did he come to reassure everybody that they were acceptable to God even if they came to God through different paths (John 8:24, 44). In fact, he said, "When you have lifted up the Son of Man, then you will know that I am the one I claim to be . . ." (John 8:28). Audaciously, Jesus said that anyone who believed in him would live forever (v. 51).

If Jesus was not raised, how are we to view this man? If in his own self-understanding his resurrection was central and integral to his whole identity as Messiah, is there any possibility of "reconstructing" a Jesus worth worshiping in the absence of that resurrection?

Can We Trust the Gospels?

The first plank in a defense of the internal witness to the Resurrection is our Lord's own self-consciousness. No modern theologian could know the inner life of Jesus other than Jesus himself. So, if he or she trusts the biblical record enough to accept the "enlightened moral principles" of the Sermon on the Mount or the commandment to love one's neighbor, he or she must also accept the self-descriptions Jesus offers in the same texts.

But that begs the question, Can we trust the Gospel accounts? Perhaps Jesus got it right, but how do we know that the authors of the New Testament did the same? Can we be sure that the ascriptions of deity, miracles, an atoning death, and resurrection are not later editorial additions that exaggerated the claims of Jesus himself? To do this, first of all, not only the New Testament writers would be called into question, but the Old Testament writers as well. As we have discussed, the Bible is a single story.

As early as Genesis 3, Scripture anticipates a Messiah who will defeat the curse of sin, death, tyranny, and hell. The Psalmist's Messiah is the Son who must be embraced in order to avoid judgment (Ps. 2). Isaiah's Servant is Yahweh himself and . . .

"Though the LORD makes his life a guilt offering,
    He will see his offspring and
    prolong his days,

And the will of the LORD
    will prosper in his hand.
After the suffering of his soul,
He will see the light of life and be satisfied"
(Isa. 53:10–11 NIV).

It is also the case that Ezekiel's Shepherd-to-come is no less than the Creator and Redeemer-God. It bears repeating: It is not only the claims of New Testament disciples, but the expectations of Old Testament prophets that must be rejected if the Resurrection is discarded.

Second, the Gospel accounts are not late editions, as much recent scholarship is beginning to concede. While the theory of the Gospels as second-generation exaggerations may have propelled the liberal movements of yesteryear (and the "Jesus Seminar" of contemporary infamy), the consensus among New Testament scholars is that the Gospels of Matthew and Luke originate no later than A.D. 85, and possibly as early as 50.

Even the arguments for the later date (A.D. 85) rest entirely on the assumption that Jesus could not have predicted the fall of Jerusalem (i.e. an antisupernaturalist presupposition), which occurred in the year A.D. 70. Matthew criticizes the powerful party of the Sadducees (they denied the resurrection of the dead), but this sect was barely known by A.D. 70 and soon passed out of existence altogether. Moreover, many scholars now believe that Matthew's Gospel is based on Mark's, and that would obviously date Mark's Gospel well within the range of thirty years after the Resurrection itself.

A popular theory among liberals, advanced also by Bultmann, is that the apostle Paul is the culprit for the alleged exaggerations. It is believed that Paul's many attributions of deity to the risen Christ created what amounted to a Jesus cult—a cult far from the original vision of even Christ himself. And yet, recent scholarship has concluded that Paul's letters are the earliest New Testament writings. Since Paul was martyred under Nero, and the Roman emperor died in A.D. 68, the dating of these letters cannot reflect a second-generation exaggeration of the actual events. Furthermore,

Paul invites skeptics to interview some of those five hundred to whom Jesus appeared at one time, "of whom the greater part remain to the present, but some have fallen asleep" (1 Cor. 15:6).

Considering these dates, there simply wasn't time to invent the sort of sophisticated Christology that we find in the New Testament. Paul can hardly be viewed as having turned a "simple teacher" into a god-man if the Old Testament anticipates a God-Man, and if Paul's letters are actually the earliest New Testament documents. But there remains another internal obstacle: the consistency of the reporting in the Gospels. John Shelby Spong spells out and defends the conventional account of the discrepancies:

> Who went to the tomb at dawn on the first day of the week? Paul said nothing about anyone going. Mark said that Mary Magdalene, Mary the mother of James, and Salome went (chap. 16). Luke said that Mary Magdalene, Mary the mother of James, Joanna, and some other women went (24:10). Matthew said Mary Magdalene and the other Mary only went (28:1). John said that Mary Magdalene alone went (20:11) . . .[8]

Ignoring the character of event reporting, Spong expects a rigid correspondence between the accounts. First, "Paul said nothing about anyone going [to the tomb]," Spong states. But Paul himself clearly tells us that he was not an eyewitness of the earthly ministry of Christ, but that the risen Lord appeared to him on the Damascus Road. Paul could only report as an eyewitness the things he himself saw. We could actually view Paul with greater suspicion if he did attempt to give reports of events as if he were an eyewitness, since we know he was not present.

Is there, then, a problem when each Gospel lists different people at the tomb? If this were a report concerning any other public event, we would probably conclude that every name mentioned in all the accounts together must have been present at the tomb. An incomplete report does not amount to a false or contradictory report. More than that, it is quite possible that there were many others besides who are not named. In any case, we do not find a contradiction.

Matthew does not say, as Spong unscrupulously slips into the account, that no one other than Mary was at the tomb. Spong himself refers to Mary Magdalene's second visit to the tomb. In reporting on a public event, especially one of such significance, it is essential to take into account the dynamic flow of activity. One would hardly expect such an event to be neat and tidy. In fact, our suspicions would be raised if the reports were neat and tidy. There is nothing that Spong has here described that would be taken as contradictory by a journalist in a similar situation.

But there is more, says Spong:

What did the women find at the tomb? [Mark] said that the women found a young man dressed in white garments who gave the resurrection message. Luke said it was two men clothed in dazzling apparel. Matthew said it was nothing less than an "angel of the Lord" who descended in an earthquake, put the armed guard to sleep, rolled back the stone, and gave the resurrection message. John began with no messenger at all, but on Mary Magdalene's second visit she confronted two angels, although they were speechless. Finally she confronted Jesus himself, whom she mistook for the gardener. From Jesus she received the resurrection message. Did the women see the risen Lord in the garden at dawn on the first day of the week? Mark and Luke said no. Matthew said yes. John said yes also, but he insisted that it was a little bit later. Where did the risen Christ appear to the disciples?[9]

Let us first reduce the discrepancies by beginning with the least difficult. As with the explanation for the different list of names at the tomb, one might easily suggest that "a man dressed in white garments" (Mark), "two men clothed in dazzling apparel" (Luke), "an angel of the Lord" (Matthew), and "two angels" (John), has a common explanation.

If one eyewitness sees one person and another eyewitness sees two, what is our usual explanation? If, for instance, an eyewitness spots a gunman aiming for a human target, does that render the testimony of another eyewitness invalid if he sees two gunmen? Such discrepancies only serve to strengthen the event character of such testimony.

Discrepancies militate against collusion and collaboration. If the disciples were to have gathered together in an effort to circulate a resurrection story that never really happened, we would expect them to give painstaking attention to the elimination of every possible difference in their reports. One would have the impression from such a project that everyone saw the same thing from exactly the same spot, but that impression is precisely what is missing from these accounts. These writings have the ring of typical eyewitness reports of actual events.

Thus, the testimony concerning the herald of Christ's resurrection at the tomb is not at all contradictory. Luke and John report two men, while Mark and Matthew refer to one. If there were two, that would obviously not rule out the one to whom Mark and Matthew referred. Furthermore, if these men were angelic beings (Matthew and John), we would hardly be surprised to find them described as wearing "white garments" (Mark) or "dazzling apparel" (Luke). There are differences, but not a single example of what Spong judges a "sea of contradictions."[10]

Can We Trust the Disciples?

We find a host of other internal evidences, only a few of which we can mention here. First, we notice throughout the Gospels that the writers hardly paint themselves and each other with pomp or majesty. Not only do they confess their sinfulness, but report the details of it as well. By their own admission, filled with grief, ignorant of what lay ahead (in spite of the Lord's many references to these events), the disciples could not even stay awake with Jesus in prayer. When he was arrested, they fled. Peter's pathetic denial of Christ is described in heart-breaking specifics, and the small band of disciples still following Jesus by the time he returns to Jerusalem for his crucifixion is weak, faithless, and utterly impotent in the face of it all.

So how could such a ragtag band, so cowardly in the face of danger, suddenly transform itself into a committee for the propaganda of false claims for which they would be martyred? They were already despairing, grieving for their Lord, so what made them change their tune so radically? One of the alternatives that has been offered to replace the Resurrection was that Jesus wasn't really dead in the first place, but was resuscitated. Emory University's Luke Timothy Johnson replied this way: "A resuscitation is excellent news for the patient and family. But it is not 'good news' that affects everyone else. It does not begin a religion. It does not transform the lives of others across the ages. It is not what is being claimed by the first Christians."[11]

Johnson's remarks could apply to all other alternative explanations for the Resurrection. Whatever happened, it had to account for the fact that cowards became martyrs. Although he denied the Resurrection, liberal theologian Adolf von Harnack understood the pivotal position of the belief itself. He wrote, "The firm confidence of the disciples in Jesus was rooted in the belief that He did not abide in death, but was raised by God. That Christ was risen was, in virtue of what they had experienced in Him, certain only after they had seen Him, just as sure as the fact of His death, and became the main article of their preaching about Him."[12]

Could the disciples have been deluded? Perhaps their grief had led to a severe case of depression that resulted in mass hysteria and the Resurrection was the only way out of it all. But is it really plausible to believe that literally hundreds of eyewitnesses were suffering from the same condition? And did masses of converts multiply because they experienced the same mass neurosis? Furthermore, this question is still left unanswered: Where was the body? Mass hysteria cannot move corpses from one place to another, particularly in this case, when both Jewish and Roman soldiers guarded the body.

External Evidence for the Resurrection

The late first-century Jewish historian Josephus recorded the following words that continue to haunt modern readers:

Now there was about this time Jesus, a wise man, if it be lawful to call him a man; for he was a doer of wonderful works, a teacher of such men as receive the truth with pleasure. He drew over to him many Jews, and also many of the Greeks. This man was the Christ. And when Pilate had condemned him to the cross, upon his impeachment by the principal man among us, those who had loved from the first did not forsake him, for he appeared to them alive on the third day, the divine prophets having spoken these and thousands of other wonderful things about him. And even now, the race of Christians, so named from him, has not died out.[13]

Although many have sought to refute the claim that Josephus is this passage's author, the passage is included in the standard Loeb edition of his works. Hardly interested in impressing the Christians, the audience for Josephus's *Antiquities* was the Roman court, and Josephus is hardly sympathetic to the Christians themselves in this work.

Much more could be said about the Jewish and Roman soldiers who had fled their post. Whatever it was that scattered them that first Easter morning, it was a greater source of fear than the certain execution appointed for Roman soldiers who deserted their posts. We could describe in great detail, from Roman military histories, the discipline of first-century Roman soldiers, and the stone at the mouth of the grave, and the way in which it was sealed to further guard its contents.

Are we really to believe that this same band of cowardly men and several women terrified the soldiers, broke the seal, removed the immense stone, and carried the region's most carefully watched body to a remote location? And what did they gain from this? How did they benefit from such an incredible theft? They were sent to their deaths—not for stealing a body, for no one even charged them with this, but for raising a seditious conspiracy against imperial power.

Surely the accusers could have come up with a better charge— all they would have had to have produced was the body of Jesus.

Instead, these early martyrs are charged with causing civil unrest. Just this sort of claim is made by the Roman historian and government official Tacitus in the year 64. Nero, he said, "justly" punished the Christians for the fire of Rome, although it was in fact Nero's own doing:

> The one from whom [the name "Christian"] originated, Christ, had been executed during the reign of Tiberius at the hands of the procurator, Pontius Pilate. For a time this pernicious superstition was suppressed, but it broke out again, not only in Judea where this evil thing began, but even in the city itself where everything atrocious and shameful from all quarters flows together and finds adherents [Rome]. To begin with, those who openly confessed were arrested, and then a vast multitude was convicted on the basis of their disclosures, not so much on the charge of arson as for their hatred of the human race. Their execution was made into a game: they were covered with the skins of wild animals and torn to pieces by dogs. They were hung on crosses. They were burned, wrapped in flammable material and set on fire as darkness fell, to illuminate the night.[14]

Gaius Pliny, Governor in Asia Minor, composed the following report to Emperor Trajan: "They [the Christians] . . . sing a hymn to Christ as to a god. . . . The matter seems to me worthy of consultation, especially because of the large number of those imperiled. For many of all ages, of every rank, and of both sexes are already in danger, and many more will come into danger. The contagion of this superstition has spread not only in the cities, but even to the villages and to the country districts. Yet I still feel it is possible to check it and set it right."[15]

Quite apart from the biblical witnesses, therefore, hostile witnesses (Jews and Romans) who had everything to gain by fashioning credible alternatives to the Resurrection claim were at a complete loss. They referred to the historical reality of Christ's death and burial. Even when they, for obvious reasons, refused to accept the Resurrection, they failed to offer Christ's body. Nor did they provide alternative explanations for the empty tomb or for the sudden tumult created by the Resurrection claim throughout the empire.

On the steps of the temple during the Feast of Pentecost, following Christ's ascension, Peter boldly proclaimed the Resurrection. And among the international community of Jews and Jewish converts gathered for the feast, the new Israel's identity was shaped. As news spread, men and women from well-educated classes as well as slaves—Jews and Gentiles—embraced a hope that they knew could seal their death. They were assured that by holding to Christ's resurrection from the dead, in the end death itself would be conquered.

SEVEN

Ascended in Glory, Returning in Judgment

+✚+ +✚+ +✚+

HE ASCENDED TO HEAVEN
AND SITTETH AT THE RIGHT
HAND OF GOD THE FATHER
ALMIGHTY. FROM THENCE HE
SHALL COME TO JUDGE THE
QUICK AND THE DEAD.

When Britain's sovereigns are crowned, a solemn question is asked of their subjects: "I present to you your undoubted king. Will you do him homage?"

In unison, Westminster Abbey's throng cheers in (it is hoped) triumphant affirmation.

In similar fashion both Old and New Testaments offer to us our King and demand our response: "Kiss the Son" (Ps. 2:12), for at his name every knee is bowed (Phil. 2:10).

With our Redeemer's glorious resurrection, his humiliation is finally concluded. Having emptied himself of the privileges of his Godhead, the God-Man has conquered death and hell. He has successfully completed his dark night in the valley of the shadow of death. Now, he has not only assumed his preincarnate glory, but has entered the gates of paradise as the conquering king who has finally imprisoned the deceiver until the day when he will crush the serpent's head forever.

Who Is This King of Glory?

It has been our practice throughout these chapters to follow each theme through the larger story of redemption, from Genesis to Revelation. And no clearer anticipation of our Lord's ascension can be found than in David's Psalms. The Second Psalm is the beginning of the so-called war songs of the Son of David:

Why do the nations conspire and the peoples plot in vain?
The kings of the earth take their stand
And the rulers gather together
Against the LORD and against his Anointed One.
"Let us break their chains," they say,
"And throw off their fetters."
The One enthroned in heaven laughs;
The LORD scoffs at them.
Then he rebukes them in his anger
And terrifies them in his wrath, saying,
"I have installed my King
On Zion, my holy hill."
I will proclaim the decree of the LORD:
He said to me,
"You are my Son;
Today I have become your Father.
Ask of me, and I will make the nations your inheritance,
The ends of the earth your possession.
You will rule them with an iron scepter;
You will dash them to pieces like pottery."
Therefore, you kings, be wise;
Be warned, you rulers of the earth.

Serve the LORD with fear
And rejoice with trembling.
Kiss the Son, lest he be angry
And you be destroyed in your way,
For his wrath can flare up in a moment.
Blessed are all who take refuge in him. (NIV)

Many readers will recall this text from Handel's *Messiah*. Its words require us to pause in sober reflection or, as the Psalmist advises, to "rejoice with trembling." While the unbelieving world seeks autonomy, God has already spoken and acted. The matter is settled: He has enthroned his King on Zion, his holy hill.

In the ancient world, the emperor would sometimes seal the treaty between his empire and a lesser kingdom by a regal ceremony in which the local king would take his place at the right hand of the emperor, the place of power and authority. Thus, he would be adopted in a sense by the great king as a son.

Some have used this psalm to justify the notion that the Messiah was merely a man who was adopted by the Father, but who in himself possessed no divine nature. But the text describes a military adoption, a governmental relationship, not a familial arrangement. Although he is the Son by eternal generation, the Messiah will be given a kingdom by the Father. Furthermore, his kingdom will not merely be a lesser realm, but will itself constitute the empire: "Ask of me, / and I will make the nations your inheritance, / the ends of the earth your possession" (v. 8). In that day, the kings and rulers will be forced to stand in line and, one by one, kiss the Son as acceptance of his reign.

Perhaps the richest Ascension Psalm is the twenty-fourth. We recall the twenty-third, a comfort to mourners for thousands of years. But now the Messiah has passed through the valley of death's shadow, and as that psalm ends with the line, "I will dwell in the house of the LORD forever," the Twenty-fourth Psalm picks up with the following:

The earth is the LORD's, and everything in it,
The world, and all who live in it;

For he founded it upon the seas
And established it upon the waters.
Who may ascend the hill of the LORD?
Who may stand in his holy place?
He who has clean hands and a pure heart,
Who does not lift up his soul to an idol
Or swear by what is false.
He will receive blessing from the LORD
And vindication from God his Savior.
Such is the generation of those who seek him,
Who seek your face, O God of Jacob.
Lift up your heads, O you gates;
Be lifted up, you ancient doors,
That the King of glory may come in.
Who is this King of glory?
The LORD strong and mighty,
The LORD mighty in battle.
Lift up your heads, O you gates;
Lift them up, you ancient doors,
That the King of glory may come in.
Who is he, this King of glory?
The LORD Almighty—
He is the King of glory. (NIV)

Many of us have heard this psalm explained as though it were somehow about us. Accordingly, if we have clean hands and a pure heart, we will ascend the hill of the LORD. But once we see the whole psalm in context, we come to realize that there is someone else in view. After all, "Who can say, 'I have kept my heart pure; I am clean and without sin?'" (Prov. 20:9 NIV).

David surely does not have himself in mind here, for he did not keep his heart pure, and his hands were stained with the blood of Uriah after having committed adultery with Uriah's wife. "Surely I was sinful at birth, / sinful from the time my mother conceived me," David confessed (Ps. 51:5 NIV). No, the one who is worthy to ascend the LORD's hill and to stand in his holy place is none other than the King of glory himself. "Who is he, this King of glory? / The LORD Almighty— / he is the King of glory" (Ps. 24:10 NIV).

But what is theLORD Almighty doing ascending his own hill and standing in his own holy place? Several intriguing features deserve mention at this point. First, this is one of the great "Psalms of Ascent" that the children of Israel sang as they made their way to Jerusalem, the earthly replica of God's holy hill.

On Mount Zion stood Solomon's glorious temple, where sacrifices would be brought. As the earthly replica of the heavenly throne room, Zion's temple was Israel's meeting place with God. Nevertheless, God's people could not enter the Holy of Holies, the place of God's Presence. Only the high priest could enter, and that only once a year and after carefully undergoing ritual cleansing. He had to bring a sacrifice not only for the people, but for himself.

The slightest violation of God's instructions meant immediate death for the high priest. No one trespassed into the Holy of Holies and lived to tell about it. Thus, "Who can stand in his holy place?" Only a perfect priest could enter the Holy of Holies behind the veil and offer a sacrifice that would forever satisfy the righteous requirements of a holy God.

The Garden of Eden was God's first temple, the Holy Land of God's Presence among his people. Before the Fall, of course, there was no need of a sacrifice for sin, and the royal couple enjoyed uninterrupted access to God's holy Presence. But the presence of God's fallen archenemy meant that there was always a threat to this kingdom. As God's underlord, Adam was to drive the serpent from the Holy Land. But instead of fulfilling his office, he joined Satan's conspiracy and God's kingdom was removed to heaven.

Generations later, God called Abraham and formed a nation for his own dwelling place. The Land of Promise was given to Abraham's offspring, but when his people finally came to possess the land, they too failed to drive out the enemies of God and his kingdom. Eventually, they settled down with their idolatrous neighbors, married unbelievers, and corrupted the land that God had given them for a dwelling place with him.

God sent Israel into exile from the Promised Land as he had Adam and Eve. Just as he had placed heavenly guards at the entrance to Eden with flashing swords, so he placed them at the gate to Solomon's temple, barring access to his holy hill. Israel cried out again to God for mercy. Her Father heard from heaven and rescued his people, returning them to the land, until her corruption once more expelled and scattered them.

"The Kingdom Is Near!"

Finally, centuries later, John the Baptist came preparing the way for God's triumphal entry into his ravaged garden: "Repent, for the kingdom of heaven is near." In fact, says Matthew, "This is he who was spoken of through the prophet Isaiah: 'A voice of one calling in the desert, "Prepare the way for the Lord, make straight paths for him"'" (Matt. 3:3 NIV). In preparation for his ministry, Jesus was led by the Holy Spirit into the wilderness where he was to face the ancient enemy of his kingdom.

Taking advantage of Jesus' humanity, Satan tempted the fasting Servant of the Lord: "If you are the Son of God, tell these stones to become bread" (Matt. 4:3). As he had tempted the first Adam so long before with the delight of forbidden fruit, so now he tortured the Second Adam's empty stomach with food. Instead of giving in, however, the Son of Adam answered with the Word: "It is written: 'Man does not live on bread alone, but on every word that comes from the mouth of God'" (v. 4). But that was not the end of the ordeal in the wilderness:

> Then the devil took him to the holy city and had him stand on the highest point of the temple. "If you are the Son of God," he said, "throw yourself down. For it is written: 'He will command his angels concerning you, and they will lift you up in their hands, so that you will not strike your foot against a stone.'" Jesus answered him, "It is also written: 'Do not put the Lord your God to the test.'" Again, the devil took him to a very high mountain and showed him all the kingdoms of the world and their splendor.

"All this I will give you," he said, "if you will bow down and worship me." Jesus said to him, "Away from me, Satan! For it is written: 'Worship the Lord your God, and serve him only.'" Then the devil left him, and angels came and attended him (Matt. 4:5–11, NIV).

In each case, even though he was himself God, the Son of Adam replied with God's Word and not in his own strength. How differently he responded to the serpent's temptation! While Adam was only too willing to accept the offer of power and glory, the Second Adam was eager to accept the offer of weakness and humiliation "for the joy set before him" (Heb. 12:2 NIV).

Every encounter with Satan and his demonic hosts thereafter was an opportunity to cleanse God's temple of the serpent, and to drive the demonic hosts from the Land: "But if I drive out demons by the Spirit of God, then the kingdom of God has come upon you. Or again, how can anyone enter a strong man's house and carry off his possessions unless he first ties up the strong man? Then he can rob his house." (Matt. 12:28–29 NIV).

Jesus was the faithful Adam, and the truly consecrated Israel:

For I endure scorn for your sake,
And shame covers my face.
I am a stranger to my brothers,
An alien to my own mother's sons;
For zeal for your house consumes me,
And the insults of those who insult you fall on me.
(Ps. 69:7–9 NIV)

Our Lord announced the arrival of his kingdom, and this time it was not merely an earthly replica like Eden or Palestine. It was the heavenly reality itself upon which even the Patriarchs had set their hopes.

Satan is bound, like the strong man who must first be chained before his house can be robbed. As David's soldiers reported astonishment at being able to subdue the Canaanites because God himself rode in battle before them, so the seventy-two disciples returned to Jesus short of breath: "Lord, even the demons submit to us in your name." Jesus replied, "I saw Satan fall like lightning from heaven," and assures them that the Gospel will now go forth with authority (Luke 10:17–18 NIV).

These are not patterns for us to imitate, but historical events—once and for all victories—that we are to joyfully accept, for they make the kingdom's success inevitable. Today, we are not intended to go about binding Satan and his minions. Instead, while he is chained, we have been given the astonishing task of untying Satan's captives and emptying his prisons by the proclamation of the Gospel.

Our Savior's victory on the Cross had secured, once and for all, the outcome of the war of the ages: "When you were dead in your sins and in the uncircumcision of your sinful nature, God made you alive with Christ. He forgave us all our sins, having canceled the written code, with its regulations, that was against us and that stood opposed to us; he took it away, nailing it to the cross. And having disarmed the powers and authorities, he made a public spectacle of them, triumphing over them by the cross" (Col. 2:13–15 NIV).

In light of this, there is a great danger in attributing to ourselves or to the church the victories accomplished by Christ's Cross and distributed by him to his apostles. It was his cross that "disarmed the powers and authorities," and it is now by the proclamation of the cross—not by naming and claiming or binding demonic forces and generational curses—that Satan's kingdom is reduced to ashes.

And so it is, that the Twenty-fourth Psalm paints the picture of the King of glory and his triumphal procession. The cheering heavenly crowds are calling for the ancient doors to be raised. And now we see the lonely, hungry, humiliated, and disgraced Servant of the Wilderness gloriously arrayed in his regal coronation robes. He who has been lifted up on the cross is now lifted up on a throne of gold, as the victim is now the victor.

But that is not all that we notice in this scene. It was customary, especially in Roman times, for conquering generals to bring in their triumphal procession their own prisoners of war. With such scenes

136

in mind, the writer to the Hebrews puts in the mouth of Jesus the words of Isaiah 8:18: "'Here am I, and the children God has given me.' Since the children have flesh and blood, he too shared in their humanity so that by his death he might destroy him who holds the power of death—that is, the devil—and free those who all their lives were held in slavery by their fear of death" (Heb. 2:13–15 NIV).

The Psalmist prophesied ultimately of this scene,

The chariots of God are tens of thousands
And thousands of thousands;
The Lord has come from Sinai into his sanctuary.
When you ascended on high,
You led captives in your train;
You received gifts from men,
Even from the rebellious—
That you, O LORD God, might dwell there. (Ps. 68:17–18 NIV)

Paul picks up on this passage in Ephesians 4:8 and 10:

This is why it says:
"When he ascended on high,
He led captives in his train and gave gifts to men."
(. . . He who descended is the very one who ascended higher than all the heavens, in order to fill the whole universe. (NIV)

So Jesus enters as the King of glory with prisoners of war in his triumphal procession. Because they are in his train, purchased by his victory, covered in his wedding garments, they are worthy to ascend the hill of the Lord with their elder brother, their greater Adam, and to stand in the holy place forever. God has finally made his dwelling among humanity without end:

The LORD says to my Lord:
"Sit at my right hand
Until I make your enemies a footstool for your feet."
The LORD will extend your mighty scepter from Zion;

You will rule in the midst of your enemies.
Your troops will be willing
On your day of battle.
Arrayed in holy majesty, from the womb of the dawn
You will receive the dew of your youth.
The LORD has sworn
And will not change his mind:
"You are a priest forever
In the order of Melchizedek."
The Lord is at your right hand;
He will crush kings on the day of his wrath.
He will judge the nations,
Heaping up the dead
And crushing the rulers of the whole earth. (Ps. 110:1–6 NIV).

Jesus Predicts His Ascension

Silent throughout his trial, Jesus finally answered Pilate's question, "Tell us if you are the Christ, the Son of God," with this bold statement:

> Yes, it is as you say. . . . But I say to all of you: In the future you will see the Son of Man sitting at the right hand of the Mighty One and coming on the clouds of heaven (Matt. 26:64).

The high priest tore his clothes, crying out, "Blasphemy!" Jesus saw his Ascension and Second Coming almost as a single event, for his enthronement at the Father's right hand is completed only when he finally subdues all enemy forces forever and judges the nations. Even as he prays to the Father before his crucifixion, Jesus is already anticipating his victory: "And now, Father, glorify me in your presence with the glory I had with you before the world began" (John 17:5 NIV).

The apostolic testimony is just as clear about our Lord's Ascension. The event itself is recorded in Luke's Gospel (24:50–53) and in Acts 1:1–11, where his angels comfort the disciples with the declaration that he will return just as he was taken, in glory and majesty. Never again would they see him with no place to lay his head, much less lifted up on a cross, except in their preaching and worship. Peter proclaimed Christ as "exalted to the right hand of God" (Acts 2:33 NIV) and even reiterated this point before the Sanhedrin: "God exalted him to his own right hand as Prince and Savior that he might give repentance and forgiveness of sins to Israel" (Acts 5:31 NIV).

Paul described God's power by referring to these events:

> That power is like the working of his mighty strength, which he exerted in Christ when he raised him from the dead and seated him at his right hand in the heavenly realms, far above all rule and authority, power and dominion, and every title that can be given, not only in the present age but also in the one to come. And God placed all things under his feet and appointed him to be head over everything for the church, which is his body, the fullness of him who fills everything in every way. (Eph. 1:19–23 NIV)

There is no doubt that the earliest Christians, who were eyewitnesses of the Lord's life and saving work, were convinced that Jesus had not only been raised, but that he had ascended to the highest position of authority in the cosmos. And yet he has never forgotten that he is our brother, with his scars and nail prints as a constant reminder. This reminder of his fellowship with us leads us to the question, What benefit do we derive from Christ's present heavenly reign?

Jesus: Prophet, Priest, and King

The best way to answer this question is by appealing to Jesus' three-fold office as prophet, priest, and king. In Christ, we have a prophet who answers temptation with God's Word, a high priest who never ceases to plead for us in the inner sanctuary, a king who fully conquers the enemies of our salvation and drives them from the Holy Land of eternal Sabbath.

By his Ascension, Jesus secured an eternal prophetic office for himself. "Do not be troubled," he told his worried disciples on the way to his cross. "In my Father's house are many rooms; if it were not so, I would have told you. I am going there to prepare a place for you. And if I go and prepare a place for you, I will come back and take you to be with me that you also may be where I am" (John 14:1–3 NIV).

Jesus tells us what the Father has in store for his children, and by leaving this earth, he is preparing for our arrival. Furthermore, he promises to return for us.

Later in the same chapter, Jesus comforts his disciples with the promise of the Holy Spirit: "All this I have spoken while still with you. But the Counselor, the Holy Spirit, whom the Father will send in my name, will teach you all things and will remind you of everything I have said to you" (vv. 25–26).

Jesus explained that it is actually good that he leaves us, because the sending of the Holy Spirit will compensate for their loss. The Spirit is sent by the Father, in Christ's name, to teach the church about Christ and to remind the church of his truth. "When the Counselor comes, whom I will send to you from the Father, the Spirit of truth who goes out from the Father, he will testify about me. And you also must testify, for you have been with me from the beginning" (John 15:26–27 NIV).

In this way, the Holy Spirit will make the church's understanding of Christ's person and work much clearer than they had known even after being at the Master's side. Furthermore, the Spirit will make the church the visible, earthly representative of Christ. It is through the church that Christ will continue to exercise his offices in the world.

In all of these statements, the Holy Spirit is presented as the messenger of Christ, not of himself. "He will testify about me," Jesus says. It is by the ministry of the Holy Spirit, even at this moment, that our exalted Lord continues from heaven his prophetic ministry among us. It is the Spirit who enables us to understand and accept our Savior's voice in his Word, and it is the Spirit who brings us from spiritual death into the kingdom of the Redeemer. "My sheep hear my voice, . . . and they follow me, and they shall never perish" (John 10:27–28). Thus, Jesus prayed before his death, "Sanctify them by the truth. Your word is truth" (John 17:17).

Not only does Jesus Christ fulfill the role of prophet, he is also a priest. The Book of Hebrews introduces us to the richest explanation of the Old Testament priesthood and its fulfillment in Christ. "The Son is the radiance of God's glory and the exact representation of his being, sustaining all things by his powerful word. After he had provided purification for sins, he sat down at the right hand of the Majesty in heaven" (Heb. 1:3 NIV).

Beginning with the exaltation of Christ, Hebrews then turns to the temple and the priesthood. Unlike the Levitical priesthood, Israel's traditional line of priests, Melchizedek is a mysterious Old Testament figure who appears in Genesis 14:18–20. Described there as both a king and a priest, his name means "king of righteousness," and he was the king of Salem, meaning "peace," a city later to become Jerusalem, the City of Peace.

Abraham accepted Melchizedek's blessing. How unusual for a patriarch who is blessed by God himself to accept a blessing from this fascinating priest! He was obviously a minister of the true God, but we hear no more of him until we get to the Psalms.

After Abraham had gone to his reward, God established the tribe of Levi as the priesthood of Israel. Under Moses, the Levites carried out their office. But the Psalmist declared in the passage prophesying the ascension and reign of the Lord at the Father's right hand, "The LORD has sworn / and will not change his mind: 'You are a priest forever, in the order of Melchizedek'" (Ps. 110:4 NIV).

Hebrews picks up this theme again, observing that ever since Moses the Levites were alone allowed to be priests. Jesus, of course, came from the messianic tribe of Judah, not the priestly tribe of Levi. How could he become high priest? Hebrews announces the fulfillment of David's prophecy: Jesus is "a priest forever, in the order of Melchizedek" (5:6). He is the King of Righteousness, Ruler of Jeru'Salem, the City of Peace. His righteousness is imputed to believing sinners, and this allows them to stand in God's holy place without fear of judgment. The redeemed make their dwelling with God in peace and safety because their mediator never sleeps, but offers perpetual and eternal intercession for sinners who trust in him. Unlike the imperfect priesthood of the Levites, says the writer to the Hebrews, our Lord's priesthood is perfect and unending.

Similarly, Paul exults,

> What, then, shall we say in response to this? If God is for us, who can be against us? He who did not spare his own Son, but gave him up for us all—how will he not also, along with him, graciously give us all things? Who will bring any charge against those whom God has chosen? It is God who justifies. Who is he that condemns? Christ Jesus, who died—more than that, who was raised to life— is at the right hand of God and is also interceding for us. Who shall separate us from the love of Christ? (Rom. 8:31–35 NIV)

Robed in His Righteousness

One of the most fascinating shadows of our Lord's priestly mediation is found in Zechariah 3:1–5:

> Then he showed me Joshua the high priest standing before the angel of the LORD, and Satan standing at his right side to accuse him. The LORD said to Satan, "The LORD rebuke you, Satan! The Lord, who has chosen Jerusalem, rebuke you! Is not this man a burning stick snatched from the fire?" Now Joshua was dressed in filthy clothes as he stood before the angel. The angel said to those who were standing before him, "Take off his filthy clothes." Then he said to Joshua, "See, I have taken away your sin, and I will put rich garments on you." Then I said, "Put a clean turban on his head." So they put a clean turban on his head and clothed him, while an angel of the LORD stood by. (NIV)

Satan is described as "the accuser of the brethren" (Rev. 12:10), which is a legal term equivalent to the title, prosecuting attorney.

While he is chained, he continues to accuse, and although he is banished from the heavenly courtroom, he seeks to renew God's prosecution of our case. But even though Joshua the high priest is dressed in filthy rags (which is how Isaiah describes our righteousness in Isaiah 64:6), God exchanges these for clean and expensive garments. And then we find an astonishing prophecy from the mouth of God: "'Listen, O high priest Joshua and your associates seated before you, who are men symbolic of things to come: I am going to bring my servant, the Branch. See, the stone I have set in front of Joshua! There are seven eyes on that one stone, and I will engrave an inscription on it," says the LORD Almighty, "and I will remove the sin of this land in a single day"'" (Zech. 3:8–9 NIV).

Later in Zechariah we read of a crown for Joshua the high priest. Joshua represents Jesus, whose name is itself a form of "Joshua," and means, "He will save his people." And God says, "Here is the man whose name is the Branch, and he will branch out from his place and build the temple of theLORD. It is he who will build the temple of the LORD, and he will be clothed with majesty and will sit and rule on his throne. And he will be a priest on his throne" (6:12–13 NIV).

Thus, we are comforted each and every moment that our high priest ministers for us in the Holy of Holies. The prosecuting attorney is ejected from the courtroom. The case against us is dismissed because our sentence was executed on our high priest himself. But we are not only exonerated, we are actually declared "righteous," as if we had lived perfectly before God. And so we have only a defense attorney before the throne of God. He pleads our case, and the Father accepts his meritorious intercession as sufficient for our right to enjoy his eternal presence forever. "Therefore, since we have a great high priest who has gone through the heavens, Jesus the Son of God, let us hold firmly the faith we profess" (Heb. 4:14 NIV).

There are no candles to light, no buttons to push, no aisles to walk, no rededications or resolutions to do better. Nothing will suffice but the intercession of the high priest whose ministry is far superior to that of Moses. For Moses brought us to Mount Sinai, where God appeared in terror, clad in lightning and surrounded by peals of thunder. "But you have come to Mount Zion, to the heavenly Jerusalem, the city of the living God. You have come to thousands upon thousands of angels in joyful assembly, to the church of the firstborn, whose names are written in heaven. You have come to God, the judge of all men, to the spirits of righteous men made perfect, to Jesus the mediator of a new covenant, and to the sprinkled blood that speaks a better word than the blood of Abel" (Heb. 12:22–24 NIV).

Jesus, our prophet and our priest, is also our king. Throughout the many passages we have seen thus far on this subject, we observe a close relationship between the Ascension and the Second Coming. Jesus returns to heaven in order to prepare a place for us, and then returns to bring us to paradise (John 14:2–4). And so it is that the Apostles' Creed closely links the two: "He ascended to heaven and is seated at the right hand of God the Father Almighty. From there he shall come to judge the living and the dead."

We have seen the prophetic expectation of a messianic king who would rule over God's house forever, his domain spreading throughout the world. We have also seen our Lord's fulfillment of these declarations. In his earthly ministry, he cast out the demons, bound the strong man, and announced the presence of the kingdom. On the cross, he defeated death, hell, and the devil once and for all. In his resurrection Jesus began his triumphal procession back into glory from shame. The period in which we are now living is described as "the last days," because it is the period between the Ascension and Return. These two events are really thought of in terms of one sweeping action of salvation and judgment.

A God Who Rescues His People

Our age has been marked by what Nietzsche identified and encouraged as "the will to power." Or, as the pop group Tears for Fears put it, "Everybody wants to rule the world." Rid of absolutist monarchs and, after two horrific wars, having vanquished totalitarian dictatorships, ours is a profoundly antinomian (antilaw) and anarchical (antiruler) period. We want to be taken care of, but we don't want to be obligated to anyone or anything. Of Israel in the period of the judges, we read, "Everyone did what was right in his own eyes. For in those days Israel had no king" (Judg. 17:6). And after the failure of Israel's kings, when they did arrive on the scene, god himself came to rule his people. The King of Zion has taken his throne among us.

Christianity stands in sharp contrast to the antinomian sentiment. As we have seen, the Old Testament is one long treaty or covenant document. God binds himself to his people, and they bind themselves to him. Should they encounter foreign attack, the Great King will rush in with his armies and sweep away all oppressors. This is what it means whenever we read in Scripture about "calling upon the name of the Lord" from the time of Seth, when "at that time men began to call upon the name of the LORD" (Gen. 4:26 NIV) to the present moment (Rom. 10:13). This is done in order to invoke that line in the treaty wherein God has mercifully bound himself to come to our rescue.

Thus, it is first and foremost good news that Christ is king. If he were not king, someone or something else would reign over our destiny, something less than the good, merciful, long-suffering God who has declared on oath that he will never forsake his people despite their unfaithfulness (2 Tim. 2:13). He rules the world for our eternal good and for his glory (Rom. 8:28; Eph. 1:11) Can you think of any ruler in all of human history who has exercised such enormous power so sacrificially and graciously? Even when we sin against his kindness, he rewards our disobedience with fatherly correction rather than rejection (Prov. 3:12).

Our Redeemer's ascension and reign at the Father's right hand is not only good news for believers in their trials; it is bad news for the unrepentant. Raising the subject of judgment is a difficult business in any period. It is especially challenging during this time when the church has vacillated between the extremes of a self-righteous spirit of judgmentalism and utter silence about the reality of the wrath to come.

It is important to say, when we talk about judgment in biblical terms, that we are not talking about Christians judging non-Christians in the world. We've seen this point in our Lord's parable about the weeds and the wheat growing up together (Matt. 13:30). Paul makes the same point: "I wrote to you in my epistle not to keep company with sexually immoral people. Yet I certainly did not mean with the sexually immoral people of this world, or with the covetous, or extortioners, or idolaters, since then you would need to go out of the world . . . For what have I to do with judging those who are outside?" (1 Cor. 5:9–10, 12).

Paul says that it is professing Christians within the church who are to be held accountable by the church (vv. 11, 13). When we talk of judgment, too often it comes off merely as scolding unbelievers, the way parents reprimand their kids for coming home late for dinner. The world is probably getting the impression that it is we and not God who are on the judge's bench. They also may believe that judgment awaits those "bad people out there" such as pornographers, gays, atheists, swindlers, and abortionists, and not all of us together.

In the first three chapters of Romans, Paul attacks this self-righteousness. First, the Gentiles are under God's judgment, despite their confidence in idols. Then the Jews are under God's judgment, despite their confidence in the Law. Nobody is left standing by the time Paul finishes. Judgment isn't limited to extraordinarily obvious manifestations of human rebellion. Sin is not only a series of acts, which a handful of bad people commit. Sin is a condition from which none of us is exempt.

The King will come to judge. In his first coming, he came to save, not to condemn (John 3:17). But in his Second Coming, he will judge according to strict justice. The time for mercy will be over:

When the Lord Jesus is revealed from heaven with His mighty angels, in flaming fire taking vengeance on those who do not know God, and on those who do not obey the gospel of our Lord Jesus Christ. These will be punished with everlasting destruction from the presence of the Lord and from the glory of His power, when He comes, in that Day, to be glorified in His saints and to be admired among all those who believe, because our testimony among you was believed (2 Thess. 1:7–10).

Thus, our Redeeming King has ascended to heaven for this two-fold purpose: to secure the everlasting safety of his people, and to execute everlasting judgment against those who do not receive him. It is good news for all who will believe, but the worst possible news for those who go on in their ignorance, apathy, and rebellion. Christ is now in heaven and he will return. Will we be among those reconciled sinners who love his appearing? Or will we be among those who are caught in terror?

We find a foreshadowing of this in Genesis 18 with the three heavenly visitors on their way to destroy Sodom and Gomorrah. We are told that "the LORD appeared to Abraham near the great trees of Mamre" (v. 1). Two of the men were angels, but one was the LORD God himself (vv. 10, 13, 17, 20, 26, 33).

Since no one had seen God's face at any time, this divine appearance was a theophany. At first, in fact, the three messengers were taken to be men. They came to assure Abraham and Sarah of the unconditional promise of a son, but they were also on their way to judge Sodom. After Abraham unsuccessfully pleaded for the wicked city, the two angels went on to carry out their mission. While they pulled Lot and his family from the scene of judgment, Lot's wife looked back and was swept into the furious sea of God's wrath. "Then the LORD rained down burning sulfur on Sodom and Gomorrah—from the LORD out of the heavens" (Gen. 19:24 NIV).

Yahweh himself (perhaps a theophany of the preincarnate Son) is present with the angels to pronounce blessing and salvation to Abraham and his seed. But now, as he marches into battle, he returns to his heavenly throne. From heaven he will execute his judgment, but it will be carried out on earth by his two avenging angels. Further, observe how the inhabitants of these two cities mock God's judgment, even to the point of demanding that the two angels from Lot's house be given to them for sexual pleasure.

This judgment presages the greater one to come. Having inaugurated his kingdom and redeemed his people, Jesus has returned to heaven from where he will himself execute the last judgment, descending to earth with his elect. The Greater David will mount his war-horse, with chariots of wrath surrounding him, and when he gives the word, his kingdom will descend on this world for the final battle. "Kiss the . . . Son, lest you perish in your way, for his wrath can flare up in a moment" (Ps. 2:12).

This is why Paul warned the Athenians that God will not overlook their superstition and ignorance. "For he has set a day when he will judge the world with justice by the man he has appointed. He has given proof of this to all men by raising him from the dead" (Acts 17:31 NIV). On that day, the army of the Lord will be arrayed against the armies of the nations, and evil will be pulled up by the roots in every part of the globe.

This final judgment is the next major event in the unfolding of redemptive history, when the graves of soil and water will give up their dead to join the living in God's court:

"Just as man is destined to die once, and after that to face judgment, so Christ was sacrificed once to take away the sins of many people; and he will appear a second time, not to bear sin, but to bring salvation to those who are waiting for him" (Heb. 9:27–28).

For the church, as with Abraham, the sight of Christ in his majestic return will bring joy. But it will bring terror to the world, where there can only be "a fearful expectation of judgment and of raging fire that will consume the enemies of God" (Heb. 10:27 NIV). God will be without mercy on that day.

Of course, there will be those who say, *That may be the belief of strange fundamentalists, and it may have even been the belief of the apostles and the church throughout two millennia, but that certainly was not the religion that Jesus taught.* In fact, we find it taught more explicitly by Jesus than by anyone else in all of Scripture. Referring to a place where the Gospel had been rejected, Jesus told the disciples, "I tell you the truth, it will be more bearable for Sodom and Gomorrah on the day of judgment than for that town" (Matt. 10:15; and again in 11:24).

We can have no idea how holy God is and how sinful we are until we are faced with this kind of judgment: "But I tell you that men will have to give account on the day of judgment for every careless word they have spoken" (Matt. 12:36 NIV). Jesus said that all judgment has been entrusted to the Son (John 5:22; 8:26; 9:39; 12:31; 16:8, 11).

Is Hell for Real?

We have already seen examples of the many places where Jesus warns that those who do not believe will die in their sins (e.g., John 8:24), and Jesus says far more about the disturbing details of hell than any person in Scripture. He warns of "the fire of hell" (Matt. 5:22), of the body being thrown into hell (Matt. 5:29–30; 18:9), and of the body and soul together being cast into the fire (Matt. 10:28). He tells the Pharisees that they travel around the world to make a single convert, only to ensure that he is as destined for hell as they are (Matt. 23:15). "How can you escape being condemned to hell?" he asks (Matt. 23:33).

In Luke 16 we have the famous parable about the rich man and Lazarus, a beggar. Both died, but Lazarus went to Abraham's bosom, while the rich man called out to Abraham from the place of torment. He looked up and saw Abraham far away, with Lazarus by his side, "Father Abraham," he pleaded, "have pity on me and send Lazarus to dip the tip of his finger in water and cool my tongue, because I am in agony in this fire" (v. 24 NIV).

Lazarus, Abraham says, is now in comfort, "and you are in agony. And besides all this, between us and you a great chasm has been fixed, so that those who want to go from here to you cannot, nor can anyone cross over from there to us" (vv. 25–26 NIV).

Hell is a place of unalterable and inescapable torment with a great chasm separating its inhabitants from hope, love, peace, and joy. No one crosses from one point to the other: there are no visitors to this prison. Therefore, the rich man begs Abraham to send Lazarus to his father's house on earth, "'for I have five brothers. Let him warn them, so that they will not also come to this place of torment.' Abraham replied, 'They have Moses and the Prophets; let them listen to them.'

'No, Father Abraham,' he said, 'but if someone from the dead goes to them, they will repent.'" Who could dismiss the appearance of a dead man at one's door, warning of hell's agony? But Abraham answered, "'If they do not listen to Moses and the Prophets, they will not be convinced even if someone rises from the dead'" (vv. 28–31).

This parable is not only the story of our Lord's neighbors, but is the story of all of us. Dead in trespasses and sins (Eph. 2:1), we are incapable of accepting the Gospel in our sinful nature (1 Cor. 2:14). We must be born again if we are to see the kingdom of God (John 3:3). And, as in the days of Sodom and the days of Jesus, our world mocks God's judgment and continues as if there were no final reckoning:

> First of all, you must understand that in the last days scoffers will come, scoffing and following their own desires. They will say, "Where is this 'coming' he promised? Ever since our fathers died, everything goes on as it has since the beginning of creation." But they deliberately forget that long ago by God's word the heavens existed and the earth was formed out of water and by water. By these waters also the world of that time was deluged and destroyed. By the same word the present heavens and earth are reserved for fire, being kept for the day of judgment and destruction of ungodly men. But do not forget this one thing, dear friends: With the Lord a day is like a thousand years, and a thousand years are like a day. The Lord is not slow in keeping his promise, as some understand slowness. He is patient with you, not wanting anyone to perish, but everyone to come to repentance. But the day of the Lord will come like a thief. The heavens will disappear with a roar; the elements will be destroyed by fire, and the earth and everything in it will be laid bare. (2 Peter 3:3–10 NIV)

The present reprieve has given scoffers the opportunity to mock. But far from being evidence of a failed promise, it is the unbeliever's only light at the end of the tunnel before total darkness. It is not slowness, says Peter, but patience. God is unwilling to suffer the loss of a single person he has chosen (John 10:27–30), and his patience has created this period in which the Holy Spirit convicts of sin, and gives repentance and faith to sinners.

However, as in the days of Noah, Sodom, and our Lord, our age is oblivious to its imminent disaster: "But the day of the Lord will come like a thief." No one expects a thief. He comes suddenly and violently. On that day, the King will end the long war. At last the new heavens and the new earth will appear—the Holy Land where God is pleased to share with us forever his peace, joy, and rest.

But until that day, the church is persecuted by the serpent, just as it has been since Cain and Abel. In a fascinating apocalyptic portrait in Revelation 12, we see the dragon. Having failed to intercept the birth of the woman's son, the evil beast is enraged. "And her child was snatched up to God and to his throne" (v. 5), but the woman herself had to escape into the desert where she was cared for by God. During the heavenly war, the dragon and his angels were "hurled to the earth" in defeat. In heaven praise filled the temple:

> "For the accuser of our brothers, who accuses them before our God day and night, has been hurled down. They overcame him by the blood of the Lamb and by the word of their testimony."
> (Rev. 12:10–11)

These are wonderful pictures of the victory we already enjoy because of Christ, but there is more to the story. Even though the worst part of the war is over, we read, "But woe to the earth and the sea, because the devil has gone down to you! He is filled with fury, because he knows that his time is short" (v. 12).

During this present time, Satan's "house arrest" keeps him from deceiving the nations, so that the Gospel has been going forward with power and success around the world for nearly two millennia. His attempts through the ages to overturn God's plan and intercept the Seed of the woman have failed, and he knows that his head is to be crushed. The only thing left to do is to take as many people with him as possible.

Spiritual Warfare: The Real Conflict

Thus, the enemy seeks out the woman (Israel, God's people, the church) who gave birth to the Son, and he torments her. Although he is no longer allowed access to God's courtroom, he continues to accuse the brethren—if not before God, then before themselves. He comes to rob them of their joy. He tries to tempt them to give up waiting for a future glory and to demand health, wealth, happiness, and fulfillment here and now.

This is where spiritual warfare becomes so important. Today, most discussions of spiritual warfare focus on the sensational: binding demonic forces by "spiritual mapping," breaking generational curses, and other practices that can only be regarded as superstition. And yet, the primary text usually cited is Ephesians 6. Remarkably, there is nothing of this sort in this passage. It does, however, support the view of spiritual warfare we have been describing here. "Put on the full armor of God so that you can take your stand against the devil's schemes," we are told (v. 11). The armor includes the following: the belt of truth, the breastplate of righteousness, the shoes of the Gospel, the shield of faith, the helmet of salvation, and the sword of the Spirit. Let us look at each of these briefly.

First, Paul frequently insists on the importance of truth over every other consideration. Even unity must be defined by truth (Eph. 4:13–16).

Second, the breastplate of righteousness must surely refer to justification by grace alone through faith alone. Paul has labored to make sure that we understand that only a perfect righteousness— alien to us and worn as a robe—can make us stand without fear in God's presence. Those who look to themselves or to their own righteousness and holiness will be doomed. Satan's arrows, either of despair or of self-righteousness, will deal a fatal blow. We need righteousness that is external, not internal; given, not inherent.

Third, there are the shoes of the Gospel. We need an objective announcement of God's saving actions, turning our focus from ourselves to Christ.

Fourth, we need the shield of faith. Our experience, emotional crises, opinions, sentiments, speculation, or mystical intuition can never defend us against Satan's devices, for he knows that when we rely on them we are only committing sabotage against our own cause. Only faith in Christ justifies. It fixes its gaze on Jesus Christ, its author and finisher, and it becomes a shield, the fifth piece of armor.

Sixth, the helmet of salvation is another way of saying the same thing: only by knowing how God saves us can we fight with confidence that we are on the winning side.

And finally, the sword of the Spirit, Paul says, is nothing other than the Word of God, the written and preached Scriptures. Through the Word, the Spirit brings death to sin and raises us in newness of life.

I hope the reader will bear with my laboring this point, but it is crucial in our day. According to recent studies, we learn the following: Most evangelicals do not believe in absolute truth, so the belt of truth is missing. Most evangelicals believe that "in salvation, God helps those who help themselves," and think that human beings are by nature good, so gone is the breastplate of Christ's righteousness. Few evangelicals define the Gospel as God's saving work. Instead they turn their focus to their own subjective experiences and activities, so gone are the shoes of the Gospel, and the shield of faith. We are far too preoccupied with practical tips on the family, finances, self-esteem, and entertainment to be interested in the doctrinal category known as "salvation," so gone is the helmet that protects our head in battle. And when it comes to popular movements in Christian circles, the objective teaching and proclamation of Scripture is too often considered less spiritual than the direct whisper of the Holy Spirit to the individual heart.

Spiritual warfare demands nothing less than "the full armor" that God has faithfully supplied. And in every age where his people have strived valiantly against Satan's devices of heresy, error, and schism, it has been because they were making full use of God's provisions. Our heavenly king sends us into battle, anticipating the final conflict that will end all warfare in heaven and on earth forever.

It is a great comfort to know that our Savior is in heaven as our prophet, priest, and king even now. He is spoken of in his heavenly session as sitting at God's right hand in kingly state, but is also said to be "at God's right hand" (Rom. 8:34; 1 Peter 3:22), and at his martyrdom Stephen saw him standing at God's right hand in the martyr's defense (Acts 7:56). In the Revelation John saw the Son of Man walking among the candlesticks, representing the churches then under persecution. Of course, these are pictures, but they give us unmistakable clues as to our Lord's present activity.

Jesus is seated at the Father's right hand in power, judgment, and rule. He is standing at the Father's right hand in defense of his people as their priest. And by sending his Spirit, he is present among his churches as they, like him, endure the cross for the joy of the crown.

EIGHT

The Dove's Descent

+‡+ +‡+ +‡+

I BELIEVE IN THE HOLY GHOST.

The story is told of a soldier whose sword was feared far and wide. Intrigued by the famous weapon, the king demanded to examine it for himself. After carefully studying the sword, the king returned it to the soldier with the note, "I see nothing wonderful in the sword; I cannot understand why any man should be afraid of it."

The soldier confidently replied, "Your Majesty has been pleased to examine the sword, but I did not send the arm that wielded it. If you had examined that, you would have understood the mystery."

Thus far we have scaled the heights of biblical redemption and have recovered a fresh glimpse of God in the face of Christ. We have seen what our Lord meant when he said that the whole of Scripture spoke about him. We have heard of his promise to send his Spirit to convict unbelievers of sin and bring them to the Savior, leading the church into all truth. It is this promise whose glorious fulfillment concerns us in this chapter, because without the work of the Holy Spirit, Christian preaching, like that sword, would be impotent.

Books, including the Bible, are often overlooked in our day. In religious matters, many would prefer to follow their own intuitions, feelings, experiences, and speculative opinions. *How could a book change my life, some ask, much less the world?* Is it not so much ink and paper? Sermons have suffered much the same fate. Should the sermon occupy so central a place in the life of God's people, when there are so many more interesting and exciting demonstrations of power available, through entertaining spectacle and dramatic signs and wonders?

Like the king in the opening illustration, we examine the sermon-sword and wonder at its simplicity. Indeed, Paul spoke of "the foolishness of preaching," because it seems so unspectacular (Rom. 1:16). But the Gospel is, in truth, the power of God to salvation for everyone who believes. In the hands of the Holy Spirit, its divine author, this mighty spiritual sword always lives up to its fame.

But there is a tendency to separate the divine soldier—the Spirit—from his sword. Some exult in the power of the Spirit, while others are content to analyze the Bible without appearing to believe in the ministry of the Holy Spirit to any degree of practical significance. When we come to church, too often we are either expecting the Holy Spirit where he has not promised to be, or we are not expecting him at all. In this chapter, we affirm once again the grand announcement of our Creed: "I believe in the Holy Spirit."

Who Is the Holy Spirit?

Many misunderstandings surround the identity of the Father and the Son, and understanding of the Holy Spirit has also been subject to distortions. Some view God as a force or universal principle, and the Holy Spirit is easily misunderstood in those impersonal terms. This is not greatly helped by the use of the impersonal pronoun, *it* (instead of *he*),which we still find in the Authorized Version, and in the many older books and liturgies that have been influenced by this.

Some interpreters, influenced by radical feminist theology, gravitate to the Holy Spirit because they believe him to be the feminine manifestation of God. In fact, as Donald Bloesch has pointed out, *The New Century Hymnal,* compiled and amended by mainline denominations, excises references in the older hymns to God as Father, King, Lord, Son of God, and so forth. In their place are such vague terms as, "All-Inclusive One," "Great Spirit," or "Source of Being." And in some circles, feminine imagery is acceptable, with "Womb of Life," "Mother," and "Partner," becoming popular replacements for the masculine terms. Similarly, the Creeds are changed to read, "God's only Child," instead of, "Son," and, "I believe in God the Father-Mother almighty." In some revised forms of the Nicene Creed, one now confesses faith in the Holy Spirit, "who proceeds from the Father-Mother, and from the Child."

In more conservative circles, the Holy Spirit is the favored person of the Trinity wherever experience is central. There is a great danger in speaking of the Holy Spirit as if he were a power source that could be tapped by "plugging in" to the electrical surge. This is a magical view of the Holy Spirit—what some have called "spiritual technology"— and its mystical tendency is to reduce the Holy Spirit to a principle of power rather than to see him as a person, the Third Person of the Holy Trinity. We will examine the effects of this view of the Holy Spirit's person in relation to sanctification.

The first thing we must say about the Holy Spirit is that he is a personal being. But second, he is a spiritual being. While God is spirit by definition (John 4:24), it is the third person who bears the name, *Holy Spirit.* From the Hebrew word for breath, *spirit* is a common Old Testament term, but the Holy Spirit is specifically mentioned frequently as well. He is active in creation (Gen. 1:2), as were the Father (v. 1) and the Son (John 1:1–3).

In creating humanity, as we have seen, God refers to himself in plurality: "Let us make man in Our own image" (Gen. 1:26). It is his Spirit who convicts of sin (Gen. 6:3). Prophets, priests, and kings of Israel are spoken of as filled with the Spirit (Exod. 31:3) or as ministering in the Spirit (Num. 11:25; Judg. 6:34; 11:29; 13:25). He speaks to his prophets (1 Sam. 10:10; 16:13; 2 Sam. 23:2) and through them spoke his Word of judgment and pardon to the people (evidenced throughout the prophetic books).

In the New Testament, we learn even more about the nature of this mysterious Spirit. He is the Comforter (John 14 and 15), and the Intercessor (Rom. 8:26–27). As a person, he is actively involved in our salvation. In Berkhof's words, "He searches, speaks, testifies, commands, reveals, strives, creates, makes intercession, raises the dead, etc."[1]

As a person, the Spirit is spoken of as being grieved by human rebellion (Ps. 106:33; Isa. 63:10), and he is poured out in both salvation (Isa. 32:15; Joel 2:28) and in judgment (Gen. 11:1–9). The same themes are reiterated in the New Testament, where these prophecies of the coming Spirit are fulfilled. He is poured out in both salvation (for believers) and judgment (for unbelievers), as we see in Matthew 3:11.

Thus, the Holy Spirit, like the Father and the Son with whom he is coequal, is personal and spiritual. Though distinct from the Father and the Son, he exists together with them in an indivisible unity of Godhead: one not only in purpose, but in essence. He is nothing less than God himself (Exod. 17:7; Ps. 139:7–10; Isa. 40:13–14; Acts 5:3–4; 1 Cor. 3:16; 12:1; 2 Tim. 3:16; Heb. 9:14; 2 Peter 1:21).

What Is the Holy Spirit's Function?

The Holy Spirit is Creator and Redeemer, together with the Father and the Son. But he also is given a particular role in the project of redemption. As the Father elects and the Son redeems, the Holy Spirit convicts of sin and unites us to Christ.

While the danger in previous generations may have been to deny any practical significance to the Holy Spirit's ministry, today we must beware of separating the Holy Spirit from the Father and the Son as if he, alone, were God. We are to worship the Holy Spirit as coequal and coeternal with the Father and the Son. Nevertheless, the ministry of the Holy Spirit is to point away from himself to Christ.

When we want to see God, worship and praise him, acknowledging his wonderful acts of salvation, we are to focus our gaze on the God-Man, Jesus Christ, who has appeared and has revealed God to us. "He who has seen me," said Jesus, "has seen the Father" (John 14:9). And when he returns to the Father and sends the Holy Spirit, it will be the Spirit's ministry to teach the church about Christ (vv. 25–26; 15:26). His purpose in coming upon the church at Pentecost is to make his people witnesses of Christ (Acts 1:8).

J. I. Packer tells the story of a lovely cathedral in Vancouver, which is spectacularly floodlit at night. One would be foolish, of course, to take a stroll by the cathedral at night and stare into the brilliant lights, and of course, that is not the intention of those who put them there. Instead, one is meant to enjoy the view of the cathedral. In the same way, says Packer, the Holy Spirit is not given so he may bring attention to himself, but in order to expose the glory of Christ amid the dark night of sin and death. We need the Holy Spirit to illuminate Christ, but it is Christ who is the focus of our wonder.

What Is the Significance of the Coming of the Holy Spirit?

Haunted by the memory of the flood, the nations came together in the Mesopotamian plains to build a massive tower reaching to the heavens. Known as a ziggurat, an ancient temple-tower of this type would have been both religious and cultural in significance, binding communities together in the attempt to control their destiny. Never again would flood-waters swallow whole populations, they reasoned, not because of God's promise in the rainbow, but because a united, international effort would eventually create a skyscraper to which they could escape high above divine judgment. Therefore, we find the following scene in Genesis 11:1–4:

> Now the whole world had one language and a common speech. As men moved eastward, they found a plain in Shinar and settled there. They said to each other, "Come, let's make bricks and bake them thoroughly." They used brick instead of stone, and tar for mortar. Then they said, "Come, let us build ourselves a city, with a tower that reaches to the heavens, so that we may make a name for ourselves and not be scattered over the face of the whole earth. (NIV)

159

Employing new technology (for instance, brick instead of stone, and tar for mortar), this international effort was a massive undertaking—far greater than the building of the Egyptian pyramids. The goal was a city and a tower reaching to the heavens, "so that we may make a name for ourselves and not be scattered over the face of the whole earth," reflecting the deeply human-centered, proud and defiant spirit of secularism. It was at this point that God broke up the party:

> But the LORD came down to see the city and the tower that the men were building. The LORD said, "If as one people speaking the same language they have begun to do this, then nothing they plan to do will be impossible for them. Come, let us go down and confuse their language so they will not understand each other." So the LORD scattered them from there over all the earth, and they stopped building the city. That is why it was called Babel— because there the LORD confused the language of the whole world. From there the LORD scattered them over the face of the whole earth. (vv. 5–9)

In this section, the story takes a sharp turn: while the nations are climbing to the heavens in triumph, God is descending in judgment. While the proud builders are building a memorial to their own greatness, God is crushing, humbling, and scattering. If he does not judge this enterprise, the collective concentration of the fallen hearts of Adam's sons in one place will only lead to another great rebellion that will require a catastrophic divine response. It is, therefore, an act of mercy that God scatters the nations by confusing their languages. But it is also an act of judgment. The proud human boast, "Come, let us build a city and a tower" (v. 4), is met with God's countermove, "Come, let us go down and confuse their language so they will not understand each other" (v. 7). Babel's ascent in pride is met by God's descent in judgment; God turns her united effort, facilitated by a common language, into confusion and scattering.

Thus began the decentralization of the postdiluvian peoples. Although the tendency of humanity in its aggressive self-assertion was to build vast empires with a common language and culture, the great empires rose and fell. Israel was never to join herself to these worldly empires. She was to be a kingdom of priests to God.

In Babylonian exile, Daniel rose in king Nebuchadnezzar's esteem and interpreted his dreams. On one occasion, God gave the king another vision that deeply confused and tormented him. In that vision there was a massive statue whose head "was made of pure gold, its chest and arms of silver, its belly and thighs of bronze, its legs of iron, its feet partly of iron and partly of baked clay" (Dan. 2:31–33 NIV). While the king's gaze was fixed on this enormous statue, "a rock was cut out, but not by human hands. It struck the statue on its feet of iron and clay and smashed them. Then the iron, the clay, the bronze, the silver and the gold were broken to pieces at the same time and became like chaff on a threshing floor in the summer. The wind swept them away without leaving a trace. But the rock that struck the statue became a huge mountain and filled the whole earth" (vv. 34–35 NIV).

Daniel interpreted the dream for the king. Nebuchadnezzar is the head of gold, representing the Neo-Babylonian empire. The silver chest and arms stand for the Medo-Persian empire, established by Cyrus in 538 B.C. The middle section of bronze represents the Greek empire created by Alexander the Great two centuries later, and the iron legs and feet stand for the Roman empire. As each kingdom diminishes in the absolutism of despotic government, so each is weaker than its predecessor. Eventually, each civilization's boasts became new strata of rock upon which other empires would build their towers to the heavens.

Daniel describes the rock that shatters this layered statue:

"In the time of those kings, the God of heaven will set up a kingdom that will never be destroyed, nor will it be left to another people. It will crush all those kingdoms and bring them to an end, but it will itself endure forever. This is the meaning of the vision of the rock cut out of a mountain, but not by human hands—a rock that broke the iron, the bronze, the clay, the silver and the gold to pieces. The great God has shown the king what will take place in

the future. The dream is true and the interpretation is trustworthy."
Then King Nebuchadnezzar fell prostrate before Daniel and paid
him honor and ordered that an offering and incense be presented
to him. The king said to Daniel, "Surely your God is the God of
gods and the Lord of kings and a revealer of mysteries, for you
were able to reveal this mystery." (vv. 44–47 NIV)

The rock in Nebuchadnezzar's dream, like the descent of God
at Babel, will dismantle all the high towers of human pride. Even
the dazzling empire of Rome, whose Caesars claimed universal
power and dubbed their seat the "Eternal City," will lie in ruins. In
contrast to these great civilizations, God's kingdom will be truly
universal and eternal. Eventually, he will bring together the scattered nations and cause them to be one flock with one shepherd.

This hope is expressed and heightened in the prophetic literature. Isaiah's Suffering Servant will come to Israel and will make
his church to be "a light for the Gentiles, / to open eyes that are
blind, / to free captives from prison / and to release from the dun-
geon those who sit in darkness" (Isa. 42:6–7 NIV). Therefore, not
only Israel, but the nations are called to burst forth in praise to the
Lord, even the remote islands, deserts, towns, and cities (vv. 10–12).

The problem is that Israel itself, God's own congregation, was
no longer faithful. She had to be raised to newness of life herself,
and this too was prophesied. In Ezekiel's vision of the valley of dry
bones (Ezek. 37), the Holy Spirit brought him to the precipice over-
looking the vast cemetery. God asked the prophet, "Can these bones
live?" "Only you know," Ezekiel safely replied, and God commanded the prophet to preach the Gospel to the sea of skeletons.
Obeying God's voice, the prophet began to preach the Good News,
telling the bones of God's word to them. "I will make breath enter
you, and you will come to life. I will attach tendons to you and
make flesh come upon you and cover you with skin; I will put
breath in you, and you will come to life. Then you will know that I
am the LORD" (vv. 5–6 NIV).

While Ezekiel was preaching, "there was a noise, a rattling
sound, and the bones came together, bone to bone," followed by the

appearance of tendons and flesh, but there was still no breath (vv. 7–8). So God commanded his servant to preach to the breath: "This is what the Sovereign LORD says: Come from the four winds, O breath, and breathe into these slain, that they may live." As a result, "breath entered them; they came to life and stood up on their feet— a vast army" (vv. 9–10).

God explained this prophecy to Ezekiel: Israel lies in the valley of death, her bones dry. But one day he will bring his people up out of their dusty grave. "I will put my Spirit in you and you will live, and I will settle you in your own land. Then you will know that I the LORD have spoken, and I have done it, declares the LORD" (v. 14).

What follows in the text links us to our previous stories about Babel, and about Nebuchadnezzar's vision. God's Word came to Ezekiel promising a day when there would be one nation, one language, and one king. The people would not accomplish this by their own efforts, skill, military might, technological sophistication, moral energy, or intelligence. "*I* will make them *one nation* in the land, on the mountains of Israel," he said (v. 22, emphasis added). "My servant David will be king over them, and they will all have one shepherd." It would be an eternal kingdom under the Davidic king, "a covenant of peace," "an everlasting covenant," in which God would place his sanctuary among his people for all time. "My dwelling place will be with them; I will be their God, and they will be my people. Then the nations will know that I the LORD make Israel holy, when my sanctuary is among them forever" (vv. 24–28).

Why should Israel trust in the idols of the nations and in their high towers? Her Rock and Redeemer alone can give her life, and this hope is held forth as a divine program for a universal and eternal empire.

Finally, God promised this coming day of the Spirit in a familiar passage in Joel:

"And afterward, I will pour out my Spirit on all people.
Your sons and daughters will prophesy,
Your old men will dream dreams,

your young men will see visions.

Even on my servants, both men and women,

I will pour out my Spirit in those days.

I will show wonders in the heavens and on the earth,

Blood and fire and billows of smoke.

The sun will be turned to darkness

And the moon to blood

Before the coming of the great and dreadful day of the LORD.

And everyone who calls on the name of the LORD

Will be saved;

For on Mount Zion and in Jerusalem there will be deliverance,

As the LORD has said,

Among the survivors whom the LORD calls. (Joel 2:28–32)

Although there have been many clues leading up to this prophecy, here it is clearly declared that God will pour out his Spirit in the last days on all people, not just on the Jews. Once again we see how the biblical drama describes the first and second comings of our Savior in one sweep, as if there were only days between them. The concern is not with the length of time, but with the fact that this whole period marks "the last days," the Age of the Spirit, when the kingdom of God comes down from heaven instead of being raised to the heavens from the earth. It will finally be a universal and eternal kingdom, embracing people "out of every tribe, kindred, tongue, people and nation" who will together become "a kingdom of priests to our God" (Rev. 5:9).

Under Moses the seventy elders prophesied as "the Spirit rested on them," and, on that sole occasion, two men who were not elders also prophesied. It was as if the Spirit's presence was so powerful that it overflowed beyond the elders to these two young men as well.

When the young man ran to Moses to inform him of this, expecting Moses to forbid the two men from prophesying, the patriarch declared, "I wish that all the LORD's people were prophets and that the LORD would put his Spirit on them!" (Num. 11:23–30 NIV). Surely Israel would be more faithful to God and less of a burden to

Moses if the Holy Spirit were poured out on the whole nation, making them witnesses of Yahweh. In Joel's prophecy, Moses' dream was transformed into a divine promise.

In all of these passages, the prophecies related to the coming of the Spirit upon all God's people are centered on the kingdom of God. Only the power of the Holy Spirit can finally secure a faithful Israel, a true church that gratefully receives new life. Only the Holy Spirit can initiate an eternal and worldwide empire in which, at last, God and his people dwell together in peace and rest forever. No more exiles, no more captivity, no more divine judgment, no more of our unfaithfulness: this is the ultimate purpose of the Age of the Spirit.

At last, Isaiah's Servant appeared. As John baptized him, the Holy Spirit descended over the sacred head of the long-awaited Davidic king. This king would finally secure an empire whose glory, though hidden to the world, would be greater than that secured by Nebuchadnezzar, Cyrus, Alexander the Great, or the Roman Caesars. He announced that he was the one who would bring the two flocks, Jew and Gentile, and make them one flock with himself as Israel's shepherd. It is he who would be Israel's temple, greater than Solomon's. This church would be his body, and unlike the statue in Nebuchadnezzar's dream, it would be fashioned out of one indestructible rock.

Jesus prepared his disciples for his departure by promising to send the Holy Spirit. So great and important was this coming Spirit's ministry that Jesus said, "It is for your good that I am going away. Unless I go away, the Counselor will not come to you; but if I go, I will send him to you" (John 16:7 NIV). This Counselor would "convict the world of guilt in regard to sin and righteousness and judgment" (vv. 8–9). Furthermore, he would bring to mind everything Christ had taught them (John 14:26), and would make them witnesses to him in the world. It is he who would turn the church's grief at her Lord's death to joy at his Resurrection. And this same Holy Spirit who raised Jesus from the dead would be given to each believer, so that the valley of dry bones would form a vast army to spread the Good News of new life.

After the Ascension, God's new Israel was sent into the "wilderness" of the upper room to wait for the coming of the Spirit. His followers remembered the risen Lord's final words to them. At that time they had still been looking for an earthly kingdom in which God would free the earthly nation of Israel from Roman oppression. The disciples had asked Jesus, "Lord, are you at this time going to restore the kingdom to Israel?" He said to them: 'It is not for you to know the times or dates the Father has set by his own authority. But you will receive power when the Holy Spirit comes on you; and you will be my witnesses in Jerusalem, and in all Judea and Samaria, and to the ends of the earth'" (Acts 1:6–8 NIV).

The kingdom was already present, but it was a spiritual kingdom, not a geopolitical one. It would advance not in the way of Babel's city and tower, nor as the empires of Nebuchadnezzar's vision did. It would be enlivened by the Holy Spirit. He would make the church witnesses to the Son; this was the purpose in sending the Spirit.

Finally, the day of Pentecost arrived. It was the Jewish Feast that celebrated the "first-fruits" of the harvest (Deut. 16:10; Exod. 23:16; Num. 28:26). Jesus had been the fulfillment of Israel's Passover Lamb, and now the Holy Spirit came in fulfillment of another feast, preparing the church to begin the harvest of the last days. Together in one hall, the disciples were suddenly aroused by a sound like violent wind from heaven, with what looked like tongues of fire resting on each person. "All of them were filled with the Holy Spirit and began to speak in other tongues, as the Spirit enabled them" (Acts 2:1–4 NIV).

What an astonishing fulfillment! As this same Holy Spirit had descended on the Tower of Babel in judgment, confusing the languages and scattering the nations, he now descended in salvation, uniting the world's languages, and calling his elect out of the nations to form one people. This was not the result of human striving, like Babel's project. The apostles were not employing spiritual technology, techniques, or "steps" for receiving the Holy Spirit and tapping into his power. But suddenly, like Ezekiel's valley of dry bones, a church was formed in that great hall by the Word and the Spirit.

Because people of many nations were in Jerusalem for Pentecost, crowds began to gather below as they heard the unusual sound. This phenomenon of "speaking in tongues" was unlike some of the phenomena associated with that term today, for "each one heard them speaking in his own language" (v. 6). These were natural languages, and those who had been scattered by language, culture, and custom were brought together in one astonishing fulfillment of prophecy. We will miss the importance of this event unless we realize that it is a *sign* in the biblical sense. Just as our Savior's miracles were signs of something greater than the miracle itself, so this scene fills us with wonder at something greater to which the sign of languages or tongues points.

As Parthians, Medes, Elamites, residents of Mesopotamia, Judea, and Cappadocia, Pontus and Asia, Phrygia and Pamphylia, Egypt and Libya, Cretans, and Arabs gathered in astonishment, it was not the phenomenon of tongues itself that captured their attention, but the message: "We hear them declaring the wonders of God in our own tongues!" (Acts 2:11 NIV). Speaking in tongues or languages was not an end in itself, but was both a sign and a means of proclaiming the Gospel to foreigners. It was neither a "heavenly language," nor a sort of "pig Latin" known only between God and the individual spirit. No one was employing it as a means of personal edification.

The first act of the church after this epoch-making descent of the Spirit was a sermon. Peter, filled with the Spirit, proclaimed the Law and the Gospel. He told the people that they were lost in their sins and without hope, even though they had come to Jerusalem for this religious feast. But then he told them the Good News of God's saving action in Christ: his life, death, burial, resurrection, ascension, and return in judgment. In other words, Peter preached the articles we find in the Apostles' Creed!

Clearly, this is the purpose of the Holy Spirit's mission, as Jesus had declared: "But you will receive power when the Holy Spirit comes on you; and you will be my witnesses in Jerusalem, and in all Judea and Samaria, and to the ends of the earth" (Acts 1:8 NIV). Although the witnesses come in weakness and humility, the Gospel comes in power through their witness, because the Spirit is present with his Word.

What Is the Role of the Holy Spirit in the Church Today?

In various periods of church history, especially when there seems to be a lack of appreciation for or awareness of the Holy Spirit in church, men and women have prophesied a new Pentecost. Claiming to be the prophet of the Holy Spirit, a second century man by the name of Montanus insisted that he was to bring the church into its third phase. Following the Age of the Father and the Age of the Son, the church was about to enter the Age of the Spirit. Two prophetesses, Maximilla and Priscilla, joined Montanus and predicted the dawn of the millennial kingdom. Judged by the church to be heretical, and crippled by countless failed prophecies, Montanism eventually died out. However, its spirit has lived on throughout church history, appearing again and again, often with the same emphases: ecstatic utterances which are said to be New Testament "tongues," prophetic revelations, and apocalyptic obsessions with the end times.

At the heart of such revivals is often the conviction, whether stated or implied, that Pentecost is illustrative rather than definitive. In other words, the Book of Acts in general and the events of Pentecost in particular are taken to be patterns for the church today rather than as once-and-for-all events. At first, this distinction may seem forced, but we can easily accept it when we apply it to the other major events of redemptive history.

Israel treasured the memory of the Exodus and guarded the tablets of the Law in the Ark of the Covenant. There were even festivals established as memorials to these past events. But Israel never saw these events as patterns that somehow called for repetition. There were no further crossings of the Red Sea, no encampments in the wilderness, for they were now in the Promised Land. As further events in redemptive history unfolded, new signs and wonders accompanied a fresh stage of revelation and prophetic activity. These were like "fireworks" that inaugurated a new stage of salvation in history. And, like fireworks, they faded from the sky.

To expect another Pentecost is similar to demanding another Creation, another Messiah, another Crucifixion and Resurrection. Like these events, Pentecost was a singular historical act of God. It serves not as the church's pattern, but as the church's empowerment. Since Pentecost, we have been living in the Age of the Spirit. Just as there is no longer any need for further sacrifices for sin, neither is there a need for further descents of the Spirit.

When our departing Lord gave his church her Great Commission, he promised, "And surely I am with you always, to the very end of the age" (Matt. 28:20 NIV). He is with us because his Holy Spirit is with us (John 14:18). Every believer receives the Holy Spirit forever (John 14:16). As Christ's body, the visible institution through which Christ's heavenly reign is exercised, the church collectively becomes the dwelling place of the Holy Spirit.

While we do not expect further stages of revelation (Heb. 1:1–4), we have the same Spirit within us, and he makes us witnesses of Christ until the end of the age. Because he was given first and foremost to create a church from the valley of dry bones and then to empower that church for its mission, it is correct to say that we are all prophets, priests, and kings in the new Israel. Like Ezekiel, we preach to those who are spiritually dead, and the Spirit breathes life into them. Our work is not prophetic in the sense that it provides new revelations, but it is prophetic because it is the proclamation of God's completed Word in this time and place. It is prophetic in forth-telling, not in foretelling.

In addition to being prophets, our office is priestly, in that we intercede for the lost in prayer and open their prison doors by the announcement of the Gospel. It also is a royal office that we share, because we have taken up the role first entrusted to Adam in his innocence, to reign in Christ's kingdom to the glory of God the Father. Peter said, "But you are a chosen people, a royal priesthood, a holy nation, a people belonging to God, that you may declare the praises of him who called you out of darkness into his wonderful light. Once you were not a people, but now you are the people of

God; once you had not received mercy, but now you have received mercy" (1 Peter 2:9–10 NIV).

Therefore, whatever grace-gifts God has given us, they must conform to this rule: They are not for our own pleasure or benefit, but to equip us in our task as the missionary people of God.

The Holy Spirit and Individual Believers

Thus far, we have described the Holy Spirit's work in relation to the corporate body of Christ, and the unfolding of the Holy Spirit's work in redemptive history. This corporate emphasis is vital in an age of individualism. Nevertheless, we must close with the equally essential news of what God has done for us personally by sending his Spirit.

First and foremost, the Holy Spirit is sent from the Father and the Son to unite us to the God-Man. What does this mean? Surely we cannot be united physically, since our Savior's body is in heaven. How can such a gulf be closed between our ascended Lord and us? In the divine economy, it is the Holy Spirit who has been given the task of bringing this union about.

By now we know that we are dead in sin, helpless to respond to God's grace. But in Romans 5, Paul announced that just as the first Adam brought us death by his disobedience, the second Adam brought us life by his obedience. We have been "baptized into Christ Jesus," so that we are made partakers of his death and life.

When the Holy Spirit comes to unite us to Christ, it is always in connection to his Word. First he "kills" us by the preaching of the Law, bringing us to despair of any hope. Giving up on the aid of our fallen nature, we sink beneath the weight of our guilt and loathe ourselves as enemies of God. But then, through his messengers, he raises us to new life through the preaching of the Gospel. He turns us from trusting in ourselves to faith in Christ, and convinces us to lay down our weapons of warfare against God.

By uniting us to Christ, he gives us every spiritual blessing in heavenly places: not only faith and repentance, but justification, sanctification, and ultimately glorification. All of these already belong to us in union with Christ, just as in marriage the treasures of husband and wife belong to each other. As our Savior inherits our debts, we inherit his riches. Paul throws all of this into the category of the indicative—what God has done to us and for us, not what he expects from us. The Holy Spirit, on the basis of Christ's saving mediation, has made us friends of God through this happy marriage. In union with Christ, we are raised from the tomb of spiritual death to enjoy the very life of Christ in heaven. Thus, he is the vine and we are the branches (John 15).

Here Paul turned from the indicative to the imperative. He tells us who we are already in Christ and then he tells us how we are to live in the light of that reality. Nowadays, these are often reversed. Many Christian self-help books promise paths to spiritual power, but Scripture assures us that spiritual power is not the Christian's goal, but rather the Christian's possession. Every believer already possesses every spiritual blessing in union with Christ, and this is the only motivation for obedience and growth in holiness. We live from Christ's victory, not for it.

And yet, as Paul continued to relate in terms of his own experience in Romans 7, every believer is still "justified yet sinful," declared righteous in God's judgment, but in constant warfare within himself or herself because of indwelling sin. There is no way to be free of this warfare in this life. However, just when this thought leads Paul toward despair, he raises his eyes from himself to Christ once more, realizing that in Christ he is already guaranteed not only justification, but glorification.

Many of us were raised in circles where we were told to "surrender" to the Spirit, to simply "let go and let God"; that is, to passively receive our sanctification by letting the Holy Spirit do it all within us. But this raises the question, When do I know whether I've done this or that "in the Spirit" rather than "in the flesh"? Fortunately, Scripture itself does not put us in this kind of dilemma. With the indicative (you are crucified and raised with Christ) and the imperative (therefore, live in the light of this), we are prepared to take our Christian responsibilities seriously.

No more of this "let go and let God" business! "Work out your salvation with fear and trembling," says the great teacher of grace, "for it is God who works in you both to will and to do for His own good pleasure" (Phil. 2:12–13). Here we see again the relationship of indicative to imperative: Do thus and so because such and such is true. Paul does not say, "Work *for* your salvation," but "Work *out* your salvation."

Sanctification is the lifelong process of discovering and putting into practice the implications of sound doctrine, especially the good news of our union with Christ and participation in all of his blessings. In this life, none of our good works—not even the best—can pass the test of purity. Once we accept that fact of our ongoing sinfulness, we can respond in obedience. Freed from the paralyzing fear that our works have to be completely free of sin, absolutely pure in motive, and entirely "in the Spirit," we begin to live in the light of what is already true about us because of Christ's saving office. Obedience is a struggle for the Christian. Don't be fooled by the simple-sounding methods of spirituality that promise easy solutions, similar to diet plans and get-rich-quick investment strategies.

Some people conclude that their disobedience means that they aren't really believers. Ironically, in most cases the children of God will be the only ones who are even concerned with such a thought. The pain of struggling with indwelling sin is peculiar to Christians. The unbeliever does not struggle with sin: he or she simply accepts it as "who I am" (i.e., the indicative definition of their identity). On the other end, the perfectionists think they've "gained victory" over all known sin, and thus "make [God] a liar and the truth is not in [them]" (1 John 1:8–9). If you are struggling with your continuing sinfulness, that is not a sign that you are not a Christian, but that you are!

Glorification is that event in which our sanctification will be immediately perfected. Although our justification is complete, immediate, and incapable of being diminished (since it is Christ's righteousness, not ours), sanctification is a lifelong process in which our best works are still contaminated by sin and require Christ's mediation. But one day, the believer will be freed not only from the guilt and dominion of sin, but from its very presence. Finally, the believer will be fully conformed to Christ's

image, forever to dwell with him in the Promised Land. The Holy
Spirit who gave us all these gifts through union with Christ will
present us complete before the Father. By indwelling us even
now, in spite of our slow growth in sanctification, the Holy Spirit
is our down-payment on final glorification (Eph. 1:13–14).

And there is more:

> The creation waits in eager expectation for the sons of God to be
> revealed. For the creation was subjected to frustration, not by its
> own choice, but by the will of the one who subjected it, in hope
> that the creation itself will be liberated from its bondage to decay
> and brought into the glorious freedom of the children of God.
> We know that the whole creation has been groaning as in the
> pains of childbirth right up to the present time. Not only so, but
> we ourselves, who have the firstfruits of the Spirit, groan
> inwardly as we wait eagerly for our adoption as sons, the
> redemption of our bodies. For in this hope we were saved. But
> hope that is seen is no hope at all. Who hopes for what he
> already has? But if we hope for what we do not yet have, we wait
> for it patiently. (Rom. 8:19–25 NIV)

As we look around our world, we see the same corruption, frustration, despair, and rebellion that is so painfully evident in our own
lives. Paul says that the same warfare that marks our lives as believers, a constant struggle with indwelling sin, also shapes the world
outside. But Jesus Christ is as much the answer to the latter as he is
to the former. At the end of the week of toil and travail, there will
be an eternal day of rest, for the people and for the land. This Age
of the Spirit is like a mother's long labor, as she relaxes and contracts in order to give birth. Paul himself uses this picture in
Romans 8, as we have seen.

Too often, Christianity is presented in a way that attempts to
tear us away from the world. Of course, "the world" as a category
is sometimes used in Scripture to refer to that which is set against
God. But the world is not always spoken of in that connection. Just
as we are not evil because of our human nature, but because of our

sinfulness, this world, which in so many ways is still a theater of God's glory, has become a stage for the acting out of human oppression, manipulation, exploitation, and pride. Nevertheless, just as God's grace will one day overcome our remaining sinfulness, so too the world that was subjected to disorder and corruption because of its human lords will enjoy its own liberation.

At last, the bloodstained ground that cries out to God for vengeance will be at rest. Its thorns will become buds for fragrant roses. The elderly will leap like lambs and the oppressed will inherit the earth. God will make all things new. But the creation must wait for the children of God to be glorified first, and the children of God must wait patiently with the rest of creation for the final stage of the Holy Spirit's mission.

As we live from our justification, through our sanctification, toward our glorification, we should eagerly see the involvement of the natural world in this sweeping vision. For although it is not the kingdom of Christ, the world will one day be made his footstool by his glorious return. As the Holy Spirit advances Christ's universal kingdom, we can expect much, but for an end to all war, poverty, immorality, disease, and evil we must wait patiently. Our own meager gains in sanctification testify to a final act in which we will be instantaneously glorified. Likewise, our slight but bitter struggles in advancing truth, goodness, and beauty in this world are sweetened by the full fragrance of the age to come. Because we are born again, we are creatures of the dawn and not of twilight (1 Thess. 5:5). The future God has planned for a new creation has already dawned in our hearts. The Spirit who will come to raise the dead and restore the earth has already come and is here at work in us.

NINE

Who Needs the Church?

✢ ✢ ✢

I BELIEVE IN . . . THE HOLY
CATHOLIC CHURCH,
THE COMMUNION OF SAINTS.

I read a recent news report of an evangelist who announced to his audience that Jesus never commanded the whole world to come to church. He had commanded the church to go into the world. After all, isn't "the church" simply the collective term for all those who love the Lord? According to this Christian leader, we need to abandon the older view that the church is somehow a unique place or institution.

In modern America, people are distrustful of institutions, and this sentiment has profoundly affected our view of the church. In one church growth study after another we are reminded that the unchurched today are not unhappy with Jesus, but with organized religion. It is the church that bothers them, so they simply do not show up. Nevertheless, they consider themselves Christians, since they say that it is spirituality and not religion that really matters.

How are we to respond to this situation? First, we have to come to terms with the sad reality that the visible church is in bad shape. Ridden with scandals, pandering after secular forms of entertainment, political power and popular fads, the church, as popularly perceived, is hardly "the pillar and ground of the truth" (1 Tim. 3:15).

Besides the condition of the visible church, we have adopted the democratic and individualistic religious outlook of our culture. I am regularly bombarded with questions about where to go to church. Even the most committed churchgoers complain that it is difficult to find a place where they will be fed with the Word. As more churches adopt an entertainment style, a growing number of believers are frustrated. I have observed even strong Christians pulling out altogether, deciding to "have church" at home rather than belonging to a community. It is my hope that this chapter will shed some light on the identity, purpose, mission, and resources of the church, thus better preparing us to contribute faithfully to the building of this divinely ordained institution.

The Father's Family, the Son's Bride, and the Holy Spirit's Home

With the promise of a Messiah made immediately after the Fall, God established his church by the Word and Spirit. Clothed in the animal skins, Adam and Eve were actually clothed with Christ, and Eve gave birth to a son. "Behold, I have brought forth a man!" she exclaimed, but after Cain grew up it became clear that he was not the Son who would crush the serpent's head. In fact, as we noted previously, he would be the first persecutor of the church and her first prophet, as Jesus observed (Matt. 23:35). But another son replaced the slain Abel: Seth, meaning, "elect one." It was Seth's descendants who began calling on the name of the Lord, while Cain's were building their city. From that point on, the rivalry between the city of man and the city of God became a running theme throughout Scripture: Two families, two seeds, two futures, two ways of salvation, two covenants, two mountains.

Again and again, God's "church" or chosen people are pursued by Satan, for he knows that she is the "woman" described in John's Revelation, who will give birth to the promised Son. This son will crush the serpent's head and will release his people from the curse (Rev. 12). God's people were often stripped, either by persecution or internal apostasy, down to only one family. But God always kept a people for himself in spite of their rebellion and unfaithfulness.

From his father's land, Abraham was called by God to become the father of all who, like him, are justified by grace alone, through faith alone, because of the redemptive work of Christ alone. While the promises of living in the earthly land of Israel, the replica of the heavenly Jerusalem, were conditioned on Israel's obedience, the promise of a Redeemer and salvation through faith in him was unconditional.

When the Father saw his children groaning in Egyptian bondage, he raised up Moses and led his church out of slavery into the wilderness toward the Promised Land. God said:

> When Israel was a child, I loved him,
> And out of Egypt I called my son.
> But the more I called Israel,
> The further they went from me.
> They sacrificed to the Baals
> And they burned incense to images.
> It was I who taught Ephraim to walk,
> Taking them by the arms;
> But they did not realize it was I who healed them.
> I led them with cords of human kindness,
> With ties of love;
> I lifted the yoke from their neck
> And bent down to feed them. . . .
> My people are determined to turn from me. . . .
> How can I give you up, Ephraim?
> How can I hand you over, Israel? (Hos. 11:1–8 NIV)

We must be careful to mark the fact that the church in the Old Testament, like the New Testament church, was a "mixed assembly."

No one was justified and accepted before God simply by being a Jew. Indeed, as the Psalmist reminds us, a whole generation under Moses was barred from God's saving rest because they doubted the promise and became cynical in the wilderness (Ps. 95:10–11; Heb. 4:1–11).

In Hebrew, *kahal* ("called"), and in Greek, *synagoge* ("gathered together"), and *ekklesia* ("called out") are various synonyms for the church which have to do with God's saving activity. The church is not a civic group or a voluntary organization that has been formed to advance human goals and longings. The church is God's idea, and he creates this church for himself and by himself.

Far from seeing themselves as isolated individuals who could worship God in their own way, the Israelites who trusted in God recognized this view as idolatry. They could only belong to God because they belonged to his covenant people, his family. Fellowship had a subjective element, but it was primarily objective: They were in union with the covenant-making God as a people, as a communion of saints.

Thus, in the Old Testament, the church is identified with a particular nation. To belong to that church one had to become an Israelite. Of course, there were Gentiles who did just that. Circumcised as adults, they joined themselves to God's people. When we get to the prophetic books, however, we find the clear expectation that, in the last days, God would extend his church beyond the borders of national Israel. And this is precisely what Jesus commanded of his church before his Ascension (Matt. 28:17–20).

The Church and the Parables

Our Lord made this plain in his teachings, especially in his parables. There, the unbelieving nation is contrasted with the new Israel Jesus was creating. He is forming this new Israel by calling both Jews and Gentiles out for his congregation, just as he had called Abram out of Ur. First, he told the parable of the sower. Some seed fell on rock, but the plant barely sprouted before it withered from lack of moisture. "Other seed fell among thorns, which grew up with it and choked the plants. Still other seed fell on good soil. It came up and yielded a crop, a hundred times more than was sown" (Luke 8:5–8 NIV). The seed is the Word, and Jesus is the good soil. This new crop, sown in him, will not only yield a crop, but will multiply it.

Later, Jesus said, "No one lights a lamp and hides it in a jar or puts it under a bed." Yet that is precisely what Israel had done. "Whoever has will be given more; whoever does not have, even what he thinks he has will be taken from him" (vv. 16–18).

In the familiar parable of the Good Samaritan, Jesus continued this theme. While the Levite priest ignored the victim's plight, a Samaritan (Samaritans were loathed as half-breeds) restores him to health (Luke 10:25–36). Jesus went on to tell his disciples that he had not come to bring peace, but a sword, to divide families over himself (Luke 12:49–53 NIV).

Later Jesus told the parable of the mustard seed and the yeast.

"What is the kingdom of God like?" Jesus asked. "What shall I compare it to? It is like a mustard seed, which a man took and planted in his garden. It grew and became a tree, and the birds of the air perched in its branches" (Luke 13:18–19 NIV). Known to the people as the smallest seed, it nevertheless became not only a plant, but a tree large enough to accommodate the birds.

"What shall I compare the kingdom of God to? It is like yeast that a woman took and mixed into a large amount of flour until it worked all through the dough" (vv. 20–21 NIV). Like the yeast, his kingdom will be worked into the "dough" of the world.

After this, Jesus warned that the door to the kingdom is narrow. One cannot assume that he belongs in the kingdom, and many who make this fatal presumption will be turned away: "There will be weeping there, and gnashing of teeth, when you see Abraham, Isaac and Jacob and all the prophets in the kingdom of God, but you yourselves will be thrown out. People will come from east and west and north and south, and will take their places at the feast in the kingdom of God. Indeed there are those who are last who will be first, and first who will be last" (vv. 22–30 NIV).

Many of the Gentiles, who are not God's people, will become God's children, while many of those who glory in being Abraham's physical descendants will be rejected because they have not entered through Christ. At this, Jesus broke down in great sorrow for the earthly Jerusalem, for he is himself a Jew and the promised Messiah of Israel. "Look, your house is left to you desolate," he lamented (v. 35).

Jesus emphasized this point again in another parable. A great wedding banquet was made ready for its guests, but the privileged invitees made excuses. Undaunted, the master sent his servant into the streets to bring in the homeless, "the crippled, the blind and the lame" (Luke 14:21 NIV). "I tell you," resolved the master, "not one of those men who were invited will get a taste of my banquet" (v. 24). This is reminiscent of God's oath that the cynical unbelievers in the wilderness would never enter his rest.

Still more parables make this point. For instance, consider the parable of the lost sheep. A good shepherd will leave the ninety-nine who are not lost in order to find one sheep who has gone astray. Or when a woman has lost a coin, does she not do everything she can to find it? Is there not rejoicing over that one coin? "In the same way, I tell you, there is rejoicing in the presence of the angels of God over one sinner who repents" (Luke 15:10 NIV).

One especially striking parable of the kingdom is found in Luke 15:11–32. A man divided his estate between his two sons. The younger son squandered his wealth in a far country in wild living, while the elder son stayed home with his father and maintained his duty to the family. When the younger son finally came to his senses, he returned home weeping. He knew he was not worthy, but the elder brother was proud and self-righteous. Willing merely to be a servant in his father's house, the younger son was nevertheless spotted by his compassion-filled father "while he was still a long way off."

The father "ran to his son, threw his arms around him and kissed him," refusing to hear about the boy's willingness to be a servant. "Quick!" he commanded his servants, "Bring the best robe and put it on him." A lost son was found and the father called for a feast, provoking the elder brother's jealous outrage.

"Look!" the other son demanded. "All these years I've been slaving for you and never disobeyed your orders. . . . But when this son of yours who has squandered your property with prostitutes comes home, you kill the fattened calf for him!"

Jesus told such parables to provoke the Jews to jealousy (Rom. 11:11). "You are the ones who justify yourselves in the eyes of men," Jesus accused, "but God knows your hearts" (Luke 16:15 NIV). The parable of the Pharisee and the tax collector makes this point (Luke 18:9–14) as well as the parable of the rich young ruler (vv. 18–30). In the parable of the tenants, Jesus tells the story of a man who sent a servant into his vineyard to collect rents, but the tenants sent the servant back empty-handed and beaten. He sent a second, then a third (figurative of the prophets), but they too were treated as the first:

> "Then the owner of the vineyard said, 'What shall I do? I will send my son, whom I love; perhaps they will respect him.' But when the tenants saw him, they talked the matter over. 'This is the heir,' they said. 'Let's kill him, and the inheritance will be ours.' So they threw him out of the vineyard and killed him. What then will the owner of the vineyard do to them? He will come and kill those tenants and give the vineyard to others." (Luke 20:13–16 NIV)

Our Lord's hearers met these remarks with horror: "May this never be!"

> Jesus looked directly at them and asked, "Then what is the meaning of that which is written: 'The stone the builders rejected has become the capstone'? Everyone who falls on that stone will be broken to pieces, but he on whom it falls will be crushed." (vv. 17–18 NIV)

No wonder the teachers of the law looked for an opportunity to arrest Jesus.

These parables drove home the point that the nation of Israel, like the fig tree that shriveled when Jesus cursed it, is no longer identified with the kingdom of God. Instead, the kingdom has been given to anyone and everyone who will come to the feast, who will return from the far country, who will receive the heir of the vineyard's master and inherit the vineyard together with him.

Reluctantly, the first Christians came to accept this universal scope of the kingdom. Peter embraced Cornelius and began baptizing Gentile converts only after God sent him a powerful dream pronouncing the end to the distinction between "clean" and "unclean" as synonymous with "Jew" and "Gentile" (Acts 10). But it was Paul the rabbi and now apostle to the Gentiles who explained "the mystery of the church," whereby, through Christ's blood, the dividing wall was torn down and peace was made.

"Consequently, you are no longer foreigners and aliens, but fellow citizens with God's people and members of God's household, built on the foundation of the apostles and prophets, with Christ Jesus himself as the chief cornerstone. In him the whole building is joined together and rises to become a holy temple in the Lord" (Eph. 2:19–21 NIV).

"If you belong to Christ, then you are Abraham's seed, and heirs according to the promise" (Gal. 3:29 NIV).

"For not all who are descended from Israel are Israel. Nor because they are his descendants are they all Abraham's children. . . . In other words, it is not the natural children who are God's children, but it is the children of the promise who are regarded as Abraham's offspring" (Rom. 9:6–8 NIV).

God has not rejected the Jews, but has chosen a remnant from among both Jews and Gentiles. Far from leading Gentiles to boast, says Paul, this should serve as a solemn warning:

> You do not support the root, but the root supports you. . . . they were broken off because of unbelief, and you stand by faith. Do not be arrogant, but be afraid. For if God did not spare the natural branches, he will not spare you either. Consider therefore the kindness and sternness of God: sternness to those who fell, but kindness to you, provided that you continue in his kindness. Otherwise, you also will be cut off. (Rom. 11:18–22 NIV)

Lessons from the Vineyard

One of the marvels of California winemaking is the fact that very old European stock was brought to the young West Coast vineyards and was grafted onto the wild indigenous vines. California's native vines were superior in both their rapid growth and their prodigious yield, but their wild character was no match for the subtlety and smoothness of French and German varietals. After a few generations, Europeans who had pioneered these California grafting projects found themselves the envy of winemakers around the world.

Similarly, we must never forget that our membership in the church is secured not because of the inherent quality of our devotion, piety, or intellect, but because God mercifully made room for us by breaking off the natural branches that did not bear faith or faith's fruit. It is the quality of the vine, not its wild branches, that yields the fruit of the Spirit. By virtue of our union with Christ, we are part of God's vineyard and belong to his church. We who were strangers to the covenant of grace are engrafted as wild vines.

We join those sons of Seth who began calling on the name of the Lord and sit around God's table as Abraham's children. We are founded on the rock of Peter's confession: "You are the Christ, the Son of the Living God." In fact, we drink from that same Rock together with our brothers and sisters in the Old Testament, says Paul, "and that Rock was Christ" (1 Cor. 10:4).

Only together, with them and with each other, collectively united to Christ, do we form the Body of Christ (Eph. 1:22–23; Col. 1:18; 1 Cor. 12:27), the Bride of Christ (Eph. 5), the Temple of the Holy Spirit and God (1 Cor. 3:16; Eph. 2:21–22; 1 Peter 2:5), the Jerusalem That Is Above (Gal. 4:26; Heb. 12:22; Rev. 21:2, 9–10), and the Israel of God (Gal. 6:16).

Many evangelical Protestants raise their eyebrows when we come to the line in the Apostles' Creed, "one holy catholic church." There is, however, wisdom in retaining this important phrase. Let's go through all three of these adjectives to get a better grasp of the identity and mission of God's people. The best way to do this is by following our own Lord's high priestly prayer in John 17, where all three elements are clearly visible.

One Holy Catholic Church

What a consolation it is for us to know that our Savior could think of nothing else before he went to the cross than the salvation, blessing, and joy of his church. If he had the good of his bride in view when he was about to suffer divine wrath for her sins, then surely he seeks only her welfare in heaven now as he enjoys his eternal reign in victory.

"Elect from every nation, yet one o'er all the earth," as Charles Wesley's hymn put it, the church was in God's mind before the creation of the world. The Father gave to the Son a people before time and made him the trustee of the church. That is why Jesus said, "All that my Father has *given* me will come to me" (John 6:37, emphasis added), and it is why here in our Lord's prayer he says to the Father, "For you granted him authority over all people that he might give eternal life *to all those you have given him.* I pray for them. I am not praying for the world, but for those you have given me, for they are yours" (John 17:2, 9 NIV, emphasis added).

Just as Abraham took it upon himself to find a bride for Isaac, the church is the Father's gift to his beloved Son. The first thing we learn about unity, therefore, is that it is given by God and not created by us. It is anchored in God's choice, not ours, and is the product of God's design, not ours. Too often we see our unity in Christ as something that we must somehow create or enforce, but we are not talking about a merger of companies. God has supernaturally united us to each other by uniting us to his Son.

What then are we to say about all the divisions? If the church is "one," why can we pick up the yellow pages in any city or town and find a bewildering array of denominations? This disunity is scandal to the watching world. But it is also evidence that our sinful condition nevertheless fails to destroy the essential unity of Christ's body. With that in mind, it is helpful to distinguish between the visible and the invisible church.

What is an "invisible" church? The Westminster Confession provides a valuable definition:

> "The catholic or universal Church, which is invisible, consists of the whole number of the elect, that have been, are, or shall be gathered into one, under Christ the head thereof; and is the spouse, the body, the fullness of Him that filleth all in all" (Chapter 25).

Although the terms may not be the best, *invisible* helps to make the point that, when we speak of the church, we do not necessarily mean the business about the yellow pages. Why does this *visible* or *invisible* church distinction matter? First, it is, as we will see below, a biblical distinction, and therefore it matters intrinsically. Second, it is immensely practical when we think, for instance, of the scandal of division.

When unbelievers see the divisions between various visible churches, Christians can point out to them that despite this tragedy, all who are united to Christ, regardless of denomination, are our brothers and sisters. It does not excuse our unfortunate divisions, but it does make the point that we do not consign people to hell because they are not in our denomination.

Thus far our attention has focused on this invisible church. But as the soul is to the body, so the invisible church is to its visible manifestation. Those who deny the importance of the visible church by appeals to an invisible church are like those who denied the importance of the body and Christ's humanity in an effort to emphasize the spirit and Christ's deity.

So what is the *visible* church? First, unlike the invisible church, it consists of both the elect and the non-elect. We have seen throughout the Scriptures how "not all who are descendants are Abraham's children," and this is as true for the church in the New as well as the Old Testament. Jesus gave us the picture of a barn in which the chaff is mingled with the wheat (Matt. 3:12). Or we recall the parable in which the enemy sows weeds among the wheat. The servants want to pull up the weeds, but Jesus warns that the wheat (hardly distinguishable in the early stages from weeds) may be pulled up accidentally. Jesus is always concerned for each grain of his precious wheat, so he (in the person of the master in his parable), instructs his servants to allow both to grow together until the harvest, when he himself will separate the wheat from the weeds (Matt. 13:25).

In all of this we see that the church is a "mixed assembly," as Augustine and the Reformers emphasized. Too often, we speak of the church as if it were composed only of regenerate Christians, but while this is true of the invisible church, it ignores the reality of the visible church and its current form. Unbelievers and believers, goats and sheep, dwell together in this field until the harvest. That does not diminish our responsibility to warn the church, nor does it forbid the discipline of members or even their excommunication.

The outward form of the church is not always clearly seen, but there is always a church, visible and invisible, among the world. While the visible church is available to our senses, the invisible church "is known only to God." We do not know who is elect and who is not, so we exercise charity toward professing brothers and sisters. The invisible church belongs to the hidden majesty and secret counsel of God in eternity. The visible church is part of God's revelation of Christ in time and space.

For Calvin, the concept of the visible church is related to the image of a mother conceiving, giving birth to, and nursing the communion of saints.

"Furthermore, away from her bosom one cannot hope for any forgiveness of sins or any salvation, as Isaiah [37:22] and Joel [2:32] testify. . . . By these words God's fatherly favor and the especial witness of spiritual life are limited to his flock, so that it is always disastrous to leave the church."[1]

In another place Calvin provides us with a helpful way of judging the so-called *visible* church:

How are we to judge the church visible, which falls within our knowledge, is, I believe, already evident. . . . For we have said that Holy Scripture speaks of the church in two ways. . . . By baptism we are initiated into faith in him; by partaking in the Lord's

Supper we attest our unity in true doctrine and love; in the Word of the Lord we have agreement, and for the preaching of the Word the ministry instituted by Christ is preserved. In this church are mingled hypocrites who have nothing of Christ but the name and outward appearance. . . .

Accordingly, the Lord by certain marks and tokens has pointed out to us what we should know about the church. As we have cited above from Paul, to know who are His is a prerogative belonging solely to God [2 Tim. 2:19]. . . . For those who seemed utterly lost and quite beyond hope are by his goodness called back to the way; while those who more than others seemed to stand firm often fall. Therefore, according to God's secret predestination (as Augustine says), 'many sheep are without and many wolves are within.' For he knows and has marked those who know neither him nor themselves. Of those who openly wear his badge, his eyes alone see the ones who are unfeignedly holy and will persevere to the very end—the ultimate point of salvation.[2]

We can begin to see the importance of the visible church, especially at a time when it has almost been lost in evangelical reflection in favor of the notion of the church as invisible. In my book, *In the Face of God,* I argued that contemporary spirituality is heavily influenced by themes that are very similar to those of ancient Gnosticism. Gnosticism was a heresy that threatened the unity of the early church, arguing that matter, history, and other marks of our physical, human existence (such as bodies) are inherently evil. In this thinking, the "prison-house" of our bodies and existence in this world had to somehow be transcended by attaining "spirit."

This kind of thinking easily shoves aside the view of the church as a visible institution, with delegated authority through human officers and ordinances (word, sacrament, and discipline). By focusing on the "spiritual," we can escape the thorny problems of accountability to an earthly institution. But Christ is not only the Mediator of the invisible church; he is the Lord of the visible church, which he established in terms of clearly defined offices and ordinances.

Thus, one has no right to regard oneself as part of "the church" in a merely vague, spiritual sense; one must belong to the visible body of Christ. Repeatedly in Scripture, we find that the church is both the invisible company of all the elect throughout all ages: "a glorious church, the bride of Christ" (Eph. 5:27; Col. 1:24), but also the visible church (Matt. 18:17; Acts 2:47; 14:23; 1 Cor. 11:22; 1 Tim. 5:16). We not only read about the invisible body, but "the Church of Corinth," Jerusalem, Rome, Ephesus, and the seven churches of the Revelation.

The Church—God's Holy People

In verses 15–19 of our Lord's high priestly prayer in John 17, we come to see the importance of defining the church as God's holy people. First, he observes that his church is "not of the world," for it has his Word, and for that reason the world hates the church. What is our Savior's prayer, then, for this conflict?

"My prayer is not that you take them out of the world but that you protect them from the evil one. They are not of the world, even as I am not of it. Sanctify them by the truth; your word is truth. As you sent me into the world, I have sent them into the world. For them I sanctify myself, that they too may be truly sanctified."

For our Lord, the critical question is not getting the world to become like the church, but keeping the church from becoming like the world. He spoke earlier of the salt losing its savor, good for nothing but to be thrown out and trampled underfoot. Just as Israel lost its hope, there continues to be danger that the visible church will become secularized. It is possible for visible churches to lose their status as such, just as the nation of Israel lost hers.

This is Paul's warning for the Galatians. It is also the warning our Savior delivered to the churches in the Book of Revelation. Candlesticks in the Holy of Holies may be removed if churches become unfaithful. And this has happened too often in church history. The early creeds were drafted to distinguish true visible churches from sects, schisms, and groups of heretics.

Similarly, even the Church of Rome, which in the early centuries did so much to uphold the truth in the face of error and division, is not immune from this warning. While individuals in that body are undoubtedly part of the invisible church, Rome's abandonment of the gospel of free justification and its determination to set itself above Scripture is a tragic warning to the rest of us. Meanwhile, Protestants have not fared much better in the modern age, as indeed contemporary evangelical (as well as Reformed and Lutheran) bodies are threatened with heresy and schism. Filled with fury after having lost the long war in heaven, Satan seeks to devour the visible church (Rev. 12), and Christ's intercession here in John 17 is that our visible churches will remain faithful to his word.

But if our Savior prays that we will not be taken from the world because of its sinfulness, how much more does he insist on our remaining in the church despite its shortcomings? After all, we are individually far from the glory that will belong to us one day.

This brings us to the sanctity or holiness for which Jesus prays here. Sanctification takes two forms, definitive and progressive. In the Old Testament, ordinary pots and pans were set apart for temple service and in this way were considered holy. It was not because there was a difference in quality or material from other household dishes, but because of the fact that God has set them apart for himself. Similarly, before we talk about sanctification as a process of growth in holiness, we must recognize that it is already a definitive reality as we belong to Christ.

We were chosen "to be holy and without blame" (Eph. 1:4), and because of our union with Christ we are already considered such: "It is because of him that you are in Christ Jesus, who has become for us wisdom from God—that is, our righteousness, holiness and redemption. Therefore, as it is written: 'Let him who boasts boast in the Lord'" (1 Cor. 1:30–31 NIV).

The Old Testament title, "The LORD Our Righteousness," is therefore applied here to our union with Christ. He *is* our holiness.

And this is precisely what Jesus intends when he prays, "For them I sanctify myself, that they too may be truly sanctified" (John 17:19 NIV). Jesus set himself apart from the world, the flesh, and the devil and consecrated himself to perfect obedience so that, in him, we too would be "truly sanctified" simply by belonging to him.

Like Noah and his family during the flood, or Israel passing through the Red Sea, the church too is saved by water and the Word (1 Peter 3:21). The church—consisting of believers and their children—is holy not because of something inherent, but because of something external: the righteousness of Christ imputed to sinners. Thus, the church as an institution as well as individual believers, is simultaneously justified and sinful. She is a holy body before God because her Head is pure and she is set apart for eternal favor because Christ is eternally loved by the Father. Nevertheless, she is often in herself a harlot; in fact God commanded Hosea to marry a prostitute to illustrate this relationship. It is not the church that separates herself from the world, but God who makes the separation in his eternal decree, executed in time through the Mediator of the Covenant.

But definitive sanctification is not all our Savior intends in this part of his petition, "Sanctify them by the truth; your word is truth" (v. 17). If we ignore the claims of truth and fail to immerse ourselves in the great treasures of biblical doctrine, we cannot grow and we will fall prey to the enemy. The part of the Word that justifies and sanctifies is the Gospel, "the power of God unto salvation."

It is the truth of the Gospel that saves the church and sets her apart from the world, not her own works or feverish posturing. We should be concerned when we hear reports of so-called "revivals" sweeping the nation in which God allegedly saves and acts apart from the ordinary means—word and sacrament. We are saved by the truth, and that truth is conveyed to us and conferred upon us by the Spirit through the means of human preaching, however unspectacular; through a book, however we might prefer exciting experiences to reading; through elements of water, bread, and wine, however common. Like Israel's pots and pans, these common elements are set aside for sacred use by the Holy Spirit. The Gospel creates the

190

church. The proclamation of justification by faith alone is not only the church's announcement; it is the church's origin, authority, and power in the world.

Christ's work not only secured the church's liberation from the curse of the Law; it secured the work of the Holy Spirit, awakening the sinner from spiritual death, granting repentance and faith, empowering the believer for new obedience. The church is God's new society, a counter culture, a sacred city set on a hill in the midst of the secular city below.

There are those who tell us that we must shape our message to suit the world. But if we do this, the church is no longer holy. It is no longer set apart from the world. Instead, in a quest for "success," it seeks to do everything it can do be like the world in its basic orientation. In doing this, it is we, rather than God, who create the church. The church is designed to be strange in an evil age, not familiar. In some cases, however, we have made truth and holiness strange in an effort to be worldly-wise.

What a remarkable petition: "My prayer is not that you take them out of the world but that you protect them from the evil one." Ironically, Christians today are often "of the world but not in it," instead of the other way around. We set up our own subculture of celebrities, rock stars, entertainers, self-help books, and cruises so we can be worldly without having to bother with the world. We are amusing ourselves to death, as Neil Postman would say, and defrocking the church of her strangeness in a perverse age.

Contrast this with the Reformation, when men and women from every walk of life, liberated by the Gospel to serve God in this world, eagerly abandoned the monastery for secular activity. They were salt and light. They were Christians "in the world, but not of it." And this energetic purity of both faith and practice revolutionized Northern Europe.

More importantly, contrast our contemporary approaches to those of the apostle Paul, who warned the Corinthians about substituting their own "excitements" for the simplicity of Word and sacrament. If we follow the biblical pattern of worship, he wrote, the unbeliever "is convinced by all, he is convicted by all. And thus the secrets of his heart are revealed; and so, falling down on his face, he will worship God and report that God is truly among you" (1 Cor. 14:24–25). It is in its strangeness that the Gospel bears the power of God unto salvation, however much it may be a stumbling block and offense to our "felt needs" (1 Cor. 1 and 2).

Holiness is not a call to become physically separated from the world, but it is a call to the very opposite: "As you sent me into the world, I have sent them into the world" (John 17:18). We are to be set apart from the world, in the world, unto God's service.

The Church—Called to Unity

It was this thought of sending his disciples out into the world that led Jesus on to the universal mission of his new society. With this in mind, he continued his high priestly Prayer:

> My prayer is not for them alone. I pray also for those who will believe in me through their message, that all of them may be one, Father, just as you are in me and I am in you. May they also be in us so that the world may believe that you have sent me. I have given them the glory that you gave me, that they may be one as we are one: I in them and you in me. May they be brought to complete unity to let the world know that you sent me and have loved them even as you have loved me. (vv. 20–23)

Curiously, most of the divisions in the church are caused by those who claim to be restoring the unity of the early church. When, for instance, Rome's greatest concern was to preserve the unity of Christendom rather than to preserve the light of the Gospel, the result was division. In our own American religious history, the nineteenth-century sects that claimed to be restoring the "original, apostolic" church of the New Testament and attacked denominations as ungodly divisions, merely succeeded in creating fresh wounds in the Body of Christ. New denominations have been born in even recent years out of movements that claimed to be nondenominational "moves of the Spirit."

A low doctrine of the church is a distinctive mark of American religion, even among American Roman Catholics, where individual tastes prevail over church dogmas. This is especially true of evangelicalism, where we have grown up believing that the church is simply a collection of individuals who have decided to follow Jesus. Christ's church is seen, in many circles, as a voluntary society, and church membership is not even required. But we must recover some sense of our catholicity, that is, some sense that we belong to one universal church through all times and in all places. We are "catholic," which means united in a visible community of the redeemed.

The word *catholic* tells us, in part, that we are connected to dead people. To borrow from a popular movie from the 1980s, ours is "the dead believer's society." Even here in our passage (John 17), Jesus moves easily from the immediate group of disciples to "those who will believe in me through their message, that all of them may be one" (vv. 20–21). The writer to the Hebrews invokes the image of a crowded stadium, filled with our brothers and sisters throughout history, cheering and guiding us as our team takes its turn on the field of history: "Therefore, since we are surrounded by such a great cloud of witnesses, let us throw off everything that hinders and the sin that so easily entangles, and let us run with perseverance the race marked out for us" (Heb. 12:1 NIV).

Our church today is answerable to the church of Pentecost, to the church of the Nicene Fathers, to the church of the Reformation, and to the church of our children and grandchildren. Wondering about the durability of a society present and future, Reggae artist Ziggy Marley warns us: "A people with no past have no future."

Ernst Troeltsch distinguished between "church-consciousness" and "sect-consciousness." The former characteristic is of churches who see themselves as part of a "communion of saints." The latter tend to regard their particular group as a restoration of true religion after its deep sleep. But today, "sect-consciousness" has devolved still further into a consumer-consciousness.

Further eroding our sense of belonging to a historical community of saints, the consumer approach that so shapes our contemporary outlook ignores roots and accountability. In spite of these trends, however, there are encouraging signs of a renewed interest in finding roots in our rootless age. Even within popular culture there are many reactions against pop culture itself.

Will the church be able to tear itself away from its present infatuations and recover its ties to the past? Genuinely catholic Christians do not start new churches from scratch, as if they had suddenly raised the *Titanic* that had been submerged in the great deep until last week. They know that belonging to their own time has its own liabilities as well as opportunities, so they stand on the shoulders of the "cloud of witnesses" to catch a better vista for the future. Furthermore, they know that passing fads are no match for the godly wisdom of the ages.

But catholicity not only means relatedness across time; geography is in view as well. Jesus spoke of bringing the Jews and Gentiles together under his own Cross. Then the Great Commission pointed to concentric circles, beginning with Jerusalem and reaching out to "the uttermost parts of the earth." The Jewish leadership of the apostolic church struggled to come to terms with the far-reaching implications of this evangelical mandate. But eventually the Spirit prevailed and by the time of Paul's death the Gospel had reached the distant borders of Europe.

The Council of Jerusalem, recorded in Acts 15, was the earliest attempt to bring the various churches together in order to resolve doctrinal and practical disputes. And throughout the first several centuries the churches enjoyed mutual respect and loyalty. It was only in the early Middle Ages when the Church of Rome began to claim primacy over all of the churches, in spite of the fact that the church fathers had condemned the notion of the supremacy of one church over the others.

The evolution of the primacy of Rome and her bishop is complicated. It was due at least in part to the fact that, initially, when heresies threatened the churches scattered throughout the empire, it was usually the bishop of Rome whose pastoral wisdom guided the churches to sound biblical exegesis. Because of repeated courageous defenses of orthodoxy, combined with the immense political importance of Rome, the bishop of Rome grew in power and authority. Even in the officially sanctioned Roman Catholic ency-clopedia, *Sacramentum Mundi,* the rise of the papacy is said to have been "accompanied by considerable resistance" within the church. However, it was seen as a way of bringing about unity.[3]

Throughout the Middle Ages the Roman bishop, now pro-claiming himself the "universal bishop," grew increasingly power-ful and this threatened to divide the church. Already in the fourth century, the bishop-patriarch of Constantinople, with the emperor's assistance, became the pope's rival. Tensions culminated in the eleventh-century schism between the churches of the East and West. By 1302, Pope Boniface VIII declared, "It is altogether nec-essary to salvation for every human creature to be subject to the Roman pontiff" (*Unam sanctam*). Eventually, there was a major division within the Roman Church itself, sometimes with two or three rival popes issuing mutual excommunications throughout the fourteenth and early fifteenth centuries. During that period, every Christian in the West was under the excommunication of at least one pope! The more Rome grew increasingly proud in her claims, the more she violated the catholic unity of the church.

But we Protestants also violate the catholic unity of the church when we show disregard for unnecessary divisions in the visible Body of Christ. Jesus prayed, "May they be brought to complete unity to let the world know that you sent me and have loved them even as you loved me" (John 17:23). If we are chosen together in Christ and redeemed by him, and if the Holy Spirit has incorporated us into that sacred body, we must long for the healing of visible fractures that continue to bring disgrace to the truth of God's Word.

Not only are we bound with the church of other times, but to the church of other places. This is sometimes forgotten, especially when we confuse our nation with the kingdom of God. Is the church an American institution, or is it a heavenly kingdom? Is it a kingdom of political power, one of the imperial layers of the statue in Nebuchadnezzar's dream, or is it the kingdom of grace whose borders reach across time and place? To be catholic is to believe—and live as though we believed—that we are more related to Christians in China, Africa, the Middle East, and Russia than we are to our own neighbors—even those with conservative moral values—who are not in union with Christ and his church.

The Protestant Reformation was not a rejection of authority, but a rejection of illegitimate authority. It was a rejection of a form of tyranny that declared the Gospel of free justification anathema. The church of the Middle Ages had refused the teaching of Scripture, teaching which the Apostles had upheld. The Reformation was not a demand for the right to private interpretation of Scripture, for, as Luther put it, "That would mean that every man would go to hell in his own way." Rather, it was a call for the whole church—not just the pope and magisterium—to read the Scriptures together and seek the mind of Christ. Far from launching modern individualism, the Reformation inspired a new era of confessions and catechisms—communal ways of reading, interpreting, and teaching God's Word, which bound together both pastor and layperson in the unity of truth.

We Believe and Confess. . . .

To the question, "Who needs the church?" introduced at the beginning of this chapter, historic Protestants have always answered with Scripture, "Whoever wishes to be saved." Not all who belong to the visible church are members of the invisible church, but one cannot choose to belong to the invisible, elect Body of Christ while refusing to belong to its visible expression. This is why the Belgic Confession (1563) of the Reformed Churches declared the following concerning the phrase, "the holy catholic Church":

> We believe and confess one single catholic or universal church—
> a holy congregation and gathering of true Christian believers,
> awaiting their entire salvation in Jesus Christ, being washed by his
> blood, and sanctified and sealed by the Holy Spirit. . . . We believe
> that since this holy assembly and congregation is the gathering of
> those who are saved and there is no salvation apart from it, no one
> ought to withdraw from it, content to be by himself, regardless of
> his status or condition. But all people are obliged to join and unite
> with it, keeping the unity of the church. . . . (Articles 27, 28).

The evangelicals did not differ with Rome in the claim that (outside the church there is no salvation) extra *Ecclesiam nulla Salus,* but in its definition of what constituted a true church. This raises the issue of unity, which is really the heart of what it means to be "catholic." Our high priest's prayer for unity in this passage (John 17) is often brandished like a sword against those who would insist on specific truths as necessary prerequisites to unity.

What is unity after all? It is the sharing of something in common. We are not united to each other by an act of our will, as if the tie that binds is that we all happen to be people who have decided to follow Jesus. We cannot simply determine to be one in Christ. Jesus prayed, "Sanctify them *by the truth;* your *Word* is truth" (emphasis added).

Similarly, Paul wrote, "Make every effort to keep the unity of the Spirit through the bond of peace." But how do we do that? Do we ignore sound doctrine? Paul replies, "There is one body and one Spirit—just as you were called to one hope when you were called—one Lord, one faith, one baptism." In fact, he adds, ministers were given to God's people "so that the body of Christ may be built up until we all reach unity *in the faith* and in the knowledge of the Son of God and become mature, attaining to the whole measure of the fullness of Christ. Then we will no longer be infants, tossed back and forth by the waves, and blown here and there by every wind of teaching and by the cunning and craftiness of men in their deceitful scheming. Instead, speaking *the truth in love,* we will in all things grow up into him who is the Head, that is, Christ" (Eph. 4:12–15 NIV, emphasis added).

Unity does not depend solely upon our faith. I cannot consider you a brother or a sister simply because you say you love Jesus and believe in him. Paul refers here not simply to *faith,* but to *the faith*—that is, an objective body of truth, and elaborates by saying that this is "the knowledge of the Son of God," which is both personal and propositional. It is not simply a common religious experience, but a common Christian confession that overcomes our worldly bigotry and knits us together into Christ.

I know Mormons who say that they love Jesus and have experienced his saving power. But since they deny essential articles of the Christian faith, they have "a form of godliness, but [deny] its power" (2 Tim. 3:5 NIV). Rejecting the catholic and apostolic faith, they are not to be regarded as part of Christ's body, visible or invisible. Our differences concern such crucial matters that we cannot call Mormons brothers or sisters despite their claims to shared experiences. As Luther put it, "Unity wherever possible, truth at all costs." Again, it is the Word that creates the church and legitimizes its existence and authority. And where this Word is not rightly preached, there is no genuine unity.

Paul insists that this one holy catholic church is "God's household, which is the church of the living God, the pillar and foundation of the truth" (1 Tim. 3:15 NIV) and warns Timothy to "guard the deposit that was entrusted to you" (1 Tim. 6:20; 2 Tim. 1:14). The Christian faith is a deposit, a treasure. This may seem like a somewhat boring word to those who would prefer to be creative and imaginative in their approach to religion. But "deposit" is nevertheless a comforting word to God's people, who have too often been victims of churchmen who sought to be wiser than God. Similarly, Jude's reference to "the faith once and for all entrusted to the saints" may sound hopelessly irrelevant. After all, he calls it the faith, assuming an objective body of doctrine, and adds, "once and for all entrusted to the saints," assuming an unchanging body of doctrine.

It is not our place to adjust the message to the audience (i.e., to be "conformed to the pattern of this age"), but rather to adjust the audience to the message (i.e., to be "transformed by the renewing of [our] mind," Rom. 12:2). We are to communicate clearly and passionately the person and work of Jesus Christ from generation to generation. As we do that, ignoring the Sirens' song of worldliness, we have the promise of the Husband to his bride: "I have told you these things, so that in me you may have peace. In this world you will have trouble. But take heart! I have overcome the world!"

TEN

Finding Forgiveness

I BELIEVE IN . . . THE
FORGIVENESS OF SINS.

"Against you and you only have I sinned," confessed the Psalmist (Ps. 51:4). That lament marks the chasm between the secular imagination of our time and the God-centered orientation of biblical history. Even though King David had committed adultery with Bathsheba and had carefully plotted the death of her husband, he realized the intensely *Godward* direction of his rebellion.

Recently, there have been numerous reports of public repentance on the part of church bodies and individuals. Various denominations have captured headlines by issuing apologies to victims regarding their explicit or implicit cooperation with oppressors. Rome has acknowledged the wrongfulness of the Crusades, Southern Baptists asked the descendants of the American slave-trade for forgiveness, and United Methodists confessed their complicity with the slaughter of American natives. Surely these are signs of a greater willingness to be self-critical and to reach out in sympathy to those who have been wronged by us.

Nevertheless, some questions are left unanswered. Is it not easier to confess the sins of our fathers than to confess our own? And is it not less offensive to us to acknowledge our mistreatment of our neighbor than to raise our eyes to heaven and say, with the Psalmist, "Against you and you only have I sinned. . . . In sin my mother conceived me, sinful from the time of birth"? In fact, it is more likely perhaps today, even in evangelical circles, to hear about the need to forgive ourselves than to hear about our need to find a forgiving God. Forgiveness, in our highly therapeutic culture, seems to have more to do with our own catharsis and psychic well-being (i.e., "getting it off our chest"), than with God.

In light of the last chapter, it is important to note that forgiveness of sins takes place within the precincts and under the ministry of the church of Christ. We begin with the so-called "marks of the church," those identifying and definitive characteristics that distinguish a true church of Christ from others that may claim to be such.

The Marks of a Church

"What are the marks of a true church?" What an odd question to ask! It sounds divisive because we believe that each congregation, perhaps each individual Christian, must determine what a true church is. After all, how can we judge? Although we can discover these signs throughout Scripture, Acts 2 places them conveniently in one place: "They devoted themselves to the apostles' teaching and to the fellowship, to the breaking of bread and to prayer" (v. 42). The importance of these qualities cannot be sufficiently stressed, for if the Gospel is confused, distorted, ignored, or denied, we close doors to the world receiving this forgiveness of sins. Thus, the marks of the true church answer this essential question: "How can sinners receive forgiveness?" By faithfully executing its ministry, the church either binds or looses things in heaven and earth (Matt. 16:19).

Historically, Protestant believers have regarded the church as the servant of the "means of grace." What is a "means of grace"? It is a way of receiving the forgiveness of sins along with all other benefits of Christ's saving work. So, as Calvin said, reflecting the conviction of Luther and the other Reformers, "Wherever we find the word of God purely preached and heard, and the sacraments administered according to the institution of Christ, there . . . is a Church of God."[1] In his dispute with Cardinal Sadoleto, the Reformer added, "There are three things on which the safety of the Church is founded, namely, doctrine, discipline, and the sacraments."[2] "As soon as we are tinctured with the contrivances of men, the temple of God is polluted."[3]

In spite of the shortcomings of Christ's visible church, these "marks"—doctrine, discipline, and sacraments—are therefore required. One may, for instance, belong to a church in which there is tremendous confusion, disorder, and even immorality, and yet it is a true church (as in the case of Corinth). But where there is an explicit denial of the Gospel a church loses its right to the title (as Paul warned in the case of the Galatian church). Jesus warns us of the possibility of true churches becoming so indistinguishable from the world that they cease to be churches at all (Rev. 2:5, 15–16; 3:1–3, 2:8–11, 14–22). What, then, can a church not live without? The answer offered by Scripture, I believe, is that given in our common evangelical confession: Word, sacrament, and discipline. Apart from the two "means of grace" (Word and sacrament) a church is not a church, for this is the ministry given to our charge.

The Importance of Sound Preaching

In his warnings to the churches in the Revelation, Jesus exercised his judgments by these criteria. Ephesus was approved for its perseverance in the Word and for its rejection of false apostles and teachers (Rev. 2:2), but the centrality of Christ was waning and they were instructed to return to their first love.

Likewise, Smyrna was commended for standing up to the legalism of the Judaizers, a church that was in truth "a synagogue of Satan" (v. 9).

Jesus encouraged Pergamum for remaining faithful to sound

teaching, despite difficulty. "Nevertheless," he said, "I have a few things against you: You have people there who hold to the teaching of Balaam. . . . Likewise you also have those who hold to the teaching of the Nicolaitans. Repent therefore! Otherwise, I will soon come to you and will fight against them with the sword of my mouth" (vv. 14–16 NIV).

The church in Thyatira was denounced: "You tolerate that woman Jezebel, who calls herself a prophetess," denoting a false teacher who led many astray (v. 20). Those "who do not hold to her teaching" he said, would be spared. "Only hold on to what you have until I come" (vv. 24–25).

Sardis was a dying church, but she could live again if she were to recover the Word: "Remember, therefore, what you have received and heard; obey it, and repent" (3:3 NIV).

Further, Jesus had seen how the church in Philadelphia had opposed the "synagogue of Satan," as Smyrna had done (v. 9 NIV).

In all these cases, Jesus concluded his admonitions with the statement, "He who has an ear, let him hear what the Spirit says to the churches." It is the Word alone that brings death and life. As Calvin reminded us, "God begets and multiplies his Church only by means of his word. It is by the preaching of the grace of God alone that the Church is kept from perishing."[4]

Scripture is called "God-breathed," and sufficient for everything, necessary for salvation and the Christian life. Thus, the church is the "pillar and foundation of the truth" (1 Tim. 3:15 NIV). As we have seen in our Lord's high priestly prayer, it is only by that Word that we are made partakers of God in Christ: "Sanctify them by your Word; your Word is truth."

So essential is the ministry of the Word that in Acts 6 we read of the apostles' establishing the deaconate to carry out the more administrative details of the church, so that the elders and ministers may be given to the Word and to prayer: "It would not be right for us to neglect the ministry of the word of God in order to wait on tables. . . . We will turn this responsibility over to them and will give our attention to prayer and the ministry of the word" (Acts 6:2–4 NIV). The seven deacons were chosen, the poor were cared for, "so the Word of God spread. The number of disciples in Jerusalem increased rapidly, and a large number of priests became obedient to the faith" (v. 7). Today, perhaps, the equivalent of "waiting on tables" might be other administrative functions. It has been widely lamented that pastors have become "managers" instead of shepherds, CEOs rather than ministers of word, sacrament, and discipline. We need to reread such passages as these from the apostolic church and be reminded of the true mission of the church.

Paul counseled Timothy to give his full attention to this ministry of the Word: "Do your best to present yourself to God as one approved, a workman who does not need to be ashamed and who correctly handles the word of truth" (2 Tim. 2:15 NIV), and calls the Word the sword of the spirit (Eph. 6:17). In Romans 10:13–17, Paul unfolds the logic of this sacred trust: "'Everyone who calls on the name of the Lord shall be saved.' How, then, can they call on the one they have not believed in? And how can they believe in the one of whom they have not heard? And how can they hear without someone preaching to them? And how can they preach unless they are sent? . . . Consequently, faith comes from hearing the message, and the message is heard through the word of Christ."

God's Word can be divided into two parts: the Law and the Gospel. Everything from Genesis to Revelation that exhorts, warns, commands, or otherwise imposes ethical obligations is "Law," and there is no mercy for those who fail at any point. Thus, the Law demands perfect compliance and attaches a curse to those who fail in this. It is not because the Law is evil that it is the enemy of our sinful nature, but because we are sinful and hostile to righteousness (Rom. 7:7).

Even as believers, after we are justified and are given new life, our budding love for the Law is always challenged by the resistance of our sinful nature. But in that exercise the Law is vital, "so that every mouth may be silenced and the whole world held accountable to God." "Therefore," Paul wrote, "no one will be declared righteous in his sight by observing the law; rather, through the law we become conscious of sin" (Rom. 3:19–20).

Fortunately, there is another "word" in Scripture: the Gospel, and Paul follows his description of the Law by a description of this other word: "But now a righteousness from God, apart from law, has been made known, to which the Law and the Prophets testify. This righteousness from God comes through faith in Jesus Christ to all who believe" (vv. 21–22 NIV). The Law kills, the Spirit makes alive by the preaching of the Gospel. "The Gospel is sheer good tidings," Herman Bavinck wrote, "not demand but promise, not duty but gift."[5]

Unless we clearly preach both Law and Gospel, we will fail in the ministry of the Word, for we must be brought to total despair of our own righteousness before we can receive the righteousness of Jesus Christ. Apart from the knowledge of our utter nakedness and corruption, we will not seek the clothing that God has provided. Who needs forgiveness but transgressors? This is why Paul declared so enthusiastically, in spite of the unpopularity of it all: "I am not ashamed of the gospel, because it is the power of God for the salvation of everyone who believes: first for the Jew, then for the Gentile. For in the gospel a righteousness from God is revealed, a righteousness that is by faith from first to last, just as it is written: 'The righteous will live by faith'" (Rom. 1:16–17 NIV).

What happens when the Word is absent or its clear teaching and preaching are somehow obscured? Through Amos God prophesied a "famine of the Word," which precedes the destruction of Israel in chapter 9. Whenever there is a famine of the Word, the church loses her vigor and becomes like those in Ezekiel's vision—a valley of dry bones. It is not because there is too much attention on the sound doctrine, teaching, proclamation, and application of God's Word, that there is dryness and a lack of enthusiasm for the things of the Lord.

"Life, not doctrine," is hardly a cliché that the prophets and apostles would have countenanced. For when the Word is faithfully preached, our misery and Christ's grace are so clearly made visible to the eyes of faith by the Holy Spirit that life cannot come without this activity. It is not cleverly invented stories that have saving power, said Peter, but the declarations of eye-witnesses about the saving work of Christ (2 Peter 1:16). Unlike the "super-apostles," said Paul, "We do not preach ourselves, but Jesus Christ as Lord" (2 Cor. 4:5 NIV). Even our testimonies to the changes Christ has made in our lives are not the preaching of the Gospel, for it is Christ's life, not ours, that is "good news" for sinners.

There is always a danger of losing our grip on the sufficiency of God's Word, especially the sufficiency of the preached Word. We seem to forget that when the minister mounts the pulpit, he is speaking to us in Christ's stead, as Christ's royal ambassador, and in his Sovereign's voice. The preacher is not there to disseminate his insights into the important needs and issues of the day, nor even chiefly to apply the Bible to daily life (although application is part of his duty).

Even if passages from the Bible are used in the sermon, it is not the saving proclamation of God's word unless it "placards" (i.e., publicly holds up, as if on a billboard) Christ (Gal. 3:1). The Pharisees had nullified the Word of God for their own commands (Matt. 15:6), but the true church hears only her shepherd's voice (John 10:27).

The Blessing of the Sacraments

So gracious is our God and so aware is he of our weakness in believing that he has added to the preached Word the visible Word in the form of two sacraments: baptism and the Lord's Supper. Not only does he announce forgiveness to our ears, he gives us his Gospel in the form of something we can see, taste, feel, and smell.

Recently, I asked a large gathering of people to name the marks of the church. Since few of us these days are taught the evangelical catechisms, where they are clearly listed, I was not expecting to hear precise responses. But I was surprised to hear a rather long list that nevertheless failed to include the sacraments.

I fear that we have so downplayed the importance of the church and its official ministry that we have deprived ourselves of the unspeakable comfort that God offers. He is the author of baptism and the Supper and we cannot dismiss the sacraments as trivial without bringing reproach to the name of their author.

Let us bear in mind that we are still talking about "the forgiveness of sins," for the sacraments, together with the Word, have more to do with this question than anything else that goes on in the church. And nothing that the church does—none of its programs, its special events, its outreaches, its community service—is as important as the forgiveness of sins.

The sacrament of initiation into the covenant community is baptism. Much can be said here with which all evangelical believers can agree, regardless of differing views on this important subject. First, it is commanded by Christ. The Great Commission is the church's missionary charter: "All authority in heaven and on earth has been given to me. Therefore go and make disciples of all nations, baptizing them in the name of the Father and of the Son and of the Holy Spirit, and teaching them to obey everything I have commanded you. And surely I am with you always, to the very end of the age" (Matt. 28:18–20 NIV).

Now seated at God's right hand, the king of the Church continues to exercise this universal authority by the proclamation of the Word and baptism. "Whoever believes and is baptized will be saved," said Jesus (Mark 16:16 NIV). After Peter preached the Gospel at Pentecost, he declared, "Repent and be baptized, every one of you" (Acts 2:38 NIV) and all "who accepted his message were baptized" (v. 41). Converts were baptized, "both men and women" (8:12). Likewise, when Paul related his own conversion, he recalled Ananias's words to him: "And now what are you waiting for? Get up, be baptized and wash your sins away, calling on his name" (Acts 22:16 NIV). As Paul comforted Timothy, so he comforts us:

> But when the kindness and love of God our Savior appeared, he saved us, not because of righteous things we had done, but because of his mercy. He saved us through the washing of rebirth and renewal by the Holy Spirit, whom he poured out on us generously through Jesus Christ our Savior, so that, having been justified by his grace, we might become heirs having the hope of eternal life. (Titus 3:4–7 NIV)

Peter made a startling parallel between the waters of the flood and the water of baptism: "There is also an antitype which now saves us—baptism (not the removal of the filth of the flesh, but the answer of a good conscience toward God), through the resurrection of Jesus Christ" (1 Peter 3:21). The sign is water, and the thing signified is regeneration and forgiveness of sins—just as the sign of circumcision was linked to the reality of belonging to God.

This is precisely the nature of a sacrament: it is the union between a sign and the thing signified. This is why the New Testament writers speak so literally about baptism washing away sins and bringing forgiveness. As Peter himself pointed out, it is not the physical washing that saves us, but rather it is Christ who saves us by washing us in his blood. And yet, in God's mysterious plan, baptism was to be the means of grace by which we are incorporated into the household of faith.

Some brothers and sisters, of course, will want to say more about baptism than that, others quite a bit less, but this seems to me to be the best way of viewing the relevant texts. Nowhere do we see baptism described as a mere symbol or a bare sign, but only as something which actually conveys and seals the thing that is promised. In fact, Old Testament circumcision was called a "seal" (Rom. 4:11), and Paul elsewhere identified baptism as the New Testament replacement of circumcision (Col. 2:11–12).

Space will not allow us to treat infant baptism with much detail, but it seems to me that we have no justification for assuming that the one covenant of grace in both Old and New Testaments includes the children of believers under the former administration, while barring them in what is ostensibly a "better covenant," as Hebrews makes plain. In his Pentecost sermon, Peter confirms the unity of the covenant by announcing that the offspring of believers are still children of the promise: "'Repent, and let every one of you be baptized in the name of Jesus Christ for the remission of sins; and you shall receive the gift of the Holy Spirit. For the promise is to you *and to your children,* and to all who are afar off, as many as the Lord our God will call'" (Acts 2:38–39, emphasis added).

If circumcision has been replaced with baptism (Col. 2:11–12), why should we deny our children the sign and seal of the covenant of grace? God is such a faithful father that he includes our children with us in the forgiveness of sins and the life in the Spirit. It would be surprising if there were no infants among the household baptisms (Acts 16:15; 16:33; 1 Cor. 1:16). In the Old Testament, the children of believers were set apart from birth as belonging to God, and this has not changed in the New Testament, for Paul says that one believing parent sanctifies the children. "Otherwise your children would be unclean, but as it is, they are holy" (1 Cor. 7:14 NIV).

If there is a clear distinction between the children of believers and those of unbelievers in the New as well as the Old Testament, what is to keep us from applying the sign and seal that God has commanded for that purpose?

The Lord's Supper

But there is a second sacrament that our Savior bequeathed to his church: the Lord's Supper or Holy Communion. We are familiar with the words of institution: "This is my body, this is my blood. Do this in remembrance of me." But perhaps the clearest exposition of this point is found in 1 Corinthians 10. As false teaching usually leads, ironically, to a greater clarity and precision, so the Corinthians' confusion is our gain, because it is to the Corinthians that Paul explained this sacrament more carefully.

First, he asked, "Is not the cup of thanksgiving for which we give thanks a participation in the blood of Christ? And is not the bread that we break a participation in the body of Christ? Because there is one loaf, we, who are many, are one body, for we all partake of one loaf" (1 Cor. 10:16–17 NIV). The word Paul uses here for "participation" is *koinonia,* often translated "fellowship." Here we discover that the cup and the bread that are blessed actually become for us a means of sharing in the benefits of Christ's saving work.

At this point, some readers will understandably say, "But I'm already saved. How does Communion make me more of a Christian afterward than before?" It is important for us not to think in terms of quantities. In other words, grace is not a substance that is poured into us like water into a cup. Rather, grace is divine favor and forgiveness in spite of our unworthiness. The problem is that we really do not believe this as fully as we should.

Although we are alive in Christ, we struggle with doubt and we still find it tempting to fall back into a form of works-righteousness that turns our attention from Christ to ourselves. If justification, sanctification, and everything else secured by Christ's death can only be given to us by grace alone through faith alone, our faith must be constantly strengthened. We do not want to be like the seed that fell on rocky ground or that was choked by the weeds. We want our roots to grow deep into the rich soil of our Savior's mercies. But if the tendency of our sinful nature is still to trust ourselves and to look within, our faith requires a constant redirection outward to Christ, and this can only come through Word and sacrament.

We never say (or at least shouldn't say) that we need to hear the good news of God's Word only once, and that after we believe it we can then get along fine without hearing it again. Although we are forever and fully absolved from our sins the moment we look to Christ and cast ourselves on God's mercy, we are always in the position of the man in Mark 9:24: "I do believe; help me overcome my unbelief!" To that end, God not only provided for our redemption, but sent his Holy Spirit to apply it. Then, as if that were not enough, he continually applies this Gospel to us and by it strengthens our faith. We are not only saved; we are being saved. We are each in a long war against our sinful heart, mind, conscience, and will. Faith receives forgiveness not only once, but throughout the Christian life.

Every time we partake of Communion, we are receiving God's grace. The same is true when we hear it in the preached Word. We hear and eat, and just as surely as we receive the bread and wine into our mouths, so we receive from heaven the body and blood of Christ for our sins. It is a real participation, according to Paul. But he goes on to add a fuller explanation: "Therefore, whoever eats the bread or drinks the cup in an unworthy manner will be guilty of sinning against the body and blood of the Lord. . . . For anyone who eats and drinks without recognizing the body of the Lord eats and drinks judgment on himself" (1 Cor. 11:27–30 NIV).

As with baptism, the Lord's Supper involves a sign, which is bread and wine. It also involves the thing signified—forgiveness by feeding on Christ's body and blood—in such close relation that to violate the Supper is a sin "against the body and blood of the Lord."

Where the Action Is

Everybody's looking for action. At sporting events at the stadium, at rock concerts, on the beach, in the mountains, on the desert, we are on the move, trying to find something truly exciting to entertain us.

This attitude also dominates our churches, so that the weekly ministry of Word and sacrament seems somehow boring in comparison to signs and wonders, praise bands, drama sketches, and other trappings of our market-driven popular culture. We are willing to set aside the biblical "means of grace" in order to institute our own, as if we were wiser than God. This was precisely the problem with the medieval church, as it has been throughout history.

If we were to recover a genuine Word and sacrament ministry, I am convinced that we would see not only many unregenerate Christians run out the back door, but we would also see the outpouring of God's Spirit in a remarkable way. After all, God has decided to bless us on his terms, not on ours. He does not just "show up" and ask us where we want him to stand. In the ministry of Word and sacrament, God is the actor. One thing both sacraments have in common is that they are from God to us, not from us to God.

For many years I thought of baptism as my sign of dedication, the token of my obedience, and a testimony to the world that I had decided to follow Jesus. But while baptism does call us to faithful discipleship, every passage we have seen on the topic has to do with what God is doing: his faithfulness, his grace, his forgiveness, his giving of the Spirit.

The same is true of Communion. No instructions are given in Scripture on how we should remember Christ's death because that is not the point. My focus at Communion used to be on the emotional state of my soul, and I saw the bread and wine as a tool or an influence to activate my piety. Now I see it as God's gift. Instead of my ascent toward God, the focus of Communion is God's descent in the person of Christ in the power of the Holy Spirit through the means of grace.

That is truly good news! It is the genuine "signs and wonders" movement, where God meets us in grace and forgiveness, raising the spiritually dead to life, giving sight to the blind, setting prisoners free! The signs may be ordinary and unspectacular: ink and paper, a simple preacher, water, bread, and wine. But God has promised to be there in the presence of weakness to display his mighty power, bringing to these signs by his Spirit the reality of the forgiveness we need and the life our dry bones crave.

The Purity of the Church

The earlier Reformed statements left out another necessary mark, but the Reformed confessions add a third mark to the Word and sacraments: church order and discipline. Not only must a true church faithfully preach the Gospel and administer the sacraments according to Christ's institution; they must also follow New Testament guidelines for order. Again, the confusion of many of the New Testament churches afforded an opportunity for great apostolic clarity for our benefit also. As a result, we have a great deal of instruction about the offices of the ministry and the qualifications for deacons, elders, and ministers. By following them, we can better avoid both tyranny and sectarian confusion.

Not only have the ministry of Word and sacrament fallen on hard times, but there is a widespread sense that our churches themselves are out of control. Scandals rock the Christian world and people wonder, "Is anybody accountable to anybody?" Doctrinal deviations are either openly tolerated or are handled by mob rule. In other cases, men and women lose their reputation to slander and gossip. Who is in charge? We are living in days like those of the judges: "In those days there was no king in Israel; everyone did what was right in his own eyes" (Judg. 21:25). But now Israel has a conquering King. And Christ reigns through the officers he deputizes through the consent of his people.

In 1 Corinthians 5, Paul commanded the church to exercise discipline of its erring flock, many of whom were engaging in open sexual immorality. He instructed that those who refused to repent must be removed from the fellowship of the church, and be treated as unbelievers. Interestingly, Paul says that this does not include unbelievers, "for then we would have to leave the world" (5:10). Rather, we cannot associate with those who claim to be Christians and yet live in flagrant disregard of biblical commands.

It is somewhat ironic that we seem to be so judgmental these days toward the immorality of the outside world while failing to exercise discipline in our own ranks. Too often, we are scolding Madonna while famous pastors and Christian celebrities turn their scandals into opportunities to make triumphant comebacks. We have clear instructions from Scripture in these matters, yet we refuse to frame our churches in such a way that our actual operating procedure is circumscribed by its limits.

It is encouraging to see in my own ministry a new generation emerging that is dissatisfied with the apathy and individualism of the eighties. Among the dissatisfied are young people—many of them considered part of the counterculture in other respects—who are weary of raising their own parents and taking up adult responsibilities while their parents indulge themselves. While this same group reacts sharply against legalism, it is eager to find some balance between form and freedom.

The reality is that churches will not always handle things as they should. If Corinth was as undisciplined as it was and was still considered a church by the apostle, then surely we must not make our judgments too quickly. "The purest churches have their blemishes," said Calvin, "and some are marked, not by a few spots, but by general deformity."[6] And further, "Very many, under the pretext of zeal, are excessively displeased, when everything is not conducted to their wish, and, because absolute purity is nowhere to be found, withdraw from the Church in a disorderly manner, or subvert and destroy it by unreasonable severity."[7]

212

We should never be surprised that the church is often assailed from within: "The Church . . . has had no enemies more inveterate than the members of the Church."[8] That which Calvin says about individual believers may be equally applied to the church generally:

> Finally, we acknowledge that this regeneration is so effected in us that, until we slough off this mortal body, there remains always in us much imperfection and infirmity, so that we always remain poor and wretched sinners in the presence of God. And, however much we ought day by day to increase and grow in God's righteousness, there will never be plentitude or perfection while we live here. Thus we always have need of the mercy of God to obtain the remission of our faults and offenses. And so we ought always to look for our righteousness in Jesus Christ and not at all in ourselves, and in him be confident and assured, putting no faith in our works. (The Genevan Confession, 1536)

What Really Matters?

If someone were to ask you, "What is the most important problem you will face in your lifetime?" what would you answer? Even when we give the correct answer, we often live and think as if it really were something else. We know what we should say, but we simply do not have this awful sense that we are under the wrath of a holy God. If we did, surely we would answer, "the forgiveness of sins." With David, we would acknowledge the Godward direction of our sinful rebellion and would be filled with a sense of our own utter lostness.

Throughout our study of the Apostles' Creed we have seen how crucial it is to understand sin and grace, how central it is to the whole Christian faith to see Christ and his Cross as the church's obsession. But then, after a diet of "relevance," where we simply parrot the interests and obsessions of the marketplace, the memory of even the correct answers fades. This is where we are, generally speaking, as recent studies indicate with frightening clarity. Surrounded by the noise of two World Wars and an exile from his homeland as an enemy of the Nazi regime, Karl Barth warned against viewing the church and her ministry as a method of helping people realize their "full humanity" and their real potential:

> The church is not a tool to uphold the world or to further its progress. It is not an instrument to serve either what is old or what is new. The church and preaching are not ambulances on the battlefield of life. Preaching must not attempt to set up an ideal community, whether of soul or heart or spirit. . . . We do not always have to bring in the latest and most sensational events. For instance, if a fire broke out in the community last week, and church members are still suffering under its awful impact, we should be on guard against even hinting at this theme in the sermon. It belongs to everyday life, but now it is Sunday, and people do not want to remain stuck in everyday problems. They want to go beyond them, to rise above them.[9]

Barth relates his own story of trying to be "relevant." After the sinking of the *Titanic* in 1912, Barth flew to the pulpit with an application, as he did two years later: "Again in 1914, when the outbreak of war left the whole world breathless, I felt obliged to let this war rage on in all my sermons until finally a woman came up to me and begged me for once to talk about something else and not constantly about this terrible conflict. She was right! I had disgracefully forgotten the importance of submission to the text. . . . All honor to relevance, but pastors should be good marksmen who aim their guns beyond the hill of relevance."[10]

Whenever we preach the Law in all of its realism and with all of its threats, followed by the Gospel in all of its sweetness, we are relevant in a way that far surpasses all attempts at meeting "felt needs." Especially we who are increasingly socialized in therapeutic categories have learned to deny our real need by simply regarding it as irrelevant.

Not long ago, a pastor told me that when he finally decided to abandon a "seeker-driven" approach, he began preaching the Law and Gospel clearly, and suddenly every sermon hit its mark. The successful businesswoman who secretly wondered whether she could be forgiven and the teenager who felt no interest in church both received what they needed. The woman received forgiveness again. The apathetic and bored teenager was suddenly shaken up and troubled at the roots, fleeing to Christ for safety. Isn't that true relevance? We cannot deny that we are naked ourselves but clothed in costly garments.

If we are to receive the forgiveness of sins as it is proclaimed and given to us from God's own lips and hands, it will be in his church. Jesus did not entrust his Word and sacraments to the media. He did not found a web of parachurch ministries. He did not turn over his kingdom to Washington, D.C. He does not expect Hollywood's entertainment writers to craft a liturgy for worship.

If reconciliation with God is the greatest need we have, and this is made available only through the ministry of the church founded by Christ, our individual churches and denominations will have to turn their backs on the diversions.

The world offers faith in anything and everything: "How to have faith in yourself," "How to have faith in the future," "How to have faith in your *possibilities*." In the face of that false hope, it is time we confessed our faith once again: "I believe in the forgiveness of sins." If there is to be any good news, any forgiveness, any hope beyond this world of immediate gratification, it will only be found in one place, however strange and flawed: in the church that our Lord founded on his prophets and apostles, with Jesus Himself as its cornerstone. It is here where frail, sinful ministers are authorized to speak for God: "Beloved, your sins are forgiven."

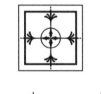

ELEVEN

Back to the Future

✦ ✦ ✦

I BELIEVE . . . IN THE
RESURRECTION OF THE BODY
AND THE LIFE EVERLASTING.

The leader of a Christian organization announced a bold new advance to his staff: "It would now be possible for us to beam our programs around the world by satellite!"

One thoughtful man, however, raised his hand: "But what if we don't have anything worthwhile to 'beam' around the world?"

This is similar to Thoreau's point in *Walden,* over a century ago. He noted that people were so excited about the new transatlantic telegraph wire that nobody had stopped to ask whether New York and London had anything important to say to each other. What would he have said if he could have seen the present deluge of information technologies, with so many people wasting their lives in swamps of data without much dry land of wisdom from which to view it all?

Our eagerness to embrace the future as an end in itself seems to have placed Americans in the forefront of technological discoveries.

And, as Albert Einstein once mused "perfection of means and confusion of ends characterize the American character." This is often true when we talk about the doctrinal confusion in the churches, for instance, and are told that we are being divisive and are interrupting the real ministry of the church. The assumption is that "the real ministry of church" has to do with means, not ends. But we have made the means ends in themselves. Preaching the Gospel, for instance, has become an end, when in Scripture it is a means to a greater end: reconciling sinners to God, which requires us to get the message right.

But this is a good place to restate our topic. Why are we here? Where are we going? Does history have any point, or is it, in the familiar words of Macbeth, "a tale told by an idiot, full of sound and fury, signifying nothing"? Because God has spoken, the Christian has a view of history that reaches beyond the events by themselves and provides the interpretation that makes sense of what might otherwise lead us to Macbeth's conclusion. Of course, there are other large-scale interpretations of history: the Marxist believes that history is the dialectical struggle of the working class; the capitalist believes that it is the triumph of the market's "invisible hand"; while artists and scientists struggle for their right to give some definition to our otherwise vaporous lives.

Only Christianity locates the meaning of history within history— the Resurrection—without abandoning belief in another world. Furthermore, Christianity maintains that through the historical event of the Resurrection we accept as God's gift the disclosure of meaning and purpose for all human and cosmic existence. Too often, current discussions of "last things" focus on speculative hunches about how the morning newspaper somehow fulfills biblical prophecy. When we concentrate narrowly on questions about the end times, we actually miss the richness of biblical teaching on eschatology.

It is time that we put last things first. In other words, we need to realize that the future—what Hebrews calls "the powers of the coming age"—is already breaking in on the present and giving shape and identity to our lives here and now. We know what it means for the present to be, in some sense, the product of the past, but how can the present be the product of the future?

"Thy Kingdom Come"

Throughout the Old Testament, believers longed for the inauguration of the New Age, the Age of the Spirit, when the serpent would finally be cast out of the garden, his head crushed, and sin, death, and suffering vanquished. In our Lord's earthly ministry, as we have already seen, this kingdom is not only announced, but is present (Luke 11:20). This means that the believer has already been transferred from the realm over which the world, the flesh, and the devil reign in death into the kingdom of Christ (2 Peter 1:11). This kingdom, however, is not merely individual, but cosmic. From a mustard seed, it grows into a mighty tree (Matt. 13:31–32). Like a dragnet, it sweeps the nations in (v. 47–50). It is the field into which the seeds of eternal life are planted, a plot of land so valuable to the farmer that he gave his greatest treasure to buy it (v. 44).

Nevertheless, the dragnet is filled with fish, which are destined to be destroyed: "This is how it will be at the end of the age. The angels will come and separate the wicked from the righteous and throw them into the fiery furnace, where there will be weeping and gnashing of teeth" (v. 49 NIV).

And the field purchased at such great expense yields both wheat and tares, some seed sown by the Spirit and others by the enemy. Nevertheless, just as the fishermen are not to separate the fish, Jesus explains that we must not "weed" God's garden yet, "because while you are pulling the weeds, you may root up the wheat with them. Let both grow together until the harvest," and then judgment will come (vv. 29–30 NIV).

Christ's kingdom, though present in the power of the Word and Spirit, is nevertheless both qualitatively and quantitatively different from the fullness of the kingdom in the age to come. Although the kingdom is spreading throughout the world, it is never identified with the world in this age, but must always be distinguished from the temporal kingdoms and cultural identities that believers share with unbelievers.

Only with the sound of the seventh angel's trumpet do we finally hear the announcement:

"The kingdom of the world has become the kingdom of our Lord
And of his Christ,
And he will reign for ever and ever."
(Rev. 11:15 NIV)

It comes as a decisive event, not as a gradual process, for it is not the church that carries the world into the Promised Land on her shoulders, but the church herself that is carried in the train of the rider of the white horse. It is he—the greater "Joshua" and the superior Davidic king—who, at the end of the age, sends his angels to drive the Canaanites out of the land, finally bringing Sabbath rest to Israel's war-weary camp.

Braving the New World

Many people are waiting for a new world. We see that longing in the clamor for "change"—anything will do, so long as it is different. Bored by the fashions that dazzled us only moments ago, our attention spans seem to be shrinking. The more addicted we are to the "new and improved," the more quickly what we have becomes tired and useless. But the promise of Scripture all along was of a New Covenant, leading God's new people to sing a new song as his new creation. That creation would be brought to life out of death, brought into the light from utter darkness and hopelessness.

None of this would have been possible apart from the resurrection of Jesus Christ. It was his resurrection as "the firstfruits of those who sleep" that guarantees the "new creation" of which we are a part (1 Cor. 15:20).

We have already taken a close look at Paul's argument for Christ's resurrection. In terms of both Old Testament anticipation and New Testament explanation, this event has cosmic significance not simply because a dead man rose from the dead. After all, God raised Lazerus from the dead, too. What makes our Lord's resurrection significant is that it was part of an unfolding plot, a plan of redemption that began in the heart of God (election) and was now worked out in human history. Jesus Christ's significance is anchored in the fact that he was the God-Man, the Mediator and Second Adam, representative head of the church.

Just as Adam's sin lost humanity its acceptance and holiness before God, Christ's obedience won for his new humanity the favor and acceptance before God. In Christ, a new world was born. In his virginal conception, a new spiritual race taken from the races of the world was made holy. In his perfect life, the church was regarded as obedient despite its perpetual harlotry. In his atoning death, his people were relieved of the burden of the debt, which they owed. Easter Sunday was the new birthday of the world:

> But now Christ is risen from the dead, and has become the first-fruits of those who have fallen asleep. For since by man came death, by Man also came the resurrection of the dead. For as in Adam all die, even so in Christ all shall be made alive. But each one in his own order: Christ the firstfruits, afterward those who are Christ's at His coming. Then comes the end, when He delivers the kingdom to God the Father, when He puts an end to all rule and all authority and power. For He must reign till He has put all enemies under His feet. The last enemy that will be destroyed is death. (1 Cor. 15:20–26)

Jesus announced the new birth (John 3:5), and Paul emphasized this as a significant reality of the future which is breaking in on the present. After driving his readers to despair of any hope in the future based on human ideals, morality, wisdom, or other "high places," Paul explained the reality of justification. Here is a future verdict that is rendered in the present because of an event in the past (Rom. 5:1).

For the believer, the judgment has already, in a real sense, taken place. It is not something to be nervously awaited, but to be joyfully anticipated. The Cross and Resurrection unite past, present, and future, bringing the future into the present. This "anticipation" is not the same thing as Old Testament longing, resting on types and shadows. Rather, it is based on the fact that we are already enjoying, in an embryonic state, the realities of the coming age. It is on the basis of our present enjoyment of this future verdict that we, therefore, endure our suffering in this life, knowing the outcome of our faith (Rom. 5:1–2).

Out of this discussion Paul then turns from the objective work of Christ for us to the subjective work of Christ by his Spirit within us. Biblical scholars distinguish between the "not yet" and the "already," as helpful guardrails against saying either that the kingdom is not present at all, or that it is so fully present that we already enjoy all of its benefits. The former denies the present reality of the kingdom, while the latter seems to impatiently insist that it is here in all its consummation and fullness.

The "already" includes not merely a future verdict rendered in the present, but a future restoration brought forward into the present as well. Unlike justification, sanctification is imperfect and incomplete in this life, according to degrees. Nevertheless, it is complete in one sense: It radically reorients the believer from self to God at the deepest level. Just as total depravity means not that we are as bad as we could be, but that sin is pervasive (leaving no faculty untouched), so regeneration means not that we are as good as we could be, but that the restoration that has taken place is just as pervasive as sin.

In Romans 6 Paul makes it clear that by baptism our death to sin has been sealed and we are alive to God in Christ. This is a completed event. Too often, we reverse Paul's indicative and imperative and create schemes of sanctification, implying that the gifts described are somehow waiting to be grasped, but only by an elite band of "spiritual" Christians. Instead, the decisiveness of baptism into Christ assures us of the decisiveness of this act of rebirth and renewal.

Sanctification overthrows the kingdom of Satan. The Christian warfare initiated by the Spirit in regeneration, however weakly endeavored, is not merely directed at some sins, but at all sins. It is determined to obedience to all divine commands. Thus, just as the future verdict is rendered in the present, so the future state (glorification) also begins to be realized in the present. So certain is Paul of this link between the future and the present that he can speak of glorification as a completed event (Rom. 8:30).

Thus, the believer is said to taste "of the powers of the age to come" (Heb. 6:5). The "age to come" is the phrase Jesus uses in Luke 18:30; 20:35, and Matthew 12:32. Paul even refers to "ages to come" (Eph. 2:7). Jesus distinguished between "the sons of this age" and "the sons of that [future] age" (Luke 20:34–35). And in Matthew 12:32 and Luke 18:29–30, our Lord again refers to these two ages. We are now, as Peter reminds us in his Pentecost sermon, living in "these last days" (Acts 2), but, as Jesus says, "the last day" (singular) refers to the very end of this age (John 6:39). Whenever someone is "born from above," he or she ceases to belong to this age and is immediately identified with the age to come (1 Peter 2:9). Miraculously, God's future is already present in embryo whenever Christ indwells his people by his Spirit.

Christ's New Creation

As Hendrikus Berkhof points out, the believer looks forward to the future blessing not out of a sense of spiritual poverty here and now, but in view of the pledge and the spiritual blessings he or she already enjoys. It is out of present abundance that the future hope is all the brighter. In Ephesians, Paul speaks of the "already" side of the equation: chosen, redeemed, forgiven, included in Christ, given the gift of faith, marked in Christ with the Holy Spirit as a seal guaranteeing our inheritance. It is this last gift especially that links the future to the present. This is why Jesus said it was better if he left, since he would then send his Spirit. His indwelling presence is the "deposit" guaranteeing that everything still laid up for us in the future belongs to us by promise, here and now.

"Therefore," Paul joyfully announces, "if anyone is in Christ, he is a new creation." It is important that we do not read this individualistically, but realize that it is part of Paul's general line of thought: The new creation is the kingdom of God! We are made new individually only as this new creation, like a luminous and fragrant cloud, envelops us. "The old has gone, the new has come!" Paul says (2 Cor. 5:17 NIV). This is stated in a triumphant indicative mood, not in the form of a command. It is not something to be attained, but a future fullness that has, by the power of Word and Spirit, broken into the present. The Resurrection of Christ in the past and the resurrection of believers in the future are not unrelated events but meet us in the present by the Spirit's presence as our "down-payment" (Eph. 1:13–14).

What Paul is announcing here is nothing short of this: The "age to come" is in some sense already present as those who are in Christ together are becoming shaped by the realities of the future world here and now. It is to that future world that we are conforming, not to the one that is passing away: the world of CNN, fashion, entertainment, and consumerism.

> Since, then, you have been raised with Christ, set your hearts on things above, where Christ is seated at the right hand of God. Set your minds on things above, not on earthly things. For you died [past tense], and your life is now [present tense] hidden with Christ in God. When Christ, who is your life, appears, then you also will appear with him in glory [future tense] (Col. 3:1–4 NIV).

This evangelical eschatological connection of the future with the present can serve as a motivation for obedience to God's commands (v. 5). But there is a "not yet" to the Christian life as well, just as with the kingdom itself. We don't have to go very far from Romans 6 to find it, in fact, as we have seen briefly in another chapter.

Just after he has announced the "already" character of our new life, Paul immediately describes the Christian life as a constant struggle, one in which obedience—however genuinely desired—is often frustrated by the believer's ongoing sinfulness. Lest the "already" of the new age in the Christian life lead to self-righteous triumphalism on the one hand, or despair on the other, Paul so emphasizes the "not yet" character of the Spirit's present work that he cries out, "O wretched man that I am! Who will deliver me from this body of death?" But his confidence is not in himself: "Thanks be to God, through Jesus Christ our Lord!" (Rom. 7:24–25). Paul's buoyancy returns, not because he has learned how to gain victory over sin in his life, nor because he has discovered hidden virtue within himself, but because he has turned outside of himself to Christ and his all-sufficient righteousness.

This is the cycle: The Law leads us to despair so that we flee to Christ. Once united to Christ, we bear fruit, since we share corporately in his Resurrection Life. Then our joy in the present realities of the age of the Spirit becomes an opportunity for our sinful hearts to regain self-confidence. We need to hear the Law again, judging our best works, so that we will flee to Christ. We also need to be reminded that it is the intrusion of the coming age into the present, not the gradual improvement of the sinful nature, that is responsible for our new life and growth in Christ.

It is not "recovery" but death, signified and sealed in baptism, that the age to come announces in our present existence. Here, the Holy Spirit is the principal actor who comes from the future, where he is shaping the "age to come" after Christ's image, into the present. He is shaping us, through suffering, into that image in anticipation of eternal glory.

Just as the resurrection of our bodies awaits a future day, so our struggle with sin will not end until the last day. But the body will be raised, says Paul: first Christ as the firstfruits, followed by those united to his flesh by faith. According to the ceremonial law, the Hebrews were to come to Jerusalem at the beginning of the harvest season to offer the first part of the harvest, recognizing that the whole harvest belonged to God.

In the New Testament epistles, Christ's resurrection and ours are so closely related that they are viewed as one single event. Our Savior's resurrection is not entirely unique: it was the "firstfruits" or down payment on the rest of the harvest. As Paul goes on to relate, our bodies will be raised in the likeness of Christ's immortal flesh (1 Cor. 15:48–49). Our divine brother now intercedes for us at the Father's right hand. He has taken our flesh into heaven beyond death and corruption, securing our own resurrection, ascension, and glorification.

In the light of all this, we should hear more than we do about the resurrection of the body. Too often, death is treated as if it were a good thing. It is sometimes considered pious to talk about the "victory" that comes at the dissolution of the body. At last, the spirit is free to fly upward to God! But this view has Plato, not Paul, as its source. It is utterly foreign to the Hebrew-Christian understanding of the body and the physical world.

While some conservative Bible teachers actually argue that the reason we continue to sin as Christians is that we live as redeemed spirits in fleshly bodies, the Scriptures affirm that our bodies are redeemed along with our souls. Both share in suffering and sanctification (Rom. 6:12–13; 12:1); only in unity together will both share in the glory which is to come (Rom. 8:23). Our great hope is not an ethereal, disembodied, "spiritlike" existence, floating on clouds while playing harps for all of eternity. Rather, "even we ourselves groan within ourselves, eagerly waiting for the adoption, the redemption of the body" (Rom. 8:23).

A Look at History

For the ancient Gnostics, history was alien. In fact, everything remotely connected to this physical world—the body, desires, time, physical space, history, rituals that involved material substances—was regarded as subspiritual and, in fact, evil. Similarly, the modern age has adopted a highly mystical theory of history, where, as Hegel's and Nietzsche's famous devotee Nikos Katzanzakis put it, "matter gives way to Spirit."

Refusing to make peace with the natural world as a given from God, our present age has been obsessed with remaking the world by escaping its realities. With the ancient Gnostic, modern men and women—illustrated in the French existentialists—seek to defy the world of space and time and escape it. Like Camus, modern men and women feel like strangers in this world, as if they were thrown mercilessly into a cosmic machine of chance. For them, meaning cannot be found in the created world of ordered events and providential direction.

Unfortunately, many Christians share this modern outlook. As it was with the ancient Gnostics, the resurrection of the body is often downplayed or even ignored. This is done in favor of the common notion that it is, after all, our physical body that keeps us tied to this sinful world, while our pure spirits enjoy unmediated access to God. In this perspective, history is as meaningless as it was for Sartre or Camus.

In such thinking, it is the suprahistorical—a Rapture, a Second Coming, or similar events—that direct the believer's understanding of the future. And yet, even here we see enormous benefits in realizing that the future return of our Lord itself is far from suprahistorical. He is going to return to the same physical world, occupying the same time line of historical events, still incarnate in the same human body that characterized his first advent. In Christianity, the goal is the salvation of the body and the world in real history.

The heart of the apostolic hope was not the escape from this world and from the physical body, but the resurrection of the body. And this is precisely where the early church ran into so many problems from their Gnostic adversaries. Many insisted, with Greek mysticism, that the body is the "prison-house" of the spirit. According to the Gnostic argument, the spirit is good, and matter is evil, so the Incarnation could never have been real. Jesus appeared to have a true human body, but it must have been a heavenly body, they said. Furthermore, the future resurrection is entirely spiritual. In fact, said many of these people, the final resurrection has already taken place as people are born again (see Paul's warning in 2 Tim. 2:18).

But Scripture is flatly opposed to this way of thinking. In 1 Corinthians 15, Paul defends our Lord's resurrection as necessary for our own. For the apostles, the resurrection of the body is not a secondary issue to salvation, but is at the heart of salvation itself. That which God saves is the person, not merely the soul or the spirit. And because of this, Paul can say in Romans 8 that our salvation is not truly complete until we receive this bodily resurrection. This, he says, is what it means for us to be revealed as God's children, and for our adoption to be at last complete.

For many conservative Christians, the "Great Escape"—a popular term for the so-called "Rapture"—does not refer to the escape from the wrath of God, but to an escape from "the late great planet earth." We must resist this unbiblical view of history and realize that God's plan is to save both individual believers and the physical creation and that the future goal must be somehow pursued in the present.

Waiting for the Rapture

At this point, let's take a brief look at the popular and quite recent theory of the Rapture. According to its proponents, there is indeed a final resurrection of the dead, but before that event Jesus will come in the clouds and the remaining believers will be "caught up" to be with him during the seven-year tribulation. At the end of that tribulation, the dead will be raised and the raptured saints will return, along with the whole church, with the Savior in judgment. The only major passage that offers even a remote possibility for such a teaching is 1 Thessalonians 4:14–18:

> We believe that Jesus died and rose again and so we believe that God will bring with Jesus those who have fallen asleep in him. According to the Lord's own word, we tell you that we who are still alive, who are left till the coming of the Lord, will certainly not precede those who have fallen asleep. For the Lord himself will come down from heaven, with a loud command, with the voice of the archangel and with the trumpet call of God, and the dead in Christ will rise first. After that, we who are still alive and are left will be caught up together with them in the clouds to meet the Lord in the air. And so we will be with the Lord forever. Therefore encourage each other with these words. (NIV)

What we notice from this passage, first of all, is that there is no mention of a "secret Rapture." Paul says that this single event is marked by "a loud command, with the voice of the archangel and with the trumpet of God." This is hardly a secret event! It is attended with penetrating sound and with pageantry. Paul also tells us that this coming he has in view is the one in which "God will bring with Jesus those who have fallen asleep in him" (v. 14). So from the very beginning of this description, it is a story about Jesus coming with his church. There is never any mention of two comings. This is one event that Paul describes, not a Rapture followed by a Second Coming.

Where do we find the seven years in between these two events in this passage? The Lord descends and the dead are raised, while those still alive will be caught up together with the resurrected saints to meet the Lord in the air. Far from saying that at this point the church is taken to heaven for seven years to return in judgment, instead we read, "And so we will be with the Lord forever." There is no way of construing a temporary interval between two comings.

Historically, Christians have looked forward to the Second Coming and not to a Rapture or any other intervening event. We are not eagerly anticipating the next end-times scenario, predicting the prophetic significance of this or that headline in the morning newspaper. We are eagerly anticipating the return of Christ. This is the next event in the unfolding of redemptive history. What an amazing thing for us to be living in this chapter of God's story, awaiting the final phase of God's saving events! We don't long to escape our bodies or to escape this world; we long for the final redemption and glorification of our bodies as well as the created world (Rom. 8:20–24).

Creature and Creation: Perfected

This passage (Rom. 8:20–24) is so pregnant that it requires some elaboration. First, the creation's bondage to decay is not seen as a natural product. It is not because creation is material, but because it was subjected to decay by a willful, unethical decision on the part of man.

Second, the whole creation will be liberated from this bondage to decay, Paul says. Where is there room for this in our view of history? Do we really believe this? Or does our future hope have to do with disembodied spirits of individual Christians?

Third, Paul argues a symmetry between the liberation of the church and the liberation of the creation. I have never met a professing American Christian who said that since he or she will be glorified in heaven, there is no use in pursuing sanctification on earth. And yet, don't we often hear that since this world is going to be judged we need not waste our time talking about the stewardship of creation? To be sure, the "not yet" of this passage is clear, as Paul goes on in the next sentence: "But hope that is seen is no hope at all. Who hopes for what he already has? But if we hope for what we do not yet have, we wait for it patiently" (Rom. 8:24–25 NIV).

We do not see the restoration of creation, but neither do we see the restoration of our bodies. We do not see the spiritual and ethical perfection for which we eagerly wait. Nevertheless, Paul says, this future hope does not mean putting present responsibilities off until the future. Quite the contrary: it means realizing that the coming age has broken in already and makes our action in this time and place in human history genuinely meaningful. Paul links the work of the Spirit to both the believer's glorification and to the creation's glorification, just as he links our adoption as sons and daughters, directly to the resurrection of our bodies.

What a radical reorientation Paul's eschatology could create if we were to recover this sense of the future's breaking in on the present. It would break up the lethargy that so often stiffens our spiritual muscles by leading us to expect very little of the joy, blessing, and spiritual power that belong to us here and now. It would also give us a new energy for relating our own sanctification to our stewardship in this world.

The believer knows how the story ends. The city of man, which persecuted the city of God with such relentless vengeance, will be defeated. Although the serpent's designs were objectively crushed already in history, we do not yet enjoy the effects of that decisive victory to the fullest. We hope, not out of blind optimism, but because of what we have already seen and heard.

The Kingdom—Right Now?

Like the early disciples, we too look for the signs of the kingdom in terms of what we can see. Not only are we used to seeing secular kingdoms born in pomp and ceremony; we have the example of Israel. "Lord, are you at this time going to restore the kingdom to Israel?" the disciples asked the resurrected Lord. Jesus answered by telling them that he would send his Spirit upon his church, as he had been sent upon Israel and into the temple. The Spirit would cause his people to become powerful witnesses to Christ throughout the world, so that the prophecies concerning this eternal kingdom spreading to all nations would be fulfilled (Acts 1:6–8).

Scripture represents the time in which we are now living as an in-between period, nestled between the first and second comings of Christ. Because Jesus himself announced the arrival of his kingdom, it must be here in some sense. Yet Scripture also points us toward the future consummation of this heavenly vision.

Carefully note how our Lord himself handled this question: "Once, having been asked by the Pharisees when the kingdom of God would come, Jesus replied, 'The kingdom of God does not come with your careful observation, nor will people say, "Here it is," or "There it is," because the kingdom of God is within you'" (Luke 17:20–21 NIV).

There is an "already" to the kingdom of God in the person of Christ and in the power of the Holy Spirit. But Jesus goes on to warn against running after signs of the second coming (vv. 22–37). He will return on schedule, but, as in the days of Noah, it will catch the world by surprise. Our goal is not to try bring the kingdom to us, but to become engrafted into the kingdom now! It is coming upon us, rushing toward us, as heaven breaks in on earth as in the days of Eden and Israel, but only the eye of faith can see it in its present form.

While the unbeliever scoffs, "Where is this 'coming' he promised?" (2 Peter 3:4 NIV), the believer sees the kingdom because he is in the presence of the great king in heaven, who "raised us up with Christ and seated us with him in the heavenly realms in Christ Jesus, in order that in the coming ages he might show the incomparable riches of his grace, expressed in his kindness to us in Christ Jesus" (Eph. 2:6–7 NIV).

This is why Jesus told Nicodemus, "I tell you the truth, no one can see the kingdom of God unless he is born again" (John 3:3). Jesus had claimed to be the long-awaited Messiah, the Lamb of God (John 1:29), the one who baptizes with the Holy Spirit (v. 33), the House of

God Jacob saw in his vision with angels ascending and descending (v. 51). He was the One who brings joy, who turns water into wine (2:1–11), he who finally drives the serpent out of the temple-garden and then announces that he is himself the temple (vv. 12–19)!

Although Nicodemus, a respected Jewish rabbi, recognized that Jesus had come from God, he was still "seeing" with a veil over his eyes so that he could not see the kingdom. Even when Jesus told him that the reason he was unable to see the kingdom was because he was not yet born again, Nicodemus further revealed his blindness by confusing spiritual and physical birth.

Jesus was not merely saying that apart from the new birth Nicodemus could not see the kingdom after he died. He was also saying that he could not see it now! It was not apparent to Nicodemus, because Jesus' kingdom, like his power and glory, were hidden. After all, what king is born in a stable, spends most of his adult life as a carpenter, and is known by everyone in the neighborhood as "the boy next door"? It is only as an adult that he began his miraculous ministry, announcing his mission as the Son of David. The kingdom is still breaking into this world, the future rushing in upon the present, as the Holy Spirit brings the dead to life through his Gospel.

Until Then: Worship in the Kingdom

What does it mean to worship as part of the "new creation"? The writer to the Hebrews tells us that through the ministry of the church, believers are enlightened, taste of the heavenly gift, share in the Holy Spirit, taste of the goodness of God's Word and the powers of the coming age" (Heb. 6:4). The scene of worship in the heavenly temple that we find throughout the Revelation is constantly interacting with the church of John's own day. Jesus walked among the heavenly candlesticks, but brought his heavenly Zion to earth in the form of the churches represented in the first three chapters.

Think of how frequently in Scripture we are described as deriving our sense of identity from our heavenly status. Surely we are not already raised physically, but somehow in the mystery of God's plan and by the power of his Holy Spirit, the future is breaking in already on the present. Paul says that we are already raised with Christ, "and seated . . . with him in the heavenly realms in Christ Jesus, in order that in the coming ages he might show the incomparable riches of his grace, expressed in his kindness to us in Christ Jesus" (Eph. 2:6 NIV).

This comforts us in our knowledge that this future hope is already certain, and it defines our lifestyle and relationship to this passing age: "Since, then, you have been raised with Christ, set your hearts on things above, where Christ is seated at the right hand of God," for now we are dead to this passing evil age now awaiting divine judgment, "and your life is now hidden with Christ in God. When Christ, who is your life, appears, then you also will appear with him in glory" (Col. 3:1–4 NIV).

It is this motivation that leads us to become sworn enemies of every desire, obsession, love, pleasure, or belief that sets itself against the coming age.

In the light of all of this, we have to ask the difficult question, "Which focus orients our worship: this present evil age or the age to come?" Style is never neutral, and it is not enough to make our decisions simply based on older versions of this evil age. Is our worship patterned on the "felt needs" and comfort zones of the unbeliever and the worldly Christian whose heart is set on things below? Or are we worshiping in heaven, in the Spirit's power, by the Word? Do we gather each week around the Lamb who was slain (Rev. 5)?

We can finally put the pieces together. Where the King is present, there is his kingdom. Although he is risen and ascended, seated at the right hand of the Father, he has sent his Holy Spirit from his throne, to convict the world of sin and to bring them to Christ the Savior (John 16:5–16).

Meanwhile, there is worship in heaven. And we who are subjects of this eternal dominion are now called to join the heavenly choir in joyful assembly. At last we see what Jesus meant by the petition, "Your will be done on earth as it is in heaven." This was the goal for Adam in paradise, for Israel in Canaan, and now it is our goal in the church, the temple-garden that is Christ's body.

233

As Israel was to be for God "a kingdom of priests and a holy nation" (Exod. 19:6), Peter says of the church, "But you are a chosen people, a royal priesthood, a holy nation, a people belonging to God, that you may declare the praises of him who called you out of darkness into his wonderful light. Once you were not a people, but now you are the people of God; once you had not received mercy, but now you have received mercy" (1 Peter 2:9–10 NIV).

Just as Israel demonstrated in her infidelity, we look to the practices of the nations and pattern our worship on what we see. Idolatry is always attractive to us, as it was to the children of Israel at Mount Sinai, when they formed the golden calf. If we cannot see the kingdom of God, we will make it visible through idolatry. We will create a kingdom through our own techniques and cleverness. However, we are called instead to pattern our worship on things above, not on things below (Col. 3:1–4). When we meet for public worship, we are part of a service already in progress.

Joining in the Heavenly Song

The Samaritan woman asked Jesus whether the correct place to worship was on Mount Gerizim, where Abraham and Jacob had built altars and the people had been blessed by God, or in Jerusalem. Jesus did not take sides in the Samaritan-Jewish squabble over holy sites. Instead, he declared, "Believe me, woman, a time is coming when you will worship the Father neither on this mountain nor in Jerusalem. . . . Yet a time is coming and has now come when the true worshipers will worship the Father in spirit and truth, for they are the kind of worshipers the Father seeks. God is spirit, and his worshipers must worship in spirit and in truth" (John 4:21–24 NIV).

No longer is there a holy place or a Holy Land. Jerusalem is no longer the Holy City, the mirror of the Heavenly Jerusalem. Instead, "a time is coming and has now come when the true worshipers will worship the Father in spirit and in truth. . . ." It is a heavenly worship that we join, fastening our hope on the world that is above and that is to come, and yet in a very real sense "has now come."

The Revelation gives us a glimpse of this kingdom:

I saw the Holy City, the new Jerusalem, coming down out of heaven from God, prepared as a bride beautifully dressed for her husband. And I heard a loud voice from the throne saying, "Now the dwelling of God is with men, and he will live with them. They will be his people, and God himself will be with them and be their God. He will wipe every tear from their eyes. There will be no more death or mourning or crying or pain, for the old order of things has passed away." He who was seated on the throne said, "I am making everything new!" (Rev. 21:2–5 NIV)

There are other scenes of heavenly worship in the Revelation, beginning with the vision of the throne. On this throne sat a radiant person, with a rainbow (symbol of peace between warring parties) encircling the throne. "Surrounding the throne were twenty-four other thrones, and seated on them were twenty-four elders. They were dressed in white and had crowns of gold on their heads" (4:4 NIV). Some commentators see this as referring to the twelve tribes of Israel and the twelve apostles. "From the throne came flashes of lightning, rumblings and peals of thunder" (v. 5), and seven lamps were blazing before the throne.

What looked like a sea of glass covered the area before the throne. Flying creatures, reminiscent of the creatures Isaiah saw in his heavenly vision (Isa. 6), were covered with wings so they could shield themselves from the glory of the throne. "Day and night they never stopped saying, 'Holy, holy, holy is the Lord God Almighty, who was, and is, and is to come.' Whenever the living creatures gave glory, honor, and thanks to him who sits on the throne and who lives for ever and ever, the twenty-four elders fall down before him who sits on the throne, and worship him who lives for ever and ever" (vv. 9–10). There was a heavenly song, a set piece, that these strange celestial creatures perpetually sang, and the elders cast their golden crowns before the one who sits on the throne. Now they have their song to sing: "You are worthy, our Lord God, to receive glory and honor and power, for you created all things, and by your will they were created and have their being" (v. 11).

After this amazing scene, a mighty angel announced the existence of a certain parchment with seven seals, each unleashing judgment on the world. "Who is worthy to break the seals and open the scroll?" the angel asked. When no one was able to even look inside the scroll, much less open it, John says he began weeping, but was consoled by an elder: "Do not weep! See, the Lion of the tribe of Judah, the Root of David, has triumphed. He is able to open the scroll and its seven seals" (5:3–5).

John reports, "Then I saw a Lamb, looking as if it had been slain, standing in the center of the throne, encircled by the four living creatures and the elders" (v. 6). The Lamb took the scroll and thus the royal company composed a new hymn:

> "You are worthy to take the scroll and to open its seals, because you were slain, and with your blood you purchased men for God from every tribe and language and people and nation. You have made them to be a kingdom and priests to serve our God, and they will reign on the earth."

A host of heavenly choristers added their voices, loudly singing, "Worthy is the Lamb, who was slain, to receive power and wealth and wisdom and strength and honor and glory and praise!" Before long, every creature, including fish, fowl, and beast, sang with their whole hearts and voices, "To him who sits on the throne and to the Lamb be praise and honor and glory and power, for ever and ever!"

As an antiphonal refrain, the four living creatures covered with wings answered, "Amen," as the elders fell prostrate before the Lamb's throne and worshiped him (5:9–14). This is the heavenly worship that our worship here on earth is supposed to join whenever we gather in the Lord's name. We are not simply to mirror it, but to participate in this heavenly service, where we are already seated with Christ.

Heavenly Impressions

We miss the whole point of this remarkable book of the Bible if we think that the Revelation is only interested in predicting end-time scenarios. If the law, the prophets, and the Gospels give us a narrative (or "storytelling") approach to redemptive history, the Revelation is more like an Impressionist painting. Belonging to the genre of apocalyptic literature, this book, far from giving us a blow-by-blow description of how things are going to come out, provides a heavily metaphorical melange.

It is redemptive history as if told by Monet or Cezanne. And it is told not simply from the perspective of its progress through linear history, but from the perspective of heaven. So when Jesus tells us to pray, "Thy kingdom come, . . . on earth as it is in heaven," he means it! We are to worship God "in the heavenlies" where God "has seated us with Christ" (Eph. 2:5). The Book of Revelation gives us fleeting and incomplete pictures of this heavenly worship, while the other portions of Scripture give us clear guidelines.

The important point here is that our worship here and now through God's ordained means of grace is the focal point for future's breaking into the present. The writer to the Hebrews, who longed to convince us that our worship is now taking place in the Holy of Holies, announced, "Therefore, since we are [present tense] surrounded by such a great cloud of witnesses, let us throw off everything that hinders and the sin that so easily entangles, and let us run with perseverance the race marked out for us," setting "our eyes on Jesus, the author and perfecter of our faith" (Heb. 12:1–2 NIV).

The image here is of a giant stadium, filled with cheering spectators. Here, however, they are called "witnesses," and they are not witnesses to our race, but to Christ and his victory that has won the race already for them as well as for us. All of the saints who have gone to their rest, whether in the Old or New Testaments, from church history down to our own immediate believing relatives, are already seated in this heavenly arena described in the Revelation. Like them, our eyes are fixed on Jesus Christ, the Lamb who alone is worthy to save and destroy.

Thus, whatever form our worship takes, it must raise our eyes to heaven rather than fixing them on this world, and it must join the choir of those who have gone before us. We cannot worship God in the present unless we clasp hands with those from the past, for only together do we enjoy the presence of God. How do we worship in this way if our orientation is toward the "new and improved" and we are fascinated with the novel? If our own individual experience is primary, we will not be able to join the heavenly choir, but will be creating our own kingdom with ourselves on the throne.

It is true that Christ's kingdom and "the powers of the coming age" are breaking into the present. But this only takes place through the office of the ministry, centering on Word and sacrament, by which Christ's set apart and officially approved ministers and elders have been given the keys to bind and loose. Our Lord could not have been clearer. After Peter confessed Christ as the Messiah, Jesus replied that he would build his church on this rock, this confession of faith. "And I will give you the keys of the kingdom of heaven, and whatever you bind on earth will be bound in heaven, and whatever you loose on earth will be loosed in heaven" (Matt. 16:19).

In the Acts and the epistles, we see this authority extended to all of the pastors and elders. Their authority is not arbitrary: God does not give it to them, but to their office. We read,

"Remember those who rule over you, who have spoken the word of God to you, whose faith follow, considering the outcome of their conduct . . . Obey those who rule over you, and be submissive, for they watch out for your souls, as those who must give account" (Heb. 13:7, 17).

According to Hebrews 6:4–5, tasting "of the powers of the coming age" comes only through baptism ("once enlightened"), the Lord's Supper ("tasted the heavenly gift and have become partakers of the Holy Spirit"), and the preached word ("tasted the good word of God"). At a time when *kingdom work* and *ministry* refer to almost anything except the ordained offices and ordinances, we desperately need to recover this biblical emphasis.

The New Jerusalem has already come down out of heaven and is even now breaking in on the world. As we have seen from previous texts, God's dwelling is now among us: we are his people, he is our God, and he is with us. Right now, the church's future glory remains hidden under suffering, like our Savior's lifelong anticipation of the cross; like our own physical bodies as well as struggling hearts. And yet, when this kingdom is finally consummated, its work on earth completed by creating a people for worship, it will be far more glorious, with death, pain, and sorrow banished from its royal precincts. "I did not see a temple in the city," John writes, "because the Lord God Almighty and the Lamb are its temple" (Rev. 21:22 NIV).

Furthermore, we see that tree of life again, the one Adam forfeited by preferring instead his own enlightenment through the tree of the knowledge of good and evil: "To him who overcomes, I will give the right to eat from the tree of life, which is in the paradise of God" (Rev. 2:7 NIV). That tree of life is in the paradise of God even now. That is to say, Jesus Christ, whose body and blood are life to our bodies and souls, is freely offered to everyone who will take and eat. It is this taking and eating, this feeding on Christ through Word and sacrament, that we are to enjoy each time we come together for worship, as those early Christians knew with such joy (Acts 2:42). The sacred branches of the Tree of Life, whose leaves bring healing to the nations, break through into our world through Word and sacrament—a taste of the age to come.

Our whole worship is to fall down before the thrones of the Father and the Son, in the power of the Holy Spirit, to receive the forgiveness of God and to bring sacrifices of praise to the Lamb who was slain. Every time we worship, we should be self-consciously committed to the ministry of John the Baptist: "Behold, the Lamb of God!" Remarkably, even in heaven the majestically enthroned Son is the slain Lamb. We never outgrow the cross. We never get beyond the need for mediation between God and ourselves—not in this life, nor in the next.

Worship: Traditional or Contemporary?

It is important here that we point out how we must be careful to allow Scripture and neither traditionalism nor contemporaneity to have the last word. While we would be foolishly proud to ignore the wisdom of those who have gone before us, and stubbornly rigid to ignore the immediate concerns of our own day, the greatest danger is to ignore the infallible pattern we find in God's Word for all generations.

Too often, debates between traditional and contemporary worship parallel the question of the Samaritan woman. I know some advocates of traditional worship forms who believe that the moving grandeur of Bach's *St. Matthew's Passion* is a divinely inspired means of grace. Many among this group will argue for such pieces not necessarily because they are the most godly and Christ-saturated music in Christian hymnody, but because the style appeals to their own tastes. They also seem to think that God has not visited the congregation in his grace unless specific words have been uttered. In short, they see their liturgies or forms of worship not as the best way of preaching Christ, but as nearly magical formulas for regulating the divine presence. So, if the standard procedures are followed, God is present. If they are not, he is absent.

Proponents of contemporary worship are remarkably like their critics. The difference is that they think they have God in their control by negating everything the traditionalist holds dear. They too seem to believe that their novel forms are the keys that unlock the Holy Spirit's gilded imprisonment in classical idioms. They believe that by not uttering specific words, by not using classic hymns or choral arrangements, by not following any particular structure or pattern, their spontaneity and honesty will be rewarded by the Spirit. They have made themselves "open" and "available" by getting rid of written prayers, learned sermons, richly biblical hymns and formal opportunities for public confession, Scripture reading, and the declaration of forgiveness.

The question is not whether we worship God on this mountain or another, whether we follow the formalism of yesterday or the novelty of today. The question is whether we are joining the heavenly choir in joyful assembly around our crucified King and ascended Lord, directed by the heavenly conductor through his Word. We should ask: Is our worship directed by this world or are we attempting to mirror that heavenly Jerusalem that is coming down out of heaven?

May we more earnestly pray, "Your kingdom come, your will be done on earth as it is in heaven."

TWELVE

Only One Way?
The Scandalous Claim

✛ ✛ ✛

Not long ago America was stunned by the news that New York's TWA Flight 800, bound for Paris, had exploded midair just beyond Long Island. As I watched the memorial service held for the victims' families, my throat tightened. I sensed a strange bond with these strangers. The state and city officials there were joined in their remarks by a priest, a minister, and a rabbi, and every speaker had something to say about the peace and joy of the departed souls. Each advanced the conviction, explicitly or implicitly, that the victims were all enjoying eternal bliss. These were, of course, our own sympathies as well.

Many people in this world are probably grateful that there are religious leaders who are willing to tell us "everything is going to be all right." But I am sure that there are others—perhaps more cynical, and questioning—who cast a suspicious glance at such blanket well-wishing.

Is there no distinction in God's judgment between one person and another? If an escaped terrorist had been on the flight, would such undiscerning kudos from the Almighty not be regarded as a travesty? Surely people want to be treated as individuals. So what if God loves "humanity"? Does he love *me*? That is not a selfish question, for the clichés of universal benevolence do not really go very far in answering our questions or calming our fears.

Although most Americans believe in eternal judgment, few entertain the slightest fear that hell is their destination. Since 77 percent of American evangelicals believe that humans are by nature basically good, the problem is not with belief in hell, but with whether we think we deserve it. According to Scripture, we are all as deserving of God's wrath as the most despised villain: "There is no one who does good; no one seeks after God, no not even one" (Rom. 3:10–12). Hell is not reserved for the eight or ten monsters of history, but is the place of judgment to which we could all be justly sentenced. But how do we actually tell people that they cannot be spared from that fate and be reconciled to God apart from explicit faith in the person and work of Jesus Christ?

Surrounded by the global village, we are confronted with more variations in lifestyles, races, religions, and philosophies than perhaps any other civilization in history. Surely it was similar in the major urban areas of antiquity, but technology has afforded us the opportunity of crying with strangers: Bosnian children wandering frantically in search of slain parents; victims of natural disasters; Rwandan orphans, wide-eyed with horror. In our popular culture, exposure to so many different worlds at the same time is almost always hailed as the way of peace and universal salvation. In fact, it desensitizes us to the very things it exposes and expects us to take seriously.

Furthermore, we all know people (or perhaps we ourselves are the people) who freely cross boundaries back and forth between religious, philosophical, vocational, or even sexual practices and orientations. The lines are blurred in every direction between right and wrong, true and false, ideal and pragmatic, objective and subjective.

In the midst of all this motion, there is this Rock jutting out of the global sea: "A stone of stumbling and a rock of offense" (1 Peter 2:8). At its sight, the ship of universal peace, prosperity, and human potential is placed in immediate danger. Like the Tower of Babel, its landlocked predecessor, this ship is destined to be shattered into fragments, its passengers scattered and lost.

To change the metaphor, there is one who comes "not to bring peace, but a sword," to divide families according to whether individuals will embrace or reject his gracious invitation. This is scandalous talk in this age of pluralism, as it was in the days of its original announcement.

Is Christianity Tolerant of Pluralism?

Today's world is made up of a vast array of cultures, races, languages, and religions. We cannot deny or reject this reality. But it is one thing to embrace pluralism as a reality and quite another to become pluralists in our own approach to questions of ultimate truth.

When it comes to cultural, racial, and linguistic pluralism, no religion has been as broadly represented as Christianity. From its earliest days, the church proclaimed the good news that God's new Israel was taken "from every tribe, kindred, tongue, people and nation" (Rev. 5:9). In the first century, many resisted the equality of Jew and Gentile, slave and free, male and female in the kingdom of God. However, "the mystery of the church" (Eph. 6) was fully revealed as it embraced its international mission in the Great Commission of the resurrected Lord: "All authority in heaven and on earth has been given to me. Therefore go and make disciples of all nations, baptizing them in the name of the Father and of the Son and of the Holy Spirit" (Matt. 28:18–19).

To some of his fellow Jews who insisted on imposing Jewish custom on Gentile Christians, the one-time persecutor of the church declared, "There is neither Jew nor Greek, slave nor free, male nor female, for you are all one in Christ Jesus. If you belong to Christ, then you are Abraham's seed, and heirs according to the promise" (Gal. 3:28–29 NIV).

Although it was a religious bond, Christianity's calling broke down the social, racial, and cultural barriers to fellowship around the risen Christ.

As Christianity expanded, it was often Christian missionaries who reconciled warring tribes to God through Christ, and to each other. For centuries, Christians have translated the Bible into the remotest dialects of the nations. There is hardly a language that is not employed in the praise and worship of the Redeemer. In fact, whenever professing Christians seek to use this faith in the service of racism or bigotry, they must necessarily refashion it entirely to suit their interests. It ceases to be Christian in substance.

Long before the United Nations and CNN, therefore, the world has known a force for cultural and racial pluralism far greater than the bureaucratic, superficial clutter of mass popular culture. While professing believers of every religion, including Christianity, have often exploited religion for evil schemes and secular projects, the message of the Bible has led to many of the advances in human rights and liberty that are enjoyed in today's world, even by atheists.

But Christianity does not consider universal peace and racial harmony to be an end in itself, as did the builders of Babel's tower. While every high tower we raise to the heavens is eventually pulled down by God, he has built a stairway down to us, to rescue us from something even more sinister than racism and strife between nations: the wrath of God which we are storing up for ourselves for the day of judgment. We are not reconciled to God so that we may be reconciled to each other. Instead, the healing of our worldly divisions is the by-product of a greater end, that healing of the greater rift between a holy God and sinful creatures.

This is where Christianity, for all of its cultural, racial, and social pluralism, becomes a scandal, and Jesus Christ becomes "the rock of offense" (1 Peter 2:8). The deity of religious universalism and pluralism is hardly offensive, but the Jesus of Scripture declares in those familiar words, "I am the way and the truth and the life. No one comes to the Father except through me" (John 14:6 NIV). "I told you that you would die in your sins; if you do not believe that I am the one I claim to be you will indeed die in your sins" (John 8:24 NIV).

Jesus was speaking to his fellow Jews, heirs to the promises. As with the other claims made by our Lord, there are two options: We can either say that Jesus Christ was a bigoted megalomaniac or he was the only hope for salvation. But, in any case, Jesus was and is the source of Christianity's insistence on this point. He himself insisted that there was only one way to the Father, and that this requires explicit trust in his own person and work. All other religions, all other ways, truths, and lives, are roads that lead to destruction. Regardless of whether we accept them, these are Jesus' claims. They are not the inventions of twentieth-century fundamentalists.

We are also faced, once again, with the fact that it is not only the New Testament, but the Jewish Scriptures that rise or fall with this claim to exclusivity. Beginning with Cain, the city of man has been built east of Eden, beyond the walls of Zion.

Throughout the Old Testament story, God brings a sword, dividing families and calling out a people for himself. While Cain's descendants were building a city, the children of Seth "began to call on the name of the Lord." From then on, the world has been divided between those who call on God's name for salvation from sin's guilt and tyranny and those who go on building secular utopias.

The religions of the nations are not treated as useful by God, but as evidence of rebellion in the human heart. In Romans 1 we see this line of argument: "The wrath of God is being revealed from heaven against all the godlessness and wickedness of men who suppress the truth by their wickedness" (Rom. 1:18 NIV).

Although those who embrace these religions are created in God's image and know right from wrong, they "suppress the truth in unrighteousness." Fashioning idols to suit their religious imagination, the nations worship created things rather than the Creator. "Although they knew God they did not honor him as God, or give thanks to him."

"Therefore," says Paul, "God gave them over in the sinful desires of their hearts to sexual impurity for the degrading of their bodies with one another" (v. 24).

But this is perfectly consistent with the Old Testament attitude toward other religions:

"This is what the LORD says—Israel's King and Redeemer, the LORD Almighty: I am the first and I am the last; apart from me there is no God. . . . Did I not proclaim this and foretell it long ago? You are my witnesses. Is there any God besides me? No, there is no other Rock; I know not one." All who make idols are nothing, and the things they treasure are worthless. Those who would speak up for them are blind; they are ignorant, to their own shame. Who shapes a god and casts an idol, which can profit him nothing? He and his kind will be put to shame; craftsmen are nothing but men. Let them all come together and take their stand; they will be brought down to terror and infamy. (Isa. 44:6–11 NIV).

Isaiah goes on to expose the idols to open mockery, describing how the craftsman fashions an idol from a piece of wood, then throws the unused portion of the wood into the fire. The only useful piece of that wood, Isaiah says, is that which he puts in the fire to warm himself. The part that became an idol is utterly useless.

Surrounded by gross superstition, Israel's true faith in God was deeply supernatural but decidedly antisuperstitious. Whenever Israel intermarried with unbelievers or adopted pagan beliefs or practices, she was judged severely. The prophets themselves attributed Israel's exile to her accommodation to the religions of her neighbors. As God spoke through Isaiah, "I am the first and I am the last; apart from me there is no God" (44:6), the New Testament repeats this claim in the person of Jesus Christ in his heavenly exaltation: "'I am the Alpha and the Omega,' says the Lord God, 'who is, and who was, and who is to come, the Almighty. . . . Do not be afraid. I am the First and the Last. I am the Living One; I was dead, and behold I am alive for ever and ever! And I hold the keys of death and Hades" (Rev. 1:8, 17–18 NIV).

As with Seth's children, only those who call on the name of the Lord will be saved (Acts 2:21). Throughout the Gospels, Jesus warns the Jews that they will die in their sins unless they accept him as their Messiah, and throughout The Acts of the Apostles the Jewish messengers of Christ boldly insist that their fellow Jews will be eternally lost unless they embrace "'the stone you builders rejected, which has become the capstone'" (Acts 4:11 NIV). After all, "Salvation is found in no one else, for there is no other name under heaven given to men by which we must be saved" (v. 12).

While the Jews thought themselves children of Abraham because of their national and ethnic heritage, Jesus told them that their real father was the devil (John 8:44). He did not say this because he sets himself against the Old Testament, but precisely because many of the Jewish people of his day were setting themselves against the fulfillment of those very prophecies: "Your accuser is Moses, on whom your hopes are set. If you believed Moses, you would believe me, for he wrote about me. But since you do not believe what he wrote, how are you going to believe what I say?" (John 5:45–47 NIV).

If Jews are not regarded as children of God apart from faith in Christ, then surely Gentiles—strangers and aliens to God's promises—can hardly find salvation in any other name.

Cornelius, a Roman centurion (captain of one hundred soldiers), is described by Luke as "devout and God-fearing," a man who "gave generously to those in need and prayed to God regularly" (Acts 10:1–2 NIV). Nevertheless, he received a vision from God telling him to send messengers inviting Peter to come and explain the Gospel to him. Reluctantly, Peter conceded because he, too, had received a corresponding vision that finally drove him to realize that Gentiles were to share with Jews in this salvation through Christ.

When Peter arrived, he preached as an eyewitness of the death, burial, and resurrection of Christ.

"'All the prophets testify about him that everyone who believes in him receives forgiveness of sins through his name.' While Peter was still speaking these words, the Holy Spirit came on all who heard the message. The circumcised believers who had come with Peter were astonished that the gift of the Holy Spirit had been poured out even on the Gentiles" (vv. 43–45).

Only when he heard this good news did Cornelius receive the gift of the Spirit and eternal life. It was not the centurion's "devout and God-fearing" life, but the announcement of Christ's perfect obedience, atoning sacrifice, and glorious resurrection that saved him.

Isn't This an Arrogant Claim?

We can clearly defend our exclusive claims. But how can we answer the critics who charge that such exclusive claims are arrogant? Let me suggest a few responses. First, we should freely and readily admit that the way in which many Christians have articulated the claims of Christ has, indeed, been arrogant. Our critics have the historical examples to make their case: the Crusades, when the Holy Roman Emperor fancied himself successor to King David driving out the Canaanites from the Holy Land. The European and American slave trade and slaughter of native Americans. South African apartheid. While critics of Christianity have greatly exaggerated and distorted history, there are tragic examples concerning certain Christian missionaries who thought that the Great Commission had as much to do with imposing cultural conformity as with announcing the Good News as Peter had to Cornelius.

We must frankly admit our failures as Christians and, especially in the face of these distortions (real and imagined), we should bend over backwards to express our convictions in as humble and gracious manner as possible. Far from giving the impression of self-righteousness, we should clearly articulate to unbelievers the biblical sense that we are ourselves part of the "mass of damnation." The only reason we are reconciled to God is because he found us and saved us, and that, in spite of ourselves. Furthermore, we must clearly distinguish the announcement of Christ as the only way to God from the ever-present temptation to regard our group as morally, intellectually, culturally, or religiously superior.

God has also found and called to himself people from every language and race. It was this love for people other than Anglo-Saxons that sent ordinary Christians to remote villages, leaving behind the comfort of western abundance for poverty, disease, and often violence. And because of those seeds that were sown so sacrificially for others, today Asia and Africa are the centers of Christian growth, while Europe and America slip into a dark night of the soul.

We must never be ashamed of the exclusivity of Christ, but we must endeavor to clearly distinguish this from a general exclusivity that fails to embrace those who, like Cornelius, are questioning and searching. In the same vein, our critics should be willing to recognize that such exclusivity is a distortion of the biblical message. A good analysis of a given religion should not be based on the misuse of its creed.

The Arrogance of Universalism

Another response is a bit more direct, and it is especially targeted for theologians who champion religious pluralism. It is important to realize that there are various types of religious pluralism. Perhaps the most common approach is represented by John Hick, who sees all religions as "fundamentally alike," since they are all concerned with the same thing: salvation/liberation/enlightenment/fulfillment.

As a doctoral student, I attended the lectures of a British theologian at Oxford who attempted to demonstrate the similarities of certain forms of Christianity, Buddhism, Hinduism, and Islam. While he eschewed the sloppy generalities previously cited, this professor nevertheless attempted to show the core commonality of these perspectives. Of course, he had to base his analysis on only particular forms of each religion and, in the case of Christianity and Islam, it was the more mystical forms.

I have no difficulty at all in agreeing that some forms of Christian mysticism have a great deal in common with non-Christian religions, but that is because these forms are removed from the biblical concentration on the historical acts of redemption. Obviously, the less distinctly Christian one's point of view is, the more easily it blends with other religious outlooks. After the lecture a group of Muslim, Roman Catholic, and Hindu students expressed outrage that an outsider was so condescending toward their respective religions. For them, his lecture was just another example of the white Northern Europeans' attempt to make the rest of the world, well, white Northern Europeans!

The claim, "We really all agree," is not only arrogant from a Christian point of view, but from the perspective of other religions as well. A Jew who takes her religion seriously should be greatly offended at the suggestion that a religion insisting upon Jesus Christ as the only Savior of the Jews is really quite similar to her own.

And a Muslim would find it condescending to be told that a religion that claims that Jesus Christ is the God-Man at whose name every knee shall bow and tongue confess as Lord (Phil. 2:10) is basically the same as his own. Such a claim (at the center of Christianity) flatly contradicts the central claim of Islam.

It is arrogant to tell Buddhists that centuries of Eastern reflection can be swept aside by some modern Christian theologian who believes that they are really Christian after all.

Universalism and religious pluralism impose upon distinct, well-defined religious beliefs and practice a brand new religion: liberal European and North American Protestantism. Roman Catholic theology has even adopted this liberal Protestant habit by officially accepting Karl Rahner's notion of the "anonymous Christian": whether they know it or not, even atheists who try to be good people show that they are Catholics. (For an example of the official adoption of this view, see the new Catholic Catechism.)

Theologians such as Hick are not simply neutral agents of reconciliation between religions. Rather, they seek to create a new religion that combines elements they find attractive. The result is a new religion that is quite contrary to any of the religions in question. Arrogance is in the eyes of the beholder, and many of us would rather side with the exclusive claims of Jesus Christ than with the founders of new religions formed by stripping major religions of their normative truth claims.

The Claim of the Resurrection

We have already argued that the Resurrection was a public event, open to the usual tests for determining the historicity of reports. Unlike the world's religions, Christianity rests its case upon an empty tomb, not on universal reason, experience, morality, values, or the like. If the Resurrection did occur, that means that Jesus was everything he said he was and that everything he said would come to pass will certainly be fulfilled.

On the temple steps at Pentecost, Peter proclaimed, "God has raised this Jesus to life, and we are all witnesses of the fact. Exalted to the right hand of God, he has received from the Father the promised Holy Spirit and has poured out what you now see and hear. . . . Therefore let all Israel be assured of this: God has made this Jesus, whom you crucified, both Lord and Christ" (Acts 2:32–33, 36 NIV).

Paul told the cultured Athenians the same thing: "In the past God overlooked such ignorance, but now he commands all people everywhere to repent. For he has set a day when he will judge the world with justice by the man he has appointed. He has given proof of this to all men by raising him from the dead" (Acts 17:30–31 NIV).

God does not overlook ignorance about the Resurrection, or the sending of its ignorant messengers to the far corners of the globe. He does not accept "seekers" who do their best and worship "God" as they know him/her/it in their own way. After all, the only God we can know "in our own way" is an idol (Rom. 1 and 2).

Furthermore, the Resurrection is the public event that secures a future public event; namely, the judgment of the world. Christianity does not claim to provide helpful insights into the human condition that support the universal notions of reason, experience, and morality. It claims to offer the only legitimate explanation for the problem and the solution of the human predicament. And it grounds this claim on a public event that is universally binding because it really happened in history. Instead of assenting to the principles of universal reason and experience, the Resurrection judges these idols and insists on being itself the universal claim that renders all rival claims null and void.

The Church's Testimony

Another response to the charge of arrogance is the testimony of the church. Israel was regarded as arrogant for not tolerating syncretistic worship. Jesus was regarded by the religious leaders as arrogant for claiming he was God's equal. The early church was considered arrogant for refusing to give up the claim, "Jesus Christ is Lord." Surely we are in good company.

The early Christians maintained their confidence in Christ and continued to model Christian charity even toward their enemies. Jesus had prepared his church well, warning them that the world would hate them because they were his disciples. Why would anyone hate a disciple of Christ if all he ever taught was universal brotherhood and harmony?

"Christianity is not a matter of persuasive words," said Ignatius in his *Letter to the Romans* (about A.D. 110). "It is a matter of true greatness as long as it is hated by the world." As the apostle Paul reminds us, "The message of the cross is foolishness to those who are perishing, but to us who are being saved it is the power of God" (1 Cor. 1:18). When the world brings these accusations against us, we can take comfort in the blessing that, by God's grace alone, he has held us fast to the unchanging Gospel.

How Do We Respond to Relativism?

In prior chapters we have appealed to the fruit of recent directions in the philosophy of science. As secular dogmatism gives way, its rival—relativism—often seems to be no greater friend to the apologetic task. But even here we find some intriguing insights from the philosophy of science. One root of relativism, which Michael Polanyi critiques, is the subjective orientation of modern culture. A bogus objectivism (i.e., presuming to see the world without any prejudices) is responsible for this subjectivism (i.e., believing that all knowledge is the product of my own assumptions). Postmodern relativists often tell us that to regard a belief-statement as "true for you but not necessarily for other people" is to presuppose that "objective" knowledge is the sort of knowledge that does not have to be actually believed by someone.

Bertrand Russell, a brilliant critic of Christianity earlier this century, represents this logical absurdity when he says that truth is the correspondence between a person's beliefs and the actual facts. But this begs the question, "How do I come into contact with an 'actual fact' and know it as such?" Where is this place, this vista from which the isolated self has access to "actual facts" that are unrelated to "beliefs" of real people on the ground? It is this logical absurdity that makes it possible for someone like Russell to relegate Christian claims to "opinion," because he has simply confused his beliefs with "actual facts." In reality, he has no better access to "actual facts" outside of his own interpretive world than does the Christian believer.

Bishop Lesslie Newbigin offers a helpful observation here: "When I say, 'I believe,' I am not merely describing an inward feeling or experience: I am affirming what I believe to be true, and therefore what is true for everyone. . . . If I refrain from the exercise, if I try to keep my belief as a private matter, it is not belief in the truth."[1]

To illustrate this point we could refer to the belief in Santa Claus versus the belief in George Washington. If I discount the reality of Santa Claus, can I nonetheless accept his existence simply because I like what he represents? Someone may easily say, "I still believe in Santa," meaning, "I still believe in the idea that Santa represents," but that is a far cry from the sort of belief one has in the historical reality of George Washington. If Christianity rests its case on public events, and those events are true, it is then public truth. It is true for everyone. It is removed from the world of ideas inhabited by the likes of St. Nick, and it becomes historical fact, like the life and death of our nation's father.

As mentioned earlier, Kant helped to launch the modern project of separating these two spheres, which he called the phenomenal (observable) and noumenal (spiritual) realms. Though he believed strongly in both the phenomenal and noumenal, Kant nevertheless stated that we can only really know the truth about things we can rationally comprehend or empirically experience. So for Kant, the Santa Claus "idea" may be true even if there is no historical phenomenon to account for it.

Liberal theology adopted this model and insisted that Christianity's historical truth claims may be false, but they contain the precious "truths" that guide Christian experience. And in this framework, "faith" came to be synonymous with the blind leap, while knowledge belonged to the province of science. In the modern world-view, the religious believer must leap across the chasm between faith on one side and reason, history, and knowledge on the other. This leap is attributed to a sheer act of will, especially as articulated by Søren Kierkegaard.

Interestingly, heresy comes from the Greek compound meaning "self-chosen." And so it is that, the heretic *chooses* for himself what he will believe by an act of will. As Peter Berger argues, this means that in the modern age everyone is required to be a heretic. Every religious belief is an act of the will rather than the embrace of public truth. If this is true, Newbigin writes, the Christian is ready with a response:

> No one, in our culture, suggests that each of us should have a physics of his own or a biology of her own. We know, of course, that there are arguments among physicists and biologists, just as there have always been arguments among biblical scholars and church theologians. But where there is a consensus among physicists, as there is across the vast range of matter which is included, for example, in a school textbook of physics, we accept that as authoritative.[2]

The relativist claims that "since all reasoning is embodied in a particular social context, no claim to know the truth can be sustained," but Newbigin replies that this is itself a claim about reality.

"What is the social context within which this claim can be formulated?" It is "that cosmopolitan world in which individuals live a rootless existence and are without a firm and stable social tradition."[3]

The Christian's task is to expose this fact of our own social conditioning and to relativize the relativist's relativism! The relativist is actually correct, in a sense, assuming that because all reasoning is socially conditioned, no truth claims can be made. So he must be made aware of the social conditioning that has made him leap from the premise to the conclusion. The premise is true enough, but to say that this means no truth claims can be made is merely to say that truth claims can only be made in a vacuum.

We would do well to follow Newbigin's warning against climbing into a warm, secluded cabin of the heart where we are safe from the questions. If Christianity really is public truth, it must live and move and have its being in the real world and stand up to real challenges in the wide-open spaces.

God's Loving Invitation

Christianity is a story about God's historical actions. It is not about principles of universal longings or experiences that somehow are reflected in religious myths. Because we require redemption, not just inspiration, we need nothing less than what we have in Jesus Christ. Because he is God, he can save us, but because he is man he is in the position to save us.

Only the appearance of the God-Man is truly "good news," and "he has appeared once and for all at the end of the age to put away sin by the sacrifice of himself" (Heb. 9:26). Appearing "once and for all at the end of the age"—a particular point in history—Jesus Christ is not merely a manifestation of God or an example of a man completely filled with the divine. He is a person who has appeared only once in history, and he came for the purpose of making his life an offering for our sins.

No one is beyond the reach of God's mercy. No racial, cultural, social, economic, or moral barrier is capable of withstanding the power of the Cross. Even though we must endure the scandal of its exclusive religious claims, we can exult in the universal scope of the risen Lord's warm invitation: "Come to me all you who labor and are heavily burdened, and I will give you rest."

NOTES

✛ ✛ ✛

Chapter 1

1. Stephen Toulmin, *Cosmopolis: The Hidden Agenda of Modernity* (Chicago: University of Chicago Press, 1992), pp. 63–65.
2. T. S. Eliot, "The Rock," *The Complete Poems and Plays* (New York: Harcourt Brace & Co., 1980), pp. 24–25.
3. Eberhard Arnold, *The Early Christians after the Death of the Apostles* (Rifton, New York: Plough Publishing House, 1970), pp. 12–20.
4. Eliot, "The Wasteland," pp. 55–56.
5. C. S. Lewis, *The Weight of Glory and Other Addresses, rev. ed.* (New York: Macmillan, 1988), p. 54.
6. G. K. Chesterton, *Heretics* (New York: Devin Adair, 1950), p. 4.

Chapter 2

1. J. B. Phillips, *Your God Is Too Small* (New York: Macmillan, 1961), p. 3.
2. Phillips, p. 9.
3. Hans Küng, *Credo: The Apostles' Creed Explained for Today* (New York: Doubleday, 1993), p. 86.
4. Küng, p. 87.
5. Sallie McFague, *Models of God* (Philadelphia: Fortress, 1987), p. 64.
6. C. S. Lewis, *The Pilgrim's Regress* (Grand Rapids: Eerdmans, 1958), p. 148.
7. C. S. Lewis, *Miracles* (New York: Macmillan, 1960), p. 94.

Chapter 3

1. I am indebted to Louis Berkhof's *Systematic Theology* for supplying these proof texts and recommend his section on the Trinity for a more thorough treatment.
2. Lesslie Newbigin, *Foolishness to Greeks: The Gospel in a Pluralist Society* (Grand Rapids: Eerdmans, 1989), p. 15.
3. Michael Polanyi, *Personal Knowledge: Towards a Post-Critical Philosophy* (Chicago: Univ. of Chicago Press, 1958).
4. Newbigin, pp. 21–22.
5. Martin Niemöller, "The Wedding Garment," in *Religion from Tolstoy to Camus,* ed. Walter Kaufmann (New York: Harper, 1964), p. 322.

Chapter 5

1. John Shelby Spong, *Rescuing the Bible from Fundamentalism* (San Francisco: HarperCollins, 1991), p. 234.
2. Clark Pinnock is a leading spokesperson for this perspective. See Clark Pinnock, ed., *Grace Unlimited* (Minneapolis: Bethany, 1975) and *The Grace of God and the Will of Man* (Grand Rapids: Zondervan, 1989).

Chapter 6

1. Bishop John Shelby Spong, *Rescuing the Bible from Fundamentalism* (San Francisco: HarperCollins, 1991), p. 236.
2. Spong, p. 242.
3. Peter Berger, *A Rumor of Angels: Modern Society and the Rediscovery of the Supernatural* (New York: Doubleday, 1990), p. 46.
4. Berger, p. 47.
5. Thomas Kuhn, *The Structure of Scientific Revolutions, 2nd ed.* (Chicago: Univ. of Chicago Press, 1970).
6. With specific reference to the application of Kuhn's view of science to religion, see Michael C. Banner, *The Justification of Science and the Rationality of Religious Belief* (Oxford: Oxford Univ. Press, 1990).
7. Hans Frei, *Types of Christian Theology* (New Haven: Yale University Press, 1992), p. 91.
8. Spong, pp. 217–218.
9. Spong, pp. 218–219.
10. Spong, p. 222.
11. Quoted in *Newsweek,* 8 April 1996, p. 68.
12. Adolf Harnack, *What Is Christianity?,* trans. Thomas B. Saunders (New York: Harper and Row, 1957), ch. 2.
13. Flavius Josephus, *Antiquities of the Jews* (London: Elwyn & Sons, 1936), 18.3.3.

14. Tacitus, *Annals,* XV.44.
15. Eberhard Arnold, *The Early Christians after the Death of the Apostles* (Rifton, New York: Plough Publishing House, 1970), pp. 64–65.

Chapter 8

1. Louis Berkhof, *Systematic Theology* (Grand Rapids: Eerdmans, 1941).

Chapter 9

1. John Calvin, *Institutes,* (Philadelphia: Westminster, 1960), 4.2.1–10.
2. Calvin, 4.2.1–10.
3. Karl Rahnerm et. al., eds. *Sacramentum Mundi: An Encyclopedia of Theology* (New York: Herder and Herder, 1972), 5:40–60.

Chapter 10

1. Calvin, *Institutes,* 4.2.3.
2. John Calvin, *Tracts* (Grand Rapids: Baker, 1982), vol. 1, p. 38.
3. John Calvin, *Corinthians* (Grand Rapids: Baker, 1982), vol 1., p. 388.
4. John Calvin, *Psalms* (Grand Rapids: Baker, 1982), vol. 1, p. 388.
5. Herman Bavinck, *The Doctrine of God,* trans. William Hendriksen (Grand Rapids: Baker, 1951), p. 56.
6. John Calvin, *Galatians* (Grand Rapids: Baker, 1982), p. 25.
7. John Calvin, *Synoptic Gospels* (Grand Rapids: Baker, 1982), vol. 2, p. 119.
8. John Calvin, *John* (Grand Rapids: Baker, 1982), vol. 2, p. 66.
9. Karl Barth, *Homiletics,* trans. G. W. Bromiley and Donald E. Daniels (Louisville, KY: Westminster/JohnKnox, 1991), p. 118.
10. Barth, p. 207.

Chapter 12

1. Newbigin, p. 22.
2. Newbigin, p. 40.
3. Newbigin, p. 57.

Acknowledgments

Special thanks to Ami McConnell, Lee Gessner, and the capable staff at Word. I am also grateful to my comrades, Kim Riddlebarger and Rod Rosenbladt, for their support, and to Lisa for her wisdom and encouragement.